War and Media Operations is must-reading for anyone who wants to understand how modern wars are sold to public opinion.

Jamie Shea, Director of Policy Planning at NATO,
alliance spokesman during the Kosovo War

Those who support or oppose "embedded" journalism will find ammunition here but Rid himself doesn't take shots.

Steven Komarow, *USA TODAY*, embedded with the US Army's V Corps
during the Iraq War

Thought-provoking, insightful, and deeply engaging.

Ikujiro Nonaka, Graduate School of International Corporate Strategy,
Hitotsubashi University, Tokyo, former Xerox Professor of Knowledge,
Haas School of Business, University of Berkeley, author of
The Knowledge Creating Company

Thomas Rid demonstrates how nimble adversaries such as Al-Qaeda are coming up with their own information strategy.

James Mann, School of Advanced International Studies,
Johns Hopkins University, author of *Rise of the Vulcans*

The best analysis I have yet seen of the role of Public Affairs within the wider context of Information Operations.

Philip Taylor, University of Leeds, UK, author of
Munitions of the Mind: A History of Propaganda

War and Media Operations

In late summer 2002 the Pentagon considered giving the press an inside view of the upcoming invasion of Iraq. The decision that followed seemed to contradict earlier more restrictive policies, and the innovative "embedded media program" itself received intense coverage in the media. Many observers denounced the program as a new and sophisticated form of propaganda. The critics' implicit assumption was that the Pentagon had become better at its news management and that the American military had learned to co-opt the media. *War and Media Operations* tests this assumption. It introduces a model of organizational learning, redraws the US military's cumbersome learning curve in public affairs from Vietnam, Grenada, Panama, the Persian Gulf, Somalia, and the Balkans to Afghanistan, and finally examines whether the lessons of the past were implemented during the invasion of Iraq in 2003. Thomas Rid argues that while the US armed forces have improved their press operations, America's military has fallen behind fast-learning and media-savvy terrorist organizations. His findings raise questions for journalists as well as for soldiers: what are the consequences for their profession if, as one Army colonel put it, "truth can be propaganda"? The book draws on new Pentagon sources, including doctrinal publications, internal messages and presentations, as well as personal interviews with spin doctors and the military's media managers.

War and Media Operations will be of great interest to students of the US Army, media and war, propaganda, political communications and security studies in general.

Thomas Rid worked for the German government's foreign policy think tank Stiftung Wissenschaft und Politik and the American Academy in Berlin. He is currently Tapir-Fellow at the Institut Français des Relations Internationales in Paris, at Johns Hopkins University's School for Advanced International Studies and the Rand Corporation in Washington, DC.

Routledge military studies

War and Media Operations

The US military and the press from
Vietnam to Iraq

Thomas Rid

Routledge
Taylor & Francis Group

LONDON AND NEW YORK

First published 2007
by Routledge
2 Park Square, Milton Park, Abingdon, Oxon, OX14 4RN

Simultaneously published in the USA and Canada
by Routledge
270 Madison Ave, New York NY 10016

Routledge is an imprint of the Taylor & Francis Group, an informa business

Transferred to Digital Printing 2008

© 2007 Thomas Rid

Typeset in Times by Wearset Ltd, Boldon, Tyne and Wear

British Library Cataloguing in Publication Data
A catalogue record for this book is available from the British Library

Library of Congress Cataloging in Publication Data
Rid, Thomas, 1975–
War and media operations: the U.S. military and the press from Vietnam
to Iraq / Thomas Rid.
p. cm. — (Routledge military studies)
Includes bibliographical references and index.
1. Armed Forces and mass media—United States—History—20th century.
2. Armed Forces and mass media—United States—History—21st century.
3. United States—Armed Forces—Public relations—History—20th
century. 4. United States—Armed Forces—Public relations—History—
21st century. I. Title.
P96.A752U67 2007
070.4'493550097309045—dc22   2006025542

ISBN10: 0-415-47209-1 (pbk)
ISBN10: 0-415-41659-0 (hbk)
ISBN10: 0-203-96452-7 (ebk)

ISBN13: 978-0-415-47209-8 (pbk)
ISBN13: 978-0-415-41659-7 (hbk)
ISBN13: 978-0-203-96452-1 (ebk)

The idea is like a pair of glasses on our nose through which we see whatever we look at. It never occurs to us to take them off.

(Ludwig Wittgenstein, 1945,
Philosophische Untersuchungen, §103)

Contents

Preface

In the summer of 2002, approximately half a year prior to the Iraq War, the Pentagon prepared to allow reporters to cover the upcoming invasion from within its military units. The decision was surprising, and the innovative "embedded media program" itself received intense coverage in the media. Its critics argued that the program was simply a new and sophisticated form of propaganda. Their common assumption was that the Pentagon had become better at its news management and that the American military had learned to co-opt the media. *War and Media Operations* tests this assumption.

Journalists react angrily when they are straightjacketed by officers, and correspondents abhor the thought of uniformed "minders" censoring their reports – safeguarding press freedom is one of the media's greatest concerns. Soldiers react angrily when press representatives suddenly come into sight in theater, and officers abhor the thought of uninformed "scribblers" reporting future plans or ongoing operations to the enemy – safeguarding an operations' security is one of the military's greatest concerns. Thus emotions often fly high in the debate about military–media relations, and scholars cannot always stay disengaged. To maintain both analytical rigor and a clear focus, this book approaches the contested issue of military media management from an unusual angle: the US military, as most government organizations, most private companies, and most of its adversaries, faces both a rapidly changing information environment and an immense learning pressure to deal with it. Media organizations, themselves in the midst of a sea change, are a critical part of that environment. With the invasion of Iraq becoming increasingly likely in the summer of 2002, how did America's military see this problem, and plan and execute its press policy? *War and Media Operations* introduces a model of strategic innovation, redraws the historical learning curve of public affairs in the US military from Vietnam to Afghanistan, and examines whether past lessons were implemented in Iraq.

This study was written for three principal audiences: for journalists and general readers interested in the new rationale of the Pentagon's media policy and its genesis; for officers and military analysts interested in media operations and processes of strategic innovation; and for scholars of knowledge management and students of organizational learning interested in the dynamics of corporate adaptation in rapidly changing, complex environments, and under conditions of high, sometimes even existential pressure. The analysis is organized in three parts: theory, history, and a case study. The book's design allows practitioners with a limited interest in the conceptual framework to go directly to the historical and empirical analyses without reading through the organizational learning chapters. Correspondingly, scholars can read the conceptual part and jump directly to Chapter 9, and only consult the empirical sections for details and illustrations. The introduction provides a first overview.

Many individuals have sharpened the text considerably with their questions. For intellectual support I am most grateful to Ariane Berthoin Antal from the Wissenschaftszentrum Berlin; without her this study would not have been completed. Herfried Münkler from the Humboldt Universität zu Berlin had a formative impact on my thinking. Presentations and conversations at the Rand Corporation in Washington, DC, at the Army War College in Carlisle, at the Stiftung Wissenschaft und Politik (SWP), at Berlin's Humboldt University, and discussions at several speaking engagements before media representatives generated invaluable thoughts and impressions. Numerous individuals have contributed useful criticism, constructive advice, and motivation when needed most. I particularly want to thank Ahmad Badawi, Christofer Burger, Janine Davidson, Gebhard Geiger, Julian Junk, Rachel Marks, Jerry Muller, Benjamin Schreer, Ursula Schröder, Lowell Schwartz, Ronald Steel, Holger Straßheim, and, above all, Annette Schulz-Baldes.

More than 40 personal conversations were the major source of insight for this book, and many officers and journalists took considerable time for interviews and follow-ups. I particularly want to thank Rear Admiral Terry McCreary, Brigadier General Vincent Brooks, Captain Brian Cullin, Colonel James DeFrank, Colonel Rick Thomas, Lieutenant Colonel Mike Birmingham, Lieutenant Colonel Scott Malcom, Victoria Clarke, William Hammond, Daniel Kuehl, and especially Mike Pasquarett at the Army War College, who provided invaluable background and contact information. I owe thanks to Squadron Leader Tom Rounds from the Ministry of Defense in London and Jamie Shea from Nato. Frank Aukofer, Peter Copeland, Joe Galloway, Donatella Lorch, Otto Kreisher, Sean Naylor, and Katherine Skiba especially helped me understand the reporters' side of the story.

For organizational support I am grateful to Peter Schmidt, Albrecht Zunker, Oliver Thränert, and Christoph Bertram from SWP, and the library and research services of Bernhard Goldmann, Axel Huckstorf, and Judith Köhler were priceless. Steve Larrabee and Jim Thomson at the Rand Corporation provided office space in Arlington with a motivating view overlooking the Pentagon. Working with Gary Smith at the American Academy in Berlin, overlooking the Wannsee, was a source of energy and inspiration. I am most grateful to Andrew Humphrys at Routledge for taking on the book, and for his useful editorial counsel. For financial support I thank the Fritz-Thyssen Foundation and the German Academic Exchange Council (DAAD).

Those and many unnamed individuals have improved the text and contributed to its strengths; mistakes and omissions remain the author's responsibility.

1 Introduction

Why did the Pentagon decide to "embed" reporters in the 2003 Iraq War? Reporters lived, traveled, ate, slept, and went to battle with military men and women. Journalists in key units attended classified meetings of their division and brigade commanders in the midst of the ongoing invasion and learned about future operations as the war plan unfolded. There was no censorship as the media covered the war and no limitation of access as the reporters broadcast live from the battlefield in one of the most ambitious military operations since World War II. Given the strained and wrangled history of military–media relations in the United States, the decision to grant journalists unfettered access by accommodating them in military units was surprising and counter-intuitive. But it paid off. In retrospect, the media coverage of the invasion phase of the Iraq War is seen as exceedingly successful, from the media's view as well as from the military's perspective. From an analyst's standpoint, the Pentagon's innovative decision in favor of the "embedded media program" is a fascinating case of organizational change in an exceptionally large, hierarchical, and presumably change-averse bureaucracy operating in a fast-paced and instable environment. How, then, was such a radical innovation possible?

Open press coverage of armed conflict used to be considered a mission-critical security risk by the American military. It undermines the support at the home front and ultimately can lose the war. This was the lesson the US military distilled from its traumatic experience in Vietnam. "Today's officer corps carries as part of its cultural baggage a loathing for the press," wrote Bernard Trainor, a former Marine Corps general and *New York Times* correspondent. "The credo of the military seems to have become 'duty, honor, country, and hate the media.'"[1] The US military came to perceive the domestic media coverage of Vietnam, particularly on TV, as a stab-in-the-back. General William C. Westmoreland, commander in Vietnam, openly blamed the "sensational media coverage" that was "piped for the first time into the homes of America" for the army's rout.[2] Military planners and political decision makers concluded after the American defeat in Vietnam to fully exclude the press from the battlefield in the next operations. The rationale was to control media coverage at the home front by limiting media access to the war front. The American electorate's support of the military effort was considered essential, and allowing reporters to roam around freely on the battlefield was considered an effective means to undermine that support. Denial of access and control of the information flow was the policy in Grenada in 1983, in Panama in 1989, and in the Persian Gulf War in 1991. In these operations reporters were either shut out completely, or they were corralled by a restrictive pool system that set narrow limits to journalists' physical mobility. The idea behind the pool was that a small group of reporters on the ground would produce news stories, which would be subject to a "security review," and then "pooled" and distributed to all the news organizations. The military's philosophy was not to control what the press could print – security reviews were hardly used to vet articles in the Persian Gulf War – but to control what the press could see, a method officially called "security at the source."[3]

Twelve years later in the 2003 Operation Iraqi Freedom, the situation on the battlefield was entirely different. As allied troops began the invasion of Iraq and crossed the border from Kuwait, approximately 775 correspondents were "embedded" with American and British troops. The predominantly American media representatives were allowed to attend classified command briefs and had access to an amount of mission-critical information that was unimaginable in earlier conflicts. But the journalists also shared the hardships of deployment and combat with the troops more than in any war in most living people's memory, and four of those embedded died between 20 March and 1 May 2003.[4] Using state-of-the-art technology such as satellite link-ups and digital videophones, the press portrayed the conflict in Iraq at an unprecedented level of transparency. Sensational pictures were again "piped" into the homes of America. This time, though, the images were piped through several hundred "soda straws," as the program's designers in the Pentagon referred to the isolated reports of single embedded journalists, who gave "a very narrow view, but rich and deep," as one of the program's managers said.[5] A quarter of a century after Vietnam, the war coverage surpassed all previous limits in scope and speed. The footage of fighting American GIs was funneled into the living rooms, offices, train stations, coffee shops, and command headquarters of neutral, allied, and adversarial countries all over the globe. And the world was getting its view without a delay of three days but in real-time and in local languages, delivered by a number of new satellite TV channels. In previous military conflicts, global live coverage would have been regarded as a dangerous source of information to the enemy and as an operational security risk by any military force. Seemingly not in Iraq.

Much had changed in the interim. Three cascading and near simultaneous developments had irreversibly altered the nature of war: the advent of modern information technology on the battlefield, the commercial media's use of that technology, and the adversaries' use of the news media. Since the late 1990s, the US Army, Navy, Air Force, and Marine Corps are undergoing a far-reaching process of modernization "from an industrial age to an information age military," internally referred to as "transformation."[6] The overhaul's objective was to harness modern information and communication technology for the purposes of military operations and to create a lean force that, as one entity on the battlefield, can act with more mobility, speed, efficiency, and precision – "interoperability" in military jargon. The new way of war would cause fewer casualties on both sides. In a transformed military, for instance, an Army Special Forces infantryman on horseback in a remote mountain range in Afghanistan could laser-pinpoint a target for an Air Force high altitude bomber to destroy it precisely and instantaneously. Information technology is the glue which connects previously disconnected units. A major ingredient of this reform was to optimize the military's "C4ISR" capabilities, the organization's ability to gather information, process it, decide, and then act promptly. The concept that formula alludes to, "Command, Control, Communications, Computers, Intelligence, Surveillance, and Reconnaissance,"[7] attempted to turn the military into a giant lethal computer network. Wars of the twenty-first century would be fought as "network-centric operations."[8]

But not only American and allied military forces were equipped with state-of-the-art weapons and networked communication technology. Both American and foreign media outlets also brought modern communication technology to the battlefield. In the Persian Gulf War 12 years earlier, the only live reporting from the war zone came from a hotel rooftop in Baghdad, and the only channel which carried the live reports was CNN. The journalists who covered the troops in 1991 were carrying typewriters, scribbled their notes on paper, then had them flown to the rear and faxed to the United States. In 2003 reporters carried laptops and mobile phones which connected them instantaneously to the internet or to their editors in Los Angeles, Berlin, Beirut, or Beijing. The media outlets carrying those vast quantities of information had equally diversified. The global media landscape was densely populated by competing satellite channels and news magazines, quoting and using each other's coverage and correspondents as sources. And the internet made the information available to consumers regardless of boundaries. An Associated Press reporter in Iraq could pinpoint a motive with a digital camera, email the picture to his agency in the United States, and find the image reproduced on the front page of the *Süddeutsche Zeitung* in Munich the same evening. Wars of the twenty-first century would not only be fought but also reported in a network-centric fashion.

The viewers and readers of this new media coverage had changed as well. Adversaries of the United States were watching and reading, too. And they were not only observing US-led military operations during the 1990s on TV. They observed keenly how America was dealing with the political challenges created by the twenty-first-century media environment in times of armed conflict. And they concluded that the decision making of a democratically elected government is vulnerable to gruesome images of accidental civilian casualties and graphic pictures of its own soldiers suffering, dying, or being tortured. As a result, Saddam Hussein in the Persian Gulf War, Mohamed Aideed in Somalia, Slobodan Milosevic during the Kosovo War, and the Taliban Regime in Afghanistan did not only watch; these regimes attempted to shape the international media coverage according to their strategic interests. New adversaries, as the strategic scholar Herfried Münkler put it, orchestrated an "offensive of pictures" against the "political and moral logistics" of democracies in an asymmetric constellation of war.[9] By exploiting the sensational reflexes of the free and competing western media outlets to break a story, they tried to break America's will. The far-reaching changes in the global information environment were playing into the hands of the west's non-democratic enemies, who were getting better at drawing media attention away from their own wrongdoings and successfully focused reports on allied mistakes and civilian casualties caused by bombs that went astray, it was argued in the Department of Defense (DoD) in Washington prior to the Iraq War. A new generation of witty and technology-savvy enemies even started to stage events for the sole purpose of exploiting their information impact upon publication: executions of US soldiers, civilian contractors, or foreign hostages in Iraq, digitally videotaped and distributed online, are cruel reminders of this development. Adversaries had become highly skilled at using "propaganda" against the United States.[10] Network-centric wars of the twenty-first century would be fought not only on the physical battle*field* but also in the virtual battle*space*.

The embedded media program was a reaction to this chain of changes in the information environment, and it fundamentally altered the way the military dealt with the press. But as a precondition to the reform of the Pentagon's media management, the mindset of uniformed planners and civilian decision makers had to undergo a fundamental transformation. In the period of only two decades, from 1983 to 2003, the Department of Defense turned from a confrontational and aggressive "denial of access" approach in media management on the battlefield to a cooperative but no less aggressive "embedded media program". The following pages depict and explain the shift of thinking that senior leaders and middle managers in the Department of Defense have performed. Some conceptual tools offered by the discipline of organizational learning and knowledge management help to unravel this mental revolution.

Scholars of organizational change have suggested different concepts to grasp the frames of reference that determine how organizations perceive and act on their environments: perception filters,[11] paradigms,[12] theories-of-action,[13] mental maps[14] or mental models,[15] interpretations,[16] and tacit knowledge.[17] All these terms describe an organization's frames of reference that predetermine the way its managers and employees interpret external challenges and react to them. A vital function of routines and perception filters is the reduction of the environment's complexity. An organization's perceptional frameworks condense the complexity of an often chaotic, fast-paced, and unstructured environment, and thus enable its members to deal with structured situations. The military needed such routines and perception filters to deal with the extremely complex advent of modern information technology on the battlefield, with the news media's use of that technology, and with the adversaries' use of the press. The embedded media program was such an innovative routine and a way of grasping the media's novel role on the battlefield. Routines are shaped by an organization's traditions and past experiences. This moves organizational memory – or, to use a more flexible term, knowledge assets[18] – into the crosshairs of research. How was the radical decision to embed reporters shaped by previous experiences with media access to the battlefield?

Three observations make the Pentagon's decision to embed reporters in the 2003 Iraq War an insightful case study of military innovation in particular, and of organizational learning in general. First, the organization embraced a new strategy with a high risk potential. Reporters would have access to mission-critical information, such as details about weapon systems, or future unit movements. In military jargon, embedding was an OPSEC risk – the "operational security" of the mission and the life of American servicemen could have been endangered. A journalist's disclosure of a unit's exact location, or signal foot-prints from the press's mobile phones, could have enabled the enemy to locate and engage the Americans. Information regarding future plans was particularly sensitive. The concern for mission security is a military reflex deeply rooted in the organization's tradition and culture. That tactical security risk was just as problematic as the strategic one. Gruesome and bloody details of combat scenes reported by the embedded journalists could have turned the American public or allied publics against the war, an intricate scenario in a prolonged con-flict.[19] The OPSEC fear was that an embedded reporter's outbound email might tactically result in an inbound Scud missile or strategically in an incoming tele-phone call from the White House. But the increased security risk the Pentagon decided to take was not the only component which made the decision counter-intuitive.

Second, embedding was a departure from previous successful strategies. In every major military operation since Vietnam, the US military and the Pentagon were reluctant to give journalists access to the battlefield. In 1983, during Opera-tion Urgent Fury, Admiral Joseph Metcalf even threatened to sink a boat hired by journalists trying to approach the shores of Grenada. Intense criticism of this rough media management triggered the creation of the DoD National Media-Pool, a suggestion of the so-called Sidle Commission to institutionalize better press access.[20] In contradiction to that stated goal, the pool was not used in sub-sequent operations to facilitate media coverage but to control where the journal-ists could go and what they could see. The military used the pool as an instrument to restrict access during Operation Just Cause in Panama in 1989 and Operation Desert Storm in the Persian Gulf War in 1991. Despite fierce criticism by media representatives, neither a public uproar nor a court ruling against the restrictive press policy ensued. As a result, the method of restriction was con-sidered successful not only by the military but in fact by the public: opinion polls had found that Americans were entirely satisfied with the coverage, and even tolerated a ban on information while the nation was at war. More than eight in ten Americans rated news coverage of the war as "good" or "excellent" just after the war in March 1991, with 45 percent rating it excellent. More than 80 percent of respondents agreed with military restrictions on war coverage.[21] After the Persian Gulf War, Pete Williams, Assistant Secretary of Defense for Public Affairs, confidently declared in the *Washington Post* that "the press gave the American people the best war coverage they ever had."[22] In a situation where past practices proved to be successful but the environment had changed markedly, organizational theory would predict a success trap, or competency trap. Such a snare occurs "when favorable performance with an inferior procedure leads an organization to accumulate more experience with it," instead of coming up with an alternative superior procedure, thus creating "maladaptive specialization."[23] The Pentagon, however, seemingly did not step into a success trap in Iraq, as organizational theory would have predicted.

Third, the new strategy of embedding conflicted with a hostile military culture. The "experiment in openness," as the *Washington Post* put it, ran "against the grain of three decades of mutual suspicion that often left journalists on the sidelines during US military operations."[24] Vietnam created a whole generation of "embittered officers" who "despised" the press, in the words of Henry Gole, an instructor at the Army War College in the 1980s. He wrote about the attitude toward the press of the young commanders after they returned home from Vietnam. "They reserved a special venomous attitude for 'the media,' a term more sneered than spoken."[25] Many of those embittered officers were in senior positions in Operation Iraqi Freedom. The implementation of the embedded media program, however, required broad support within the military and the willingness to trust journalists on operational-security-relevant information. It could not have been forced upon senior and mid-level military leaders against their will. The Assistant Secretary of Defense for Public Affairs, the ASD/PA, traditionally a civilian official with a background in journalism rather than a career in the armed services, has no authority to pass orders down the formal chain-of-command. Sitting in a Washingtonian office, the spokesperson tends to be perceived by soldiers as detached from the realities of war. If a civilian assistant secretary recommends a risky and innovative public affairs policy, this by no means implies that the generals and colonels on the battlefield will follow – even if the policy had the explicit support of the Secretary of Defense. Military culture and the commanding officers, the majors, captains, and lieutenant colonels who actually implement policy, must be supportive of such an innovation if it is to work. Cultural support is particularly essential when an innovation is not based primarily on new technological equipment, like a new tank or targeting system, but exclusively on new mental equipment, like a new type of informal After Action Review or a new approach toward dealing with the press. One of the most critical components of the embedded media program was a change of the military mindset, which meant that a generally accepted and culturally robust bias against the media needed to be overcome. Those three reasons – the high risk the military was taking, the deviation from the successful policies of past, and the seemingly hostile but all-important military culture – make it appear puzzling that the Pentagon would and could successfully embed reporters in the Iraq War.

To narrow the shutter and to increase the sharpness of the emerging picture, it needs to be clear what this study is *not* about: it is not about journalism, and it is not about politics. Much has been said about the journalistic quality of the Iraq War's coverage. Several media outlets, most prominently the *New York Times*, after re-examining and reflecting on their reportage during the conflict's controversial prelude, regretted their lack of criticism during the build-up to war as well as during the invasion phase. Did journalists come too close to their official sources, both in Washington and in the desert of Iraq? Has the quality of the war coverage increased or decreased as a result of embedding? Were the reporters co-opted? Those are much debated questions that drew broad attention, and they are important ones. But this study does not look at the embedded media program's consequences or effects; it does not attempt to judge whether the arrangement was satisfactory from the media's or the public's perspective. The empirical foundation of a study attempting to assess the media coverage would be an extensive review of articles and news broadcasts of various outlets, not interviews and documents that the Department of Defense used in the decision-making process during the preparation for war. This study does, though, shed light on the Pentagon's intentions for the embedded media program.

Furthermore, the *political decision* to deploy the American military and invade Iraq was made by the political leadership of the United States: the White House of President George W. Bush, the Vice President, the Secretaries of Defense and State, their deputies, the National Security Advisor, and the head of the CIA.[26] Claims about Weapons of Mass Destruction (WMD) and al-Qaeda ties of the Iraqi regime were part of the political public relations campaign that accompanied the decision to go to war. This decision needed to be justified and communicated to the American and international public, as vocalized most memorably in Secretary of State Colin Powell's speech before the UN Security Council on 5 February 2003. The present study does not rely on any assumptions about the truthfulness, the intentions, or the integrity of those controversial claims. Once the war began, military routines would dominate action on the ground, the details of which are difficult to manage for political leaders from Washington. The government actors responsible for communicating the decision to go to war are distinct from those responsible for communicating the ongoing war. This study focuses on military learning, and on the discourse and decision within the Department of Defense about an appropriate public affairs strategy and the best way to handle journalists on the battlefield – independent of the broader political decision to invade Iraq.

Although the final decision to embed the media with the troops was a political one, authorized by civilians at the top of the chain-of-command, it had a complex military prelude that predates the G.W. Bush administration by more than three decades. The period covered here begins with the last US helicopter taking off from the roof of the American embassy in Saigon at the wind-up of the Vietnam War in April 1975; and it ends with President Bush's landing on the USS *Abraham Lincoln* on 1 May 2003, and his declaration that "major combat operations have ended" after the invasion of Baghdad by US troops. Two sets of questions will be asked to explore the history and story of the decision-making process in the US armed forces that ultimately led to the embedding of journalists in the Iraq War. First, why was the embedded media program implemented, and what was the military rationale for the new public affairs strategy? Second, how did the Department of Defense change its public affairs policy? What were program's enablers and obstacles?

The first question examines the decision's background. The program's intentions, its objective, and concrete arrangements will be revisited, as discussed in key meetings in the Pentagon, on PowerPoint slides, in informal conversations, as well as in the formal guidelines and official internal communications issued by the Secretary of Defense, his public affairs office, or the Joint Chiefs of Staff (JCS). While the first question is about the new policy's content and rationale, the second question aims at the innovation's form and trajectory. It explores, based on the recent history of media operations, how the arguments in favor of embedding were generated and where they derived from. Through the lens of organizational theory it is possible to see whether embedding evolved out of reflections on past experiences, or whether it was simply the brainchild of a small and powerful group of leaders in the mood for an experiment. Both questions, why and how the new media strategy was designed, need to be answered to understand what the press coverage of future wars may look like.

Neither question, however, can be answered from an outside perspective. Any statement about an actor's strategy is essentially a statement about adopted intentions, framesets, perception filters, and theories-of-action. The efficiency of an organization's instrumental knowledge is a function of its adaptability, flexibility, and learning ability. This thought has far-reaching consequences. The making of strategy has an intimate relationship to organizational learning, a link neglected in both disciplines.

Learning, be it individually or organizationally, uses knowledge derived from previous experiences to choose among a set of present alternatives, or to expand the spectrum of available options.[27] This process involves the storage as well as the retrieval of information, and sometimes the creation of new knowledge. In order to learn, an organization needs to act, then capture its experience, store it in its internal knowledge assets, and retrieve the lessons learned from its memory when it confronts a new situation in which it wants to achieve a given objective without repeating past mistakes. Organizational learning, accordingly, can be defined as the development of insights, knowledge, and associations between past actions, their perceived effectiveness, and future actions[28] – strategy, as Carl von Clausewitz defined it, is "the use of engagements for the object of the war."[29] The Prussian philosopher of war has had an inestimable influence on US military thought. The US armed forces understand strategy as the art and science of developing and employing instruments of power in a synchronized and integrated fashion to secure a set of objectives.[30] The development and employment of instruments involves the creation of knowledge about causal relations, the basis of any pragmatic and effects-oriented approach to problem-solving. Strategy, consequently, relies on the development of both abstract assumptions and concrete logistics to maximize the effectiveness of available military means to achieve given political objectives. In a word, strategic innovation is a subset of organization learning.

The case of the Pentagon's innovative media strategy and its evolution serves as an illustration. The process was one of organizational learning, its output was the most sophisticated communications strategy ever put into practice in a modern war: *The US Department of Defense stopped perceiving journalists' access to the battlefield as a vulnerability and learned to use the mass-media coverage as a force multiplier.* That statement gives a first idea of what decision makers in the Pentagon and commanders in the armed services have adopted as a frame of reference, as a mental map, or as the clue that guided their approach to media management on the battlefield. How they got that clue, and how they were able to put it into practice, is what this book is about.

The United States Department of Defense qualifies as a complex umbrella organization, of which the Army, the Air Force, the Navy, and the Marine Corps are the biggest sub-organizations.[31] The task of the Joint Chiefs of Staff is to represent the services and prepare them for joint warfighting. Each of the services is a massive organization on its own, with a particular history, experience, doctrine, and culture. And with its own organizational memory and knowledge repositories. The commonly best-known form of organizational memory is an archive. But military commanders rarely browse archival records when in need of guidance for immediate action. Another part of the military's organizational memory – more applicable in decision making – are doctrinal publications and the doctrinal debate that takes place in military journals. Each service publishes several periodicals where professionals and, occasionally, external authors contribute to the debate, and reflect on past performance and new developments.[32] The magazines are an open forum for doctrinal debate, and the ideas that are discussed in professional journals contribute to the development of new doctrine. Each of the services has its own body of doctrinal publications, dealing with everything from the philosophy of war down to the nuts-and-bolts of actual deployment. A complex and standardized doctrinal review process is supposed to guarantee a constant updating as well as a synchronization of each service's doctrine with joint doctrine, published by the Joint Chiefs of Staff. Both doctrinal debate in periodicals and the authoritative doctrinal regulations are the most obvious part of what could be called the military's memory. But military commanders do not read doctrine when in need of guidance for immediate action.

This study offers a model to understand how military organizations incorporate past lessons into their institutional memory, and how these lessons impact organizational performance and actual behavior under stress. The model introduced here is inspired and built on the grounds of the "dynamic theory of organizational knowledge creation," proposed by the Japanese management scholar Ikujiro Nonaka.[33] It is based on the distinction of two fundamentally different forms of organizational memory: tacit knowledge assets and explicit knowledge assets. Doctrine as well as doctrinal debate in journals is part of the explicit organizational memory. It can be stored in physical archives, libraries, and databases. Tacit knowledge, by contrast, cannot be reposited as systematically. Routines, action-based procedures, implicit norms, the "usual way of doing things," work attitudes, and the specific organizational culture – all of which have a strong and sometimes decisive influence on actual battlefield perform-ance – are not cached in files and dossiers. Humans are the medium of storage for tacit knowledge. An example of tacit organizational knowledge is the pre-vailing negative attitude many soldiers had towards the press after their defeat in Vietnam. Though never mentioned in official doctrinal publications, this hostile attitude was a culturally inherited part of the US military's organizational memory. As a result of this deeply rooted and rather sticky tacit lesson, the explicit recommendations of the Sidle Commission after the public relations mishap in Grenada were not implemented in Panama six years later. A model of organizational learning, it is clear, has to take into account the dynamics created by the interplay between tacit and explicit knowledge assets. The following model, somewhat simplified, assumes a cyclical pattern of knowledge creation: organizational *action* is followed by *reflection* of the performance, which is *reposited* as new knowledge in its institutional memory, *retrieved* from that cache if needed, and eventually put into *action*.

The embedded media program would qualify as the outcome of organi-zational learning and as a strategic innovation if the Department of Defense has performed the following three-step process. First, the public affairs lessons from past operations had to have been recorded in the organization's memory, explic-itly or tacitly. Second, those lessons must have also been *retrieved* from the institutional memory during the operation's planning phase to choose among present alternatives, such as either opening up media access by embedding jour-nalists, or denying media access through a restrictive pool system. The most sophisticated doctrinal publications, DoD-directives or orders, however, are pointless if the relevant commanders are unwilling or unable to put them into practice. Drafting and authorizing innovative paperwork is not sufficient: effect-ive learning only takes place when performance and action changes. Hence, third, the knowledge that was first recorded and second retrieved needed to be implemented on the battlefield. The ultimate test of whether an organization has learned is not whether it succeeded to get new knowledge into its memory; learning is getting it out again and using it.

The argument is organized in three sections. The first part, *The military as a learning organization*, contains two chapters. Chapter 2, *Perspectives on mili-tary learning*, reviews the state of research on martial innovation and finds that the conceptual foundation of many studies on military learning leaves room for improvement. Most studies do not use the powerful tools provided by the increasingly rich discipline of organizational learning. Chapter 3, *A model of strategic innovation*, draws on that discipline and introduces a spiral model of organizational change. The model identifies several drivers of innovation, exter-nal as well as internal ones, and distinguishes different forms of institutional memory. Accordingly, three types of organizational learning are introduced: experiential, conceptual, and systemic learning, differentiated by the level of hierarchy on which the new knowledge is created, stored, and used.

The second section, *The history of media operations*, focuses on how the Pentagon granted (or denied) media access to the theater of conflict. Three chapters systematically analyze the US military's practice of managing press access to the battlefield from Vietnam to Iraq. Chapter 4, *Disastrous public affairs*, reviews the US military's experience with the press in Vietnam, the body-counts, the "five-o'clock-follies" as well as the Tet offensive, and discusses the lessons the armed services learned from that experience. Chapter 5, *Restrictive public affairs*, explores how Vietnam's major lesson, "keep the press out," was applied in the operations in Grenada, Panama, and the Persian Gulf War. In all three interventions the US military exerted a high level of control over the operation's media coverage. A strict denial-of-access policy dominated Operation Urgent Fury in Grenada, a badly planned pool system and unforeseen incidents with public affairs implications beset Operation Restore Hope, and a stark contrast in media savvy between the Army and the Marine Corps characterized Operation Desert Storm. The lessons learned from each operation are reviewed based on extensive research of primary sources. Chapter 6, *Experimental public affairs*, looks at the turbulent period at the turn of the century. Several small-scale military operations were rich in lessons for public affairs officers and commanders. Somalia demonstrated that the media – and the enemy – could penetrate the American decision loop; in the wars in the Balkans various ways to react to the new information environment were experimented with; and Afghanistan saw a reluctant test of the idea to embed the media with military units.

The third part, *A case study of strategic innovation*, looks in detail at media access to the battlefield in the first phase of Operation Iraqi Freedom in 2003. The historical second part scrutinizes the explicit forms of the military's organizational memory, and showed how public affairs lessons from past conflicts were stored and recorded; it does not examine the retrieval process. Chapter 7, *Retrieving past experiences?*, attempts just that. It first dissects the body of doctrinal knowledge on public affairs management at the onset of the Iraq War, the condensation of the organization's explicit lessons of the past. In a second step it examines if this body of knowledge was used in the public affairs planning process of Operation Iraqi Freedom. Based on extensive interviews with decision makers and planners in the US military, it analyzes the prelude to the embedded media program, its origin, the development of new guidelines, orders, discussions, communications, and its internal obstacles. Chapter 8, *Strategic public affairs*, reviews the implementation of the embedded media program during the Iraq War's first phase. Based on interviews with soldiers and journalists, first-hand accounts and memoirs, this case study of the media management in Operation Iraqi Freedom looks at the three levels of war and their public message, the strategic, the operational, and the tactical.

The fourth part, *Discussion and outlook*, will put the history and the case study back into the model's perspective and illustrate its practical relevance. Chapter 9, *The friendly learning loop*, discusses the book's findings in the light of the spiral model. Its core insight contradicts conventional wisdom on two accounts. The embedded media program was not an instrument of sophisticated co-option and it was not a top-level initiative by cunning politicians or senior officers; the innovation was a slow and reluctant reaction of the military's middle-management to fundamental changes in the information environment. While the book's main theme is the US military's "friendly" learning loop that led to the embedded media program, Chapter 10, *The adversarial learning loop*, looks at its opponents' reactions to essentially the same challenges. Radicalized militant networks, it argues, have equally adapted, and are using and exploiting the modern information environment in a more sophisticated and advanced way than traditional military and intelligence organizations.

Part I

The military as a learning organization

The old saying "live and learn" must be reversed in war, for there we "learn and live"; otherwise we die.

(US War Department, Washington, DC, 1945)[1]

2 Perspectives on military learning

Modern military establishments are complex organizations. The main characteristic which distinguishes them from other large bureaucracies is that military organizations are "functionally specialized in the institutional application of violence."[2] Today's conflict environment is extremely complex, quickly changing, and difficult to predict. For an organization that counts combat operations to its core tasks, the worst case scenario of failure does not mean red numbers at the end of the fiscal year or bankruptcy. Failure can mean defeat, and its consequences could imply large-scale loss of human life and political disaster. Thus military organizations confront an exceptionally high pressure to learn from past mistakes and improve organizational performance. "If we have to learn lessons all over again," illustrates Daniel Kuehl, coauthor of the Air Force's Gulf War Air Power Survey, "the price for learning is blood."[3]

But bureaucracies are not designed to change. Max Weber, one of the first sociologists to study public-sector organizations, argued that the essence of a bureaucracy was its reliance on routine, repetitive, and orderly action.[4] Military organizations, some argue, are especially prone to this behavior and hence resistant to change.[5] Militaries have developed a unique organizational culture that is geared to guarantee stable organizational performance under the conditions of extreme strain and stress encountered on the battlefield. This culture is characterized by rigid adherence to rules, clear chains-of-command, and a hierarchical rank system, the ideal of strict obedience and discipline, high levels of physical fitness, and full commitment of its soldiers, sailors, or airmen. Procedures, norms, and routines have evolved over time and are deeply rooted in the organization's history. Armies, though, confront a dilemma. While their characteristic culture of strict rule adherence creates a form of procedural conservatism, procedural flexibility is required to deal with a fluid and fast changing operational environment. The accelerated speed of technological change in the information age aggravates this dilemma. The ability to innovate is therefore critical to maintain a modern army's competitive edge. In order to deal with this problem and maintain what can be called *flexible conservatism*, contemporary armed forces have created a set of procedures to guarantee constant innovation by learning not only from their own mistakes or successes, but also from their allies' and adversaries' experiences.

Tactics and procedures are constantly tested in training situations, simulations, and rehearsals, as well as in actual military operations. Military campaigns of other armies, service branches, and competing units are eagerly observed and carefully analyzed. After an exercise, the performance is immediately evaluated. So-called "After Action Reviews," AARs, are an instrument to assess organizational performance immediately. Informal, on-the-spot AARs are an instant oral reflection on an exercise, not unlike the feedback a dancer or a wrestler receives after each rehearsal, to use a Clausewitzian metaphor.[6] Formal reports then provide elaborate written assessments and capture insights. Those formal After Action Reviews are part of an army's institutional memory. But yet another form of military memory has drawn most scholarly attention – doctrine.

The Army's field manuals, the Air Force's airpower doctrines, or the Joint Staff's publications are authoritative documents with institutional blessing. Doctrinal publications constitute, conserve, and internally communicate an army's knowledge about how to do things. Many researchers and a few officers share the common understanding that doctrine determines the way an army fights and operates. Doctrinal publications, as an officially sanctioned form of organizational memory, seem to be an easy indicator for scholars of political or social sciences to detect and observe organizational change.

But what exactly is doctrine? The term doctrine is notoriously elusive. The reason for many misconceptions is that doctrine tends to have two different meanings in the civilian and the military world. In a political and non-military context, the term is used in a rather abstract way. The word, for instance, describes the habit of American presidents of trying to establish a history-proof catch-phrase to permanently mark one of their policies, such as the "Truman doctrine" or the "Monroe doctrine." As the presidential nomenclature indicates, the direction and content of those grand strategies is defined by the senior political leadership rather than by their uniformed subordinates in the armed services.

In its military usage, the term doctrine is more specific and contains more detail. In order to understand its practical meaning in the armed services, it is helpful to recall the origins and initial functions of doctrine. The term's etymology contains a clue: "doctrine" is derived from the Latin word *doctrina*, which means "teaching," Historically military doctrine has its roots in early drill manuals. At the beginning of the seventeenth century, Maurice von Nassau outlined the precise tactical procedures in which troops should be trained.[7] Colonel Robert Cassibry, from the US Army's Command and General Staff College, emphasized in 1956 that doctrine is essentially a body of knowledge that is taught and disseminated.[8] In a widely received article in *Air University Review* in 1984, Major General I.B. Holley tried to clarify the terminology: "Doctrine is what is being taught, i.e. rules or procedures drawn by competent authority," he states reaching back to the word's semantic origins. "Doctrines are precepts, guides to action, and suggested methods for solving problems or attaining desired results."[9] In a recent article in *Parameters*, a Canadian Air Force Captain, Paul Johnston, offers a similar definition: "Doctrine is what is written down, usually at the highest levels, for dissemination throughout an army, the usual intention being therefore to instruct and to standardize."[10] The purpose of Army field manuals or joint doctrinal publications is to create and synchronize the practical knowledge needed by men and women in arms. The Pentagon's *Dictionary of Military and Associated Terms*, which lists consolidated and authoritative definitions for internal use, defines doctrine as "fundamental principles by which the military forces or elements thereof guide their actions in support of national objectives."[11] An Army manual adds that doctrine is "rooted in time-tested principles but is adaptable to changing technologies, threats and missions" and that it provides "the basis for a common vocabulary across the force."[12] FM 100–5 *Operations* – the Army's supreme doctrinal manual and thus itself part of what it describes – emphasizes doctrine's role of standardizing and disseminating knowledge within the organization: "Doctrine touches all aspects of the Army. It facilitates communications between Army personnel no matter where they serve, establishes a shared professional culture and approach to operations, and serves as the basis for curriculum in the Army school system."[13] In the Army, therefore, doctrinal publications have a more appropriate name: field manuals. These manuals cover almost every facet of Army life. FM 23–35 *Pistols and Revolvers* describes in detail how to clean, fire, assemble and disassemble a .45 caliber pistol.[14] The entire body of doctrines and manuals in the US armed services and their ongoing review processes on various organizational levels absorb significant resources and create considerable bureaucratic inertia. "Changing any military's doctrine," Alvin and Heidi Toffler point out in their influential book *War and Anti-War*, "is like trying to stop a tank armor by throwing marshmallows at it."[15] Armed services, just like all vast bureaucracies, resist reform, particularly if the proposed change implies the downgrading of influential sub-units, the need to acquire new skills, and to overcome service rivalries.

The majority of academic analyses on military innovation are focused on doctrinal change. Scholars implicitly seem to agree on the dependent variable, on what to explain – doctrinal change. Most scholars, however, disagree on the independent variables, on how to explain doctrinal change. For purposes of clarification the scholarly research on doctrinal change will be categorized in two groups. Authors in the first group tend to emphasize the importance of factors external to the military, for instance political leadership, civilian intellectuals, technology, battlefield geography, resources, or the international state system; the second group of scholars focuses on internal factors, such as individual officers, be it "mavericks" or lower-level officers with hands-on experience, organizational structure, culture, or self-interest.

External factors

Organizations operate in a given environment over which they have only limited control. For the armed services the external environment consists of international threats to the nation's or an ally's security, but also of its own government,[16] newly developed technology, or the global mass media. Several scholars who understand doctrine in the more abstract civilian sense have pondered on the influences of the "structure of the international system" on doctrinal change.[17] But international influences – other than bombardment, maybe – need to be perceived, interpreted, and communicated internally to have impact on the concrete behavior of an organization. Analysts emphasize several other factors external to the organization as drivers of institutional change and innovation, notably the civilian political leadership, resources, and technology.

Civilian leadership

Civil–military relations are one of the oldest subjects of political theory. It has two adverse dimensions: civilian control of the military, with the goal of preventing an armed takeover of the state;[18] and civilian management of the military, with the purpose to optimize the military's performance as a political instrument. Are civilians or officers the better reformers and decision makers? The question is contentious in the literature on military innovation, and the answer seems to depend on the case studied. The critics of civilian involvement in military affairs point to two problems. First, civilians often lack the detailed experiential and technical knowledge necessary to make the right decisions. Samuel Huntington, who set the standard of the debate, argued in *The Soldier and the State* in favor of a sharp separation between military expertise and political knowledge. The "criteria of military efficiency are limited, concrete and relatively objective; the criteria of political wisdom are indefinite, ambiguous, and highly subjective."[19] Officers, in this view, have superior technical and strategic expertise that enables them to make better decisions than civilians in the business of "managing violence." Second, civilians lack legitimacy within the military community. Stephen Peter Rosen has articulated this argument most eloquently by pointing out that initiatives historically tend to come from within the military rather than from civilians. The role of civilians, he argues, is limited to either support or not support senior officers in implementing an innovation: "A civilian's impact on innovation is strongest if he concentrates on reinforcing those senior officers who already have legitimate power and who are already committed to the struggle for innovation."[20]

Several authors, on the other hand, are skeptical about the ability of military organizations to create conceptual change on their own.[21] Barry Posen argued in favor of civilian-induced innovation by pointing out the military's inherent reluctance to change: first, militaries, like every bureaucracy, have vested interests in the organizational status quo; second, organizations abhor uncertainty, and changing traditional ways of doing things creates uncertainty; third, military organizations are hierarchical, and the flow of reformist ideas from lower levels to higher levels is restricted; and fourth, inter-service rivalries make an agreed multi-service strategy rather unlikely, as each service is concerned for its own autonomy and resources. The effect is stasis and inertia, which can only be resolved through either significant failure or the intervention of civilians from outside the organization. The appointment or removal of general officers is a tool by which political leaders can influence military decisions. "Thus," Posen argues in his study of grand-strategic doctrine in France, Germany, and Britain during the interwar period, "innovation should occur mainly when the organization registers a large failure, or when civilians with legitimate authority intervene to promote innovation."[22] A strong proponent of political intervention in military decision making in times of war is Eliot Cohen. In *Supreme Command*, he blames the US failure in Vietnam on both the political "inability to pick the right generals" and a lack of political interference by not asking the hard questions.[23]

Resources

Several scholars posit a correlation between budgets and doctrinal change. Their argument is that resources affect procurement and the acquisition or maintenance of capabilities, which in turn affects doctrinal conceptions. In western societies armies do not have control over their financial resources. Budget decisions are made in the government or the legislature, and they are monitored by the government's watchdog organizations. Hence Stuart Kaufman pointed out that budgets can be used politically as a tool to induce organizational change: "Budgets sometimes act as policy handles for changing military policy."[24] Others argue along similar lines. Graham Allison regards "prolonged budgetary famine" as a major incentive for reform in large public organizations otherwise averse to change (the other incentive being disaster).[25] The budget handle's leverage, it should be noted, is a function of the costs of an innovation. The replacement of traditional fighter jets by sophisticated unmanned aerial vehicles, such as the Global Hawk for instance, is a very costly decision with economic and political consequences. The introduction of an embedded media program, for the most part a change of mindset, does not require significant resource allocations. Its total costs for the government were a mere 1.2 million dollars, a minuscule sum if compared to the operation's total expenses.[26] The present analysis can therefore neglect the resource variable, which often conditions innovative decisions.

Technology

Technology is an essential driver of doctrinal change. In 1977 David Macmillan highlighted technology as a decisive factor of doctrinal change. The Air Force officer uses examples from the history of his own service branch. The evolution of tactical air warfare illustrates the impact of technology. The experiences of four major wars led to the creation of several sub-specializations within the Air Force, such as counterair, air interdiction, close air support, aerospace surveillance and reconnaissance, airlift, and special operations. At first, airplanes were merely used to assess the enemy's force disposition. But soon aircraft would be able to carry heavy workloads and drop bombs to support land forces. The possibility to attack or defend against enemy aircraft eventually led to the concept "counterair." Technological improvements made it possible to incrementally develop the equipment to perform those specialized missions.[27] In twenty-first century warfare unmanned aerial vehicles roam the skies above the battlefield and perform unprecedented functions in joint operations. Stephen Cimbala and James Tritten, in an article in *Joint Forces Quarterly*, ask what use technological innovation has if the military is not trained to use it to its fullest advantage. "Preparing for the optimal use of technology requires clear organization, planning, and training to impact all aspects of doctrine," they argue.[28] Tritten, in an earlier article, underscored that the link between technology and doctrine is not a one-way street. So-called revolutions in military affairs, characterized by rapid technological reform, "are also stimulated by doctrinal development, which can create a 'vortex' or begin a new cycle, during which doctrine pulls on the future development of technology."[29] Doctrinal concepts evolve hand in hand with technology, one shaping the other.

Internal factors

Political leadership, resources, and technology can be potent drivers for organizational and doctrinal change. But external stimuli are neither sufficient nor necessary conditions for reform. Both are possible, doctrinal change without external pressure, and doctrinal continuity despite external pressure. Internal organizational influences, in other words, must be taken into account. A second group of analysts focuses on internal stimuli for change, such as senior officers, mid-level officers, and organizational culture.

Senior officers

General officers play a vital role in promoting military change. A prominent proponent of this argument is Rosen. The author holds that "militaries" – and the same applies to the single service branches, Army, Navy, Air Force, and the Marine Corps – cannot be treated as monolithic units. Each service is composed of sub-units. Because the conglomerate of services and sub-units is a complex community of organizations, successful innovation requires an "ideological struggle." Rosen showed in detail the significance of what he called the "intellectual redefinition of the way the entire military organization conceived of the tasks it had to perform in the next war."[30] Thereby he emphasized the role of inner-organizational discourse and communication. In an effort to justify and legitimize innovation, the new requirements and tasks have to be tied to a common objective. Since the objective of a military organization is to win a war, Rosen thinks that a successful innovation must be internally communicated as a "new theory of victory."[31] The new thinking needs to be translated into concrete new tasks, in order to affect the behavior of the officers that need to train and execute them. Finally, newly created career paths can solidify the new approach. Only senior officers have the power within a professional military to shape ideas and careers: "Civilians, acting alone, are not entirely 'legitimate' political players when they attempt to interfere in the promotion of officers," he wrote.[32]

Civilians can only favor their innovation-minded protégés. Rosen concludes that successful innovation starts within the senior officer corps and "proceeds upward through the advancement of young officers into higher ranks."[33]

Mid-level officers

Descending further down in the hierarchy, to the major and captain level, Keith Bickel points to the importance of "lower and midgrade officers" in the organizational learning process.[34] He studied the Marine Corps' development of the small wars manual between the two world wars. The academic literature on military learning tends to analyze "the doctrinal product, and not the doctrinal process," Bickel points out. The effect is that the significance of doctrinal publications is overemphasized. He sees a level-of-aggregation problem: academic scholars tend to find that learning took place at higher levels of an institution simply because the documentation of the informal processes of intra-organizational discussion and negotiation is missing. It is difficult for researchers of military innovation to find archival accounts of individuals and on how those individuals shaped organizational change. Adding to this problem, the majority of the literature on military innovation studies historical cases, the most recent case studies deal with the Army or the Marines in Vietnam more than 20 years after the events. Informal discussions and debates, however, often take place on lower levels, where documentation is imperfect. There are good reasons to assume that the most useful ideas for improvement indeed come from lower levels: it is the level of battalion commanders, company commanders, and even platoon leaders, the middle-management of battle, that experiences problems most pressingly and has to react instantly.

Strategic culture

Culturally transported and historically determined rules, norms, and values produce the pre-eminent feature of bureaucracies' behavior, their programmed character, what March and Simon called the "logic of appropriateness."[35] Challenges in the face of nonstandard problems and unprecedented situations are approached by members according to standard rules of procedure and routines. Several scholars of innovation in the armed forces emphasize military culture's preeminent role. Williamson Murray is one of the most outspoken proponents of culture as a driver or blocker of innovation:

> Institutional culture shapes the understanding of the strategic, operational, and tactical choices before the professional soldier, and it implants as well broader assumptions concerning the historical framework in which those choices find their meaning. It is a process that proceeds by means of formal education, informal acculturation, and practical experience.
>
> (W. Murray, "Clausewitz out, Computer in: Military Culture and Technological Hubris," *The National Interest*, 1997, vol. 48, Summer, p. 57)

In an article in *Joint Forces Quarterly* Murray defined military culture as "the sum of intellectual, professional, and traditional values possessed by an officer corps. It is key to how officers assess the external environment and respond to threats."[36] According to this view, organizational culture guides interpretations, filters perception, and predetermines action. Scholars with a military background tend to share Murray's conclusions and emphasize an army's strategic culture as the most significant blocker or enabler of adaptation. In 2005 Brigadier Nigel Aylwin-Foster, a general of the British Army responsible for training and organizing Iraq's Armed Forces, published a widely received article, based on his one-year experience "at the heart of a US dominated command" in Iraq. The general draws a dark picture of American strategic culture with its strong predisposition to use massive offensive firepower as the only way to quick results, and concludes that "the [US] Army's organisational culture has discouraged adaptation to non-conventional roles."[37]

Questioning doctrinal assumptions

Most scholarly research on military innovation implicitly contains two assumptions. First, it is assumed that doctrinal change foreshadows and conditions change in an organization's behavior. Authorized change in doctrine, sanctioned either by the civilian or the senior military leadership, is expected to automatically translate into a change of organizational action and behavior. From this follows the second assumption. Doctrine, it is often implied, is a sufficient representation of an army's organizational memory.[38] The first assumption is problematic from an empirical point of view; the second assumption is questionable from an analytical standpoint.

Formal and informal doctrine

In his book *Mars Learning*, Keith Bickel distinguishes between formal and informal doctrine: "Doctrine is most often associated with the training manuals published for school and field use. Manuals are the most visible manifestation of doctrine and, by their revision, doctrinal change."[39] Manuals, training circulars, and pamphlets are part of what he calls formal doctrine. But the informal processes in which ideas are developed and disseminated are an essential part of the doctrinal process as well: "The most common method of idea exchange," writes Bickel, "is writing articles for professional journals, such as the *Infantry Journal*, the *Marine Corps Gazette*, and the *Naval Institute Proceedings*."[40] The author also points to field orders that analyze situations as well as to the way soldiers socialize, which are central but usually lost to history. Professional articles, field orders, and personal letters are part of informal doctrine. In the 1950s, the Army's main intellectual forum for debate, *Military Review*, explicitly mentions the journal's mission on each edition's first page. The passage illustrates the way informal doctrine works: "the *Military Review* has the mission of disseminating modern military thought and current Army doctrine concerning command and staff procedures of the division and higher echelons and to provide a forum for articles which stimulate military thinking." Lieutenant Colonel Dennis Drew, for instance, replied to Holley, who was quoted earlier, in the subsequent issue of *Air University Review*, and argued that "informal doctrine" would usually be underestimated. His main argument was speed and timeliness: "One might also assume that these informal beliefs are more timely, more accurate, and more useful than officially sanctioned doctrine, which must suffer through the travails of bureaucratic coordination and compromise before publication."[41] While informal doctrine is developed much easier, Drew points out, it also has a higher propensity for error. It is therefore essential that informal doctrine is evaluated and tested. As a result, Drew recommends, the official doctrine should "'bubble up' from below rather than be imposed from the top."[42]

An understanding of doctrine that focuses solely on the product, that is the authorized written manuals or principles, is conceptually blindfolded. Doctrine means teaching. Bickel studied the development of the Marines' Small Wars Manual. By the time the first edition was published, its authors and promoters had already been *teaching* the principles of small wars in military schools and academies, even before the document had been officially published: "They apparently needed no higher authority to teach officially what they knew versus writing officially what they knew."[43] This shows that doctrine can have influence on action even when it is still informal. The central feature is that formal doctrine has been sanctioned by the organization's leadership. Formal doctrine is authoritative and has institutional blessing as it is disseminated officially among officers, often as required reading material for training and educational courses. Informal doctrine, by contrast, often does not have support from the top of the hierarchy. It might only be known to a very specialized group of officers or employees, but nevertheless informal knowledge has an essential function in many organizations.

Doctrine in action

Academic debates and research designs seem to assume that formally written and authorized doctrine effectively prescribes organizational action – almost in the same way in which software syntax determines the behavior of a computer. "Is that true?" asks Paul Johnston in an article in *Parameters*, the Army War College's journal.[44] He questions the link between doctrine as the officially blessed organizational memory and the actual behavior of units on the battlefield. Several arguments call into question that doctrinal documents can be treated as if they were software syntax that determines the behavior of the armed forces. Cimbala and Tritten give two main reasons. First, official regulations are often drafted and phrased in a one-size-fits-all manner which is difficult to reconcile with tactical commander's broad spectrum of experiences. Doctrine, and particularly joint doctrine, tends to be abstract and general, and often makes it difficult to derive concrete guidance from it. Second, once the manuals are authorized and disseminated, they are difficult to replace. Doctrine, they write, "takes on inertia that can defy changes in the geopolitical, technological, and social environments of war."[45] The top-down approach's tendency to be both too abstract as well as too slow to adapt call its practical significance into question: "Fundamentally, how armies fight may be more a function of their culture than of their doctrine," writes Johnston.[46]

While authorized doctrine is indeed part of the organizational memory, it is only a small part of it. And, as the following case study in strategic innovation will show, it is often bypassed in critical situations. A wider and more sophisticated understanding of organizational memory is needed which extends the concept beyond officially sanctioned and designated doctrine. Both problematic views, the doctrine–action link and the narrow understanding of organizational memory, can be tackled by introducing some helpful concepts from the literature on organizational learning.

3   A model of strategic innovation

In the skies above Korea during the war in the early 1950s, American pilots in F-86 "Sabre" jets engaged Russian-built MiGs. The young US pilots who fought in Korea were victorious far beyond their own expectations. The official count after the war maintained that 792 MiGs were shot down by 78 Sabres, despite the fact that the MiG could out-accelerate the F-86, make harder turns, and perform better in high altitudes. That stunning "kill ratio" of one to ten caused some confusion in the Air Force's ranks. Neither superior training nor better technology could explain the lopsided numbers. John Boyd was one of the successful US pilots. Years later, as a retired colonel and civilian analyst, Boyd came up with an explanation: the so-called OODA-loop, today praised as one of the most significant contributions to strategic theory by an American thinker. The abbreviation stands for "Observe – Orient – Decide – Act." The Sabre had both better visibility, through a protruding bubble-shaped cockpit, and more sensitive controls, allowing faster maneuver changes. The US pilots were thus able to run faster OODA-loops than their adversaries, and to get themselves into the shooter's trailing position more quickly, the enemy's "six" in pilot speak: they visually observed the opposing pilot's behavior, oriented themselves about possible maneuver options, made a decision, and took action. In Boyd's more general thinking, the loop's orientation phase is the most critical, and tactically most relevant – here the adversary's decision loop can be penetrated. The aim is to get inside the adversary's decision cycle by creating a maneuver environment in which he is constantly dealing with outdated information and struggling to update, thereby denying him the time necessary to orient his decision. At the same time, the friendly commander should speed up his own orientation phase and minimize the time between observing a situation and taking action, thereby compressing his own time while causing his opponent's time perception to stretch. The OODA-loop is a tactical decision model on an individual level, and in essence it is about a pilot's or a small unit's ability to adapt to a swiftly changing operational environment in maneuver warfare. But what if an operation's environment is not a single opposing pilot's aggressive aerial maneuver, but an entire opposing regime's aggressive exploitation of a complex twenty-first century media landscape? To seek out this question, Boyd's model of individual and tactical innovation will be lifted onto an organizational and strategic level.[1]

Modern militaries confront an unstable and unpredictable operational environment. Pressure to adapt is high. The US armed forces – and many other armies – have created methods, procedures, instruments, and even sub-organizations to facilitate continuous individual as well as organizational learning. Computer-based simulations, After Action Reviews, lessons-learned processes, doctrinal review processes, or institutions like the Center for Army Lessons Learned (CALL) or the Training and Doctrine Command (TRADOC) all serve the purpose of making a large bureaucratic organization more adaptable, flexible, and innovative while maintaining a high standard of performance. In the early 1980s, Alvin Toffler, author of the influential futurist management book *The Third Wave*,[2] was approached by Don Morelli and Donn Starry from TRADOC. The officers were in charge of a major doctrinal overhaul and wanted the well reputed management writer to develop their vision of "third wave warfare." The military reformers were eager for external inspiration and out-of-the-box thinking. In 1993, the Tofflers' book *War and Anti-War* was published. It became required reading at service schools and war colleges. A flood of student papers and articles in military periodicals explored the book's ideas and related them to new concepts in US military thought.[3] "As in business," the Tofflers describe a development of which they had just became part, "learning, de-learning, and re-learning has become a continuous process in every occupational category in the military."[4] On the following pages a model will be developed which conceptually grasps this continuous organizational process of learning, de-learning, and re-learning.

As talk of the knowledge society and the information age gained currency in the 1970s, management scholars had already begun to explore organizational learning and to examine companies managing their knowledge. One of the discipline's most influential lines of thought was stimulated by the Japanese scholar Ikujiro Nonaka. In a 1994 milestone article in *Organization Science*, he quotes Alvin Toffler to highlight the increasing importance of knowledge creation as opposed to industrial production and calls for "a shift in our thinking concerning innovation in large business organizations – be it technical innovation, product innovation, or strategic or organizational innovation."[5] His 1995 book *The Knowledge-Creating Company* attempts such a shift of thinking.[6]

Two dimensions of knowledge

The philosopher Michael Polanyi has articulated a conception of knowledge that turned into the epistemological foundation of many of today's contributions to organizational learning literature (John Boyd also read Polanyi). The notion of "tacit knowing" lies at the center of his understanding of knowledge. Polanyi's pivotal argument is that "we can know more than we can tell."[7] According to this philosophy, all knowledge is rooted in action and experience, and the act of knowing is always carried out by an actor. The title of his main work, *Personal Knowledge*, mirrors Polanyi's conviction that knowledge always has to be understood as attached to a performing person who knows. As a consequence the philosopher, who turned to epistemology at the age of 50 after a successful career as a physical chemist, rejects the traditional distinction between theoretical and practical knowledge, and between objective and subjective knowledge. One of his popular examples is that of a cyclist. Polanyi argues that the principles by which cyclists keep their balance are not generally known to cyclists. The rider of a bike keeps balance by winding through a series of curvatures. But most cyclists do not explicitly know that, when their vehicle starts falling to the right, they have to turn the handlebar to the right so that the bicycle's course is deflected along a right curve. But they do it anyway. Cyclists tacitly know how to ride without knowing the underlying rule of physics they are actually applying. That rule can be stated explicitly: "For a given angle of unbalance the curvature of each winding is inversely proportional to the square of the speed at which the cyclist is proceeding."[8] Obviously such a rule can be helpful, but it is of little use for someone attempting to learn to ride the bicycle. The example illustrates that cyclists know more than they can tell. Polanyi uses several similar examples to show that explicit rules have little effect on practical action unless they are assimilated and interiorized by the user as "tacit knowing." Readers who have a driver's license are encouraged to remember their early practical lessons in order to get a feeling for how it was like to learn textbook knowledge, "interiorize" it, and finally come to "dwell" in it.[9]

On an organizational level, the concept of tacit knowledge is juxtaposed to explicit knowledge. Organizational knowledge is called "explicit" when it is transmittable in a clear and formal language. In manuals, regulations, job-descriptions, and standard operating procedures, explicit knowledge is codified mostly in a written way. It is accessible in documents, memoranda, reports, reviews, articles, or statistics and data. In the case of the US military, the entire hierarchy of doctrinal publications – field manuals in the Army or airpower doctrines in the Air Force – are an ideal example for codified explicit knowledge.[10] The difference between such doctrinal training manuals on the one hand and an air force pilot being trained and skilled in actually flying aerial maneuvers on the other hand, is analogous to the difference between explicit and tacit knowledge in Polanyi's examples of cycling or driving a car.[11] Explicit knowledge captures only a tiny fraction of the overall body of an organization's knowledge: "Knowledge that can be expressed in words and numbers represents only the tip of the iceberg of the entire body of knowledge," Nonaka argues.[12] The underwater chunk of this iceberg consists of tacit knowledge. Actions, routines, procedures, but also the skills, values, attitudes, the commitment and involvement of the organization's members are an expression of their tacit knowledge.

Craft-based organizations rely more heavily on tacit knowledge than bureaucracies.[13] Military organizations are both craft-based and bureaucratic. Tommy Franks, who later commanded the invasion of Iraq as a four star general, illustrates the army's craft-based character in his memoirs. He describes his training to become a second lieutenant of the field artillery early in his career. As a young Private, First Class (PFC) in the officer candidate school he had spent weeks in classrooms learning the theory underlying accurate and effective artillery fire, understood the moving parts of the guns, the energy of propellant charges, the muzzle velocity, the weight of projectiles, and "all the hundreds of other complex facts involved with firing big guns in combat."[14] But apart from those facts he had to memorize from source of explicit knowledge, the young officer had to internalize the tacit knowledge needed to fire big guns in combat, the practical skills necessary to handle the artillery. Hands-on experience was essential. Franks describes a field exercise as a Forward Observer, where his task was to determine the target coordinates and communicate them to the gunner:

> We had stopped looking at the landscape like civilians. Now we instinctively saw the world around us in terms of six-digit coordinates on military maps or firing charts. Our visual perspectives automatically measured distance left (west) to right (east) and bottom (south) to top (north). Normal people saw rows of barracks, the commissary, or the softball diamond. We saw target coordinates.
>
> (T.R. Franks, *American Soldier*, New York: HarperCollins, 2004, p. 80)

Only the tacit knowledge Franks had interiorized and come to dwell in through training and practice enabled him to speedily observe, orient, decide, and fire in stressful combat situations, of which there would be plenty in Vietnam. Reflecting on this learning experience, Franks wrote later: "I recognized this mental readjustment as a necessary and valuable adaptation to our situation."[15] Tacit experience can be acquired without the use of language, by imitating and copying procedures and routines from colleagues and comrades. If all members of an organization would instantly be fired, or if an entire artillery battery would be killed in combat, its explicit knowledge would still be retrievable in training manuals. Its tacit and personal knowledge, however, would be lost together with its human bearers.

Organizations and their members need to reduce the environmental complexity in order to be able to act. This is especially true for the immensely complex and ephemeral "information environment" military organizations operate in, as joint doctrine acknowledges.[16] In the military, routines, norms, common interpretations, and world views act as attention-directing mechanisms and as perception filters that enable the organization's members to cope with environmental complexity. Organizations develop standard operating procedures to direct search and problem identification,[17] to map their environments and to infer causal relations with the help of those filters: "The real world provides the raw material of stimuli to react to, but the only meaningful environment is the one that is born when stimuli are processed through perceptual filters."[18] When an employee or decision maker deals with a concrete situation, the complexity-reducing perceptual filters determine the way the situation is structured as tacit knowledge, like a pair of glasses on the decision maker's nose through which he sees whatever he looks at. If a document, manual, or doctrine merely states how things should be perceived and dealt with, but the relevant actors have not read and internalized its contents, trained the use of their knowledge, and undergone a "mental readjustment", then perception filters do not exist.

The spiral model

The two dimensions of knowledge, tacit knowledge and explicit knowledge, can be combined dynamically. The resulting four fields represent four modes of knowledge conversion: the conversion of tacit knowledge into tacit knowledge is called *socialization*; tacit knowledge is turned into explicit knowledge through *externalization*; explicit knowledge is processed with more explicit knowledge by *combination*; and organizational members acquire tacit knowledge from explicit knowledge by *internalization*. In Nonaka's model,[19] these four forms of knowledge conversion depend on several conditioning factors. Conversion of knowledge, and hence organizational learning, is facilitated or inhibited by different structures and actors on all levels of an organization's hierarchy, as well as by outside factors. The knowledge conversion takes place on specific platforms, called "*ba*" in the Japanese author's native language. *Ba* does not necessarily mean just a physical room: "It is a concept that unifies physical

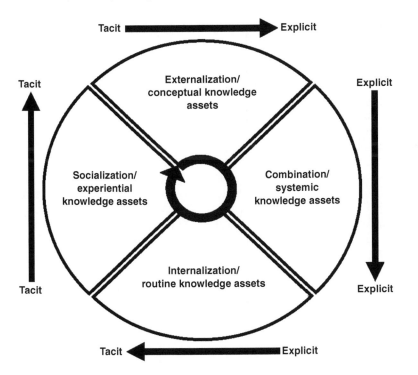

Figure 1 Nonaka's cyclical model of knowledge creation in its abstract form, and the four corresponding forms of knowledge assets.

space such as an office space, virtual space such as e-mail, and mental space such as shared ideals."[20] Examples for such spaces are drafts, review processes, statistical calculations, presentations, meetings, conferences, working lunches, coffee breaks, evaluations, training and simulations, exercises, organizational action and practical performance, and others. *Ba* means both repositories of the various forms of knowledge and the framework for knowledge conversion. In the following paragraphs, the model will be discussed and illustrated with examples from military organizations.

Internalization and routine knowledge assets

Internalization is the adoption of tacit knowledge from formalized explicit knowledge: "Internalization is the process of embodying explicit knowledge as tacit knowledge."[21] This is the closest resemblance to learning in an everyday sense, like learning to drive a car or to fly an airplane. If members of an organization learn routines and work procedures according to curricula, manuals, or formalized rules, they internalize explicit knowledge. Traineeships, internships, professional education, and seminars, but also practical experience, exercises, on-the-job-training, simulations, or physical training are examples. Internalization can happen through active or passive learning, verbally or non-verbally, involving professional education or merely ad-hoc familiarization with new ways of doing things. Internalization creates or changes *routine knowledge assets*.[22] "Through continuous exercises, certain patterns of thinking and action are reinforced and shared among organizational members."[23] Complementary to the example of a retiree who takes valuable tacit knowledge assets away from an organization, firms or bureaucracies try to acquire routine knowledge assets by hiring newcomers with a sufficiently long record of work-experience.

An example of internalization and the creation of routine knowledge assets in military public affairs can be found at DINFOS, the Defense Information School. Every public affairs officer of the US armed services has to take at least one course on military public affairs at the joint schooling facility at Fort Meade in Maryland. For one part, officers attend classroom seminars where they learn about the history of public affairs and the relevant doctrinal regulations. The reading list of the Joint Public Affairs Supervisor Course, that targets mid-level and senior public affairs specialists, include the Panama After Action Report, Lessons Learned Reports from the Persian Gulf War, various DoD directives, doctrinal publications, but also treatises of the theory of war such as Carl von Clausewitz's *On War* and Sun Tzu's *The Art of War*.[24] The uniformed students of public relations not only read and discuss texts in their classrooms; every-day problems and routine situations encountered by media officers in real-life military contingencies are simulated as well. Students interview each other and try to give their comrades a hard time by playing journalists and grilling them in front of a camera. Members of so-called "Combat Camera" units practice to take photos in the idyllic meadows surrounding the school in the village-like Fort Meade. In actual combat and war those units will visually document the performance of other units and disseminate a selection of their digital imagery for public affairs usage and release to the commercial media.[25]

Socialization and experiential knowledge assets

If tacit knowledge is adopted or invented from tacit knowledge, *socialization* takes place. "Socialization is the process of bringing together tacit knowledge through shared experiences."[26] Because tacit knowledge resides in routines and procedures, an important precondition for communicating tacit knowledge is that the organization's members share the same experiences. Socialization takes place when a team or a group of people who share specific experiences interact and reflect their work. Due to its informal nature, tacit knowledge is often articulated in analogies and metaphors – which only intuitively make sense to people who share the same experiences and make no sense to outsiders.[27] At this stage, knowledge is not corroborated or tested yet, and there is a high propensity for error. Military examples for socialization – in the model's use of the term – are informal meetings in an officers' club, discussion rounds in educational facilities, conferences, informal After Action Reviews, and the like. It is in this conversion mode where new concepts, ideas, and perspectives usually *originate*. Such new, untested, and undocumented ideas are called *experiential knowledge assets*.[28] The medium for storage for experiential knowledge is the personnel, which makes it difficult be sold or purchased or imitated easily. Levinthal and March argue that the innovative potential of an organization can be increased if it deliberately avoids socializing all new members as quickly as possible.[29] While new members of an organization learn the dominant routines and ways of doing things from colleagues, the codes and routines, in turn, "learn" from new members who might deviate from the norm in a useful way.

An example from the US Army's War College in Carlisle, Pennsylvania, illustrates socialization. From 3 to 5 September 2003, the Center for Strategic Leadership at the war college hosted a conference entitled: *Reporters on the ground: the military and media's joint experience during Operation Iraqi Freedom*. More than 100 representatives from different command levels of the Army, the Marines, and the DoD were brought together with embedded reporters, unilaterals, and news editors. Almost all participants shared personal media-military experience in the recent Iraq operation, although in different positions. The event had the purpose to reflect upon the war and its coverage. Lead questions were whether the objectives for DoD and the media were achieved; whether military–media relations were improved; and what could be done to enhance the program in future. Discussions in the After Action Workshop were highly detailed, long, honest, remarkably open-spirited, constructive, and sometimes rather emotional.[30]

Externalization and conceptual knowledge assets

If explicit knowledge is distilled and extracted from tacit knowledge, so-called *externalization* takes place. "Externalization is the process of articulating tacit knowledge as explicit knowledge," in Nonaka's words.[31] Dialogue triggers the articulation of new explicit concepts, and this fragile new knowledge is then documented and recorded. If a team of skilled workers sits down and puts its experiences into a memo, a presentation, or a manual, the workers externalize their tacit knowledge, but also reduce it through abstraction. As soon as new knowledge is made explicit, it can be shared by third persons, such as colleagues in other units, superiors, or external onlookers like researchers of organizational change. It can also be sold, stolen, or reproduced. Discussion rounds, presentations, email-conversations, or taking down protocols during meetings and workshops are other examples of turning tacit knowledge into explicit knowledge in a process of externalization. Examples from a military context are what earlier have been called "informal doctrine": presentations, drafts, conference reports, transcripts, curricula in academies, articles in military periodicals. These documents constitute *conceptual knowledge assets*. Conceptual knowledge assets are, by definition, not authorized and broadly disseminated. A new idea or concept originates as an experiential knowledge asset, then it is discussed and debated and made explicit, for instance in a presentation, in an essay, or in an online forum. Before an idea or a concept in the next step can become a systemic knowledge asset, such as a manual, guideline or a patent, it needs to be tested, consolidated, and authorized. This involves a review process by subject matter experts and the organizational hierarchy's higher echelons.

A military example of a conceptual knowledge asset is an After Action Review. Such reviews are feedback mechanisms that primarily provide information to commanders, but also help reflect all participants on their own performance. Once a unit has completed training or a mission, the AAR tries to capture the deficiencies and to identify the mistakes encountered by the unit. Error detection is the method's main purpose. A similar feedback tool, the so-called battle summary, used after trainings and simulations, is the main part of a "take-home package" used to identify and assess the "mission essential task list."[32] Colonel Gunzelman, senior trainer in a US Combat Maneuver Training Center, argues that the summaries should be drafted and processed as quickly after the training as possible: "O/C [observer/controller] teams must be able to create summaries as soon as possible after a fight concludes while their impressions are clear and focused – catching up with the paperwork at the end of a rotation is unacceptable."[33] In the official language of doctrine, "the purpose of the AAR is to provide feedback essential to correcting training deficiencies. Feedback should be direct and on the spot."[34] The demanded speed in order to capture the impressions of fresh experiences highlights the importance of tacit experiential knowledge.

Combination and systemic knowledge assets

Explicit knowledge can be merged and integrated with already existing explicit knowledge through *combination*: "Combination is the process of connecting discrete elements of explicit knowledge into a set of explicit knowledge that is more complex and systematic than any of its parts."[35] This phase of the model's cycle is often performed in a formalized and even technical manner, for instance by using computing systems and databases, such as in a financial report. In practice, combination entails three components. First, explicit knowledge has to be gathered from inside or outside the organization; second, it needs to be disseminated among the relevant organizational members; and finally the explicit knowledge is edited in order to increase its applicability. Systematized and packaged explicit knowledge is called *systemic knowledge assets*. Of all four forms of knowledge assets, the systemic kind is most easily accessible and retrievable. Systemic knowledge assets can be data-sets, official documents, specifications, manuals, guidelines, or, in the military, doctrinal publications and directives. These records can be sold, purchased, published, or stolen. In organizations in the security sector like the military and intelligence services, and in firms that try to hide newly developed technical know-how, such knowledge is often protected and classified. The process of creating, testing, authorizing, and disseminating systemic knowledge assets involves power. This is particularly evident in the case of documents that have a law-like character, such as constitutions, binding internal rules, or directives. The authority of the person signing, issuing, or developing such a document weighs its significance.

The model illustrates the role of culture. Organizational culture is part of an organization's tacit knowledge assets and thus a medium that records the lessons from the past. Consequently, scholars of organizational learning described culture as a form of memory. Ariane Berthoin Antal speaks of "organizational culture as a medium of storage."[36] Edgar Schein argues that "culture is an accumulation of past learning."[37] This logic also applies to military organizations: "Specific military organizations certainly have specific organizational cultures in the same sense that business theory describes corporate cultures," writes Johnston in *Parameters*. He argues that "an army's behavior in battle will almost certainly be more a reflection of its character or culture than of the contents of its doctrinal manuals."[38] The officer considers the soldiers' mindset more important for an army's performance than the content of a book or manual. Mindset change, Johnston contends, is a reaction to vivid experience. He introduces the term "doctrinal dissonance" to refer to the difference between what is written in field manuals and the way that an army actually behaves on the battlefield. The model sheds some light on doctrinal dissonance. Official doctrinal publications are, in the model's terminology, authoritative systemic knowledge assets. The problem with explicit knowledge assets is their retrieval. They might not be active organizational knowledge in the heads of current decision makers but only passive organizational knowledge that is stored in some rarely visited library or archive, with little effect on actual performance. Routine knowledge assets, in contrast, do not have to be retrieved, because they are the working memory of the organization's members. On a tactical level, routines predetermine a decision's orientation phase, and thus the speed of action. Routine knowledge assets by nature are engrained in experience and traditions. And traditions can be a significant hindrance to learning and a source of cultural conservatism. If change and reform of systemic knowledge assets does not translate into a change of tacit routines and standard procedures, then we observe what Johnston called "doctrinal dissonance."

Spinning the spiral

So far the distinction in tacit and explicit knowledge has been outlined and four forms of knowledge assets were discussed. The model, until now, was described in a rather structuralistic fashion. The role of agency in the organizational learning process as well as the influence of the external environment remained underemphasized: who does the actual work and what are the concrete real world challenges? Individuals who learn and act as well as external pressures on individual and organizational action are crucial facilitators (or interrupters) of innovation and learning. Several studies on doctrinal change and military innovation identified a list of external as well as internal factors necessary to facilitate change. Those drivers will now be incorporated into the spiral model. The environment, technology, leadership, teams, and the ability to unlearn are seen as the principal drivers (or blockers) of strategic innovation.

The environment

Public sector organizations operate in a convoluted environment. They not only have to deal with citizens and customers, technological change, other bureaucracies, parliamentary turnover, and evaluations. Public sector organizations in a democratic system operate in a normative environment with complex relations of accountability and subordination to other institutions – the executive, the legislature, the judicative, the electorate, and the fourth estate. The situation in the case of military organizations is even more complex, adding the defense industries, the vast web of security organizations, foreign allied militaries, potential and actual adversaries, foreign populations, and even geography or the weather to the environment. This complexity makes it difficult to outline environmental influences in a systematic manner. Therefore only the environment that is of immediate importance for the DoD's public affairs performance will be considered here.

External influences are an important driver of change. Most models of organizational learning see the external environment as the major trigger of innovation.[39] A complex and continuously changing environment requires a much faster and more innovative learning behavior of an organization than a stable one. But environments do not only motivate change, they also constrain organizational behavior, and exclude certain options from the spectrum of possible reactions. For the US military, some of the operational environment's features are stable, some are following a trend, some are not predictable at all and

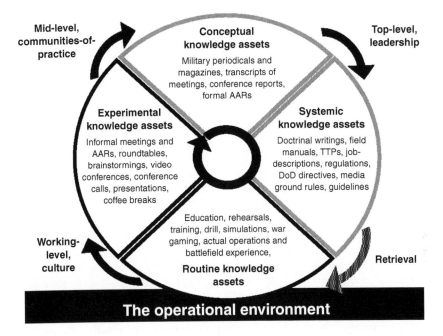

Figure 2 The abstract cyclical learning model applied to military organizations, including determinants and drivers of the learning process.

highly case dependent. To understand this, it is necessary to distinguish at least
four types of external environments.

The *normative environment* constrains behavior. Political and public organizations, by design, are accountable to a range of individuals and other institutions. Government accountability, and therefore military accountability, is
ultimately grounded in the American constitution, and the country's constitution
and legal code. The public affairs offices and sub-organizations of the US armed
forces are the institutional reaction to the military's accountability towards the
American people and their elected representatives. The most important military
publication, Joint Publication 1, illustrates this:

> We in the Armed Forces of the United States must account for our actions
> with the American people whom we serve, by dealing openly and well with
> the representatives of the nation's free press. We are also responsible for
> protecting classified or sensitive information related to the national security
> and will be challenged by the news media concerning such information. It is
> our duty as members of the Armed Forces to balance these demands in a
> responsible and intelligent fashion.
>
> (US Department of Defense, *Joint Warfare of the Armed Forces of the
> United States*, JP 1, 1995)

Though legal obligations could never be used by media organizations to appeal against the military in court, they influence military public affairs significantly.[40] The Smith-Mundt Act of 1948 and two subsequent amendments, as the Department of Defense makes clear, "prohibit PA operations from using propaganda techniques to intentionally misinform the US public, Congress, or US media about military capabilities and intentions in ways that influence US decision makers and public opinion."[41] The internal military distinction between "psychological operations," targeted at adversarial audiences, and "public affairs," directed at the American public, is legally grounded.

Particularly in the case of military organizations, the *political environment* is a second constraint. Clausewitz wrote in 1832 that "war is not merely an act of policy but a true political instrument, a continuation of political intercourse, carried on with other means."[42] War, that is, is not an activity controlled exclusively by the military. The US President's byline "commander-in-chief" epitomizes the primacy of politics even in times of war. It is the political leadership in the White House that makes personnel decisions, that determines the grand-strategic direction of national security, and sometimes demands its share of operational and tactical decisions as well. This is where the media comes in: "Dramatic media coverage at the outset of a military action can rapidly influence public and political opinion and affect strategic decisionmaking," doctrine makes unmistakably clear.[43] Talking to the media, soldiers have learned, can be like talking to your superiors in Washington. Colonel Guy Shields, the director of the Coalition Press Information Center in Kuwait during the war in 2003, explained: "Because of instantaneous reporting from the battlefield, the media were inside our decision cycle."[44] News management and pubic affairs, therefore, can be regarded as a major effort to "negotiate the political environment" by trying to manage the reactions of external actors the military has to deal with.[45] Those actors include not only the domestic and international electorates but also the legislature, the executive, allied governments, and the adversary's civilian and military leadership: public affairs is not merely about the public.

A third external influence of eminent importance is the *conflict environment*. One of the conflict environment's determinants is geography. For the British in the Malvinas/Falklands conflict, for instance, it was possible to control the journalists' access as well as the information the press tried to relay to London because the conflict took place at such a geographically remote location. Things clearly look different if a military operation takes place in a densely populated urban area. The Joint Chiefs of Staff recognize that the news media coverage of operations in a city is more intense than in other environments. They point to the relative proximity of civilian sources and communications facilities that are easily available to journalists.[46] Another important characteristic of the conflict environment are the platforms and weapon systems that are being used by the US military. The Nato campaign Allied Force in Kosovo in 1999 was rather unusual in that it was an operation conducted solely airborne. This had obvious repercussions for the conflict's media coverage: journalists could not accompany ground troops – be it embedded or with a pool – because there were no ground troops.

Technology

Finally, the *technological environment* is a determinant of public affairs innovation. Technological sophistication of both the media's and the military's communication equipment grew rapidly, and will continue to do so. Technology's influence does not remain external to an organization. Armies have to reconcile a rapid and revolutionary technological change with a traditional, conservative, and rigid organizational culture. Accordingly the information revolution is pushing the organization into two ways: it creates external pressure to act, and it enables new instruments and means to react. The initial version of the *Joint Doctrine on Information Operations*, a 130-page document published in 1998, illustrates both.

In the Department of Defense, the term "information environment" refers to the aggregate of all individuals, organizations, and systems that collect, disseminate, or process information. That information environment is understood as immensely complex, without fixed boundaries, and multi-dimensional. Interconnected systems, predominantly of a technical nature, coalesce into an expanding "Global Information Infrastructure" (GII):

> The GII is the worldwide interconnection of communications networks, computers, data bases, and consumer electronics that make vast amounts of information available to users. It encompasses a wide range of equipment, including cameras, scanners, keyboards, facsimile machines, computers, switches, compact disks, video and audio tape, cable, wire, satellites and satellite ground stations, fiber-optic transmission lines, networks of all types, televisions, monitors, printers, and much more. The GII includes more than just the physical facilities used to store, process, and display information. The personnel who make decisions and handle the transmitted information constitute a critical component of the GII.
>
> (US Department of Defense, *Joint Doctrine for Information Operations*,
> JP 3–13, 1998, p. I-13–14)

The described technological developments are not under the control of the Department of Defense, and they constitute a drastic change for the organization. The reaction had to be just as profound in order to ensure success and survival.

Technology as enabler

Technology, more specifically information technology, creates not only pressure and vulnerabilities for the US military: "The growth of information systems and technologies," the Joint Chiefs of Staff in the Pentagon point out, "offers continuing potential for exploiting the power of information in joint warfighting."[47] The definition of information operations (IO) includes an offensive as well as a defensive dimension. The Pentagon defines IO as "actions taken to affect adversary information and information systems while defending one's own information and information systems."[48] On page one of the Air Force's doctrine on Information Operations, it is argued that information is itself "a weapon and a target." The list of such weapons that were created and enabled by advances in communication technology is long: electronic warfare, computer network attack and computer network defense, new ways of physical attack, counterpropaganda operations, information assurance, and public affairs operations. The embedded media program was not merely a reaction to technological environmental pressure, the new policy was also enabled by the latest advances in modern communications technology. In 2003, for the first time in history, the technological equipment at the hands of the commercial media outlets was sophisticated enough to allow live coverage of rapid front-line movements and combat scenes without creating logistical problems for the military.

Leadership

Both sets of drivers identified so far, environments and technology, are not actors. If an organization – be it a private company, a military bureaucracy, or a loosely defined terrorist network – is meant to implement change, somebody has to make decisions and take action. In management studies and organizational theory, large organizations and bureaucracies were traditionally regarded as hierarchical, rational, information-processing machines.[49] Accordingly agency-based approaches focus on the top-management and generally assume that change can only be created from the top-down, particularly in rigidly hierarchical organizations. Military organizations are often invoked as prototypes of hierarchical and change-averse organizations in order to underscore the role of leadership.[50] The same focus on leadership can indeed be observed in the body of literature on military innovation, where – as discussed earlier – the debate is focused on the civilian leadership's influence versus the military's top brass, though the tendency to neglect mid- and lower-levels of the organizational hierarchy has been recognized in both research areas.[51] Recent approaches in the literature on management and organizational behavior have begun to overcome that narrow view and started to focus on the middle-management and employees with front-line contact as sources of problem-solving practical knowledge. A leader, then, needs to be open for input from lower levels. Berthoin Antal *et al.*, for instance, discuss this openness as "polycentric learning forms" in organizations in which decision makers draw the inspiration for their decisions from informal meetings and internal oral communications. In "monocentric organizations," by contrast, formal and written forms of communication structures are dominant.[52]

Communities-of-practice

Lower- and mid-level employees have few chances of becoming agents of organizational change or organizational learning as long as they act individually.

Therefore motivated individuals often group autonomously in so-called "communities-of-practice." The defining feature of a community-of-practice is that it is self-emerging rather than created in a top-down manner. Members of such communities find themselves in similar situations, share the same practical experiences and often a penchant for pragmatic problem solving. Through their front line contact, communities-of-practice foster out-of-the-box thinking. Their problem exposure enables them to recognize changes in the environment often before the leadership higher up the hierarchy does. Communities-of-practice, moreover, can span organizational boundaries and even include outside actors, and are in a position to ignore established patterns, precepts and traditional expectations.[53] Brown and Duguid emphasize this deviation from the organizational norm as an asset: "Communities-of-practice ... develop a rich, fluid, noncanonical world view to bridge the gap between their organization's static canonical view and the challenge of changing practice. This development is inherently innovative."[54]

The term community-of-practice has gained popularity beyond the field of management studies. Today the US Army is not only acquainted to the concept, the Pentagon even spends money to create the infrastructure to foster communities-of-practice, shortened somewhat martially to COPs.[55] Scholarly research on military innovation neglects the role such self-organized groups play. An example for a community-of-practice is an officer's club, where informal lunchtime discussions often foster creative team-spirit and innovative ideas.[56] A more peculiar example is the companycommand.com website. It began as a private project and was later sponsored by the Army. The online-forum's main target group are company-level commanders. In on-screen discussions they share recent experiences, stories, anecdotes, and ideas for improvement. Commanders can post a problem and invite answers from other members of the online community. On its entry page, the welcome message read as follows: "If you are a past, present, or future company commander, CompanyCommand.com is your professional forum! Join with us, tap into the experience of others, share your knowledge, participate, make a difference, and improve the profession!"[57] Early 2004, when the US army did a massive troop rotation into and out of Iraq, with 250,000 soldiers either returning home or going to Iraq, the website was extensively used for the transfer of expertise. In sometimes relentless but valuable detail, the internet forum helped to transfer knowledge from one shift of soldiers to the next. One commander, Captain Morgan, advises online that every soldier in the unit should carry a tourniquet sufficiently long to cut off the gush of blood from major leg wounds inflicted by roadside bombs: "Trust me," he adds, "it saved four of my soldiers' lives."[58]

In an article in *Military Review* in 2002, Major Peter Kilner discussed the website as an example of communities-of-practice (his terminology). He argued that communities-of-practice perform an important function by speeding up and shortening the link between hands-on experience in the field and formalized techniques and procedures that are put into manuals:

Army doctrine writers could leverage COPs to decrease the time it takes to develop and field new doctrine. COPs make possible an integrative model of knowledge management that would speed the flow of knowledge between leaders in the field and doctrine developers in the schoolhouses.[59]

The doctrinal process, the author argues, is in dire need of an overhaul and could be speeded up with the help of such new methods: "Those who write doctrine could then learn in real time as the field is learning." According to Kilner, it is "not an overstatement" to say that communities-of-practice have the potential to transform the way the Army works, "helping it to become a knowledge-based learning organization that is even more able to educate and train its leaders, develop its doctrine, and inspire commitment from its people."[60]

Unlearning and culture

Many corporations and some public sector organizations strive to optimize their performance. But concentrating on a particular successful competence and gradually improving time-tested routines or technologies may lead to competency traps. Success can weaken the ability of an organization to unlearn and reorient rapidly: "When actions yield apparently good results, organizations tend to repeat them, and repeated actions eventually become standard operating procedures," Starbuck and Hedberg point out, two of the idea's pioneers.[61] That risk highlights the need for organizations to unlearn. But long-term success often has the opposite effect, as it weakens an organization's ability to thoroughly unlearn and reorient its strategy, thus blinding an organization to both superior approaches as well as new threats and risks.[62] This warning holds true for military organizations as well. In an article in *Joint Forces Quarterly*, Barry McCaffrey, one of the Persian Gulf War's most aggressive generals who led the Army's 24th Mechanized Division, echoes the concern about competency traps, though without using the scholarly terminology: "Focusing doctrine on past successes can blind commanders to rapidly evolving asymmetrical threats which may target predictable US military doctrine, leadership, and equipment in the future."[63] Unlearning is conceptually subsumable under learning.[64] While learning is an increase in the choice of options, unlearning decreases the choice of potential behaviors.

If an organization faces a rapidly changing environment, adherence to formerly successful routines can become particularly risky and dangerous. Exposed to tactical stress, its members, lacking appropriate routines, will be disoriented and produce flawed or slow decisions. When the Tofflers were approached by officers Morelli and Starry and asked to do some out-of-the-box thinking, it was precisely to break the standard and routine way of thinking about war and to offer an alternative perspective. To maintain its flexible conservatism, an army needs to acquire both stable routines, enabling continuity of performance under extreme conditions, as well as stable routine-breaking routines, enabling discontinuity of performance and innovative behavior if external conditions change too significantly to continue as before. Routine-breaking means that obsolete and discarded standards are intentionally abandoned.[65] As a first step, disconfirmation of the seemingly successful procedure has to set in; a flaw first needs to be recognized.[66] Once the problem is identified, decision makers can apply different methods to implement unlearning. An extreme way of unlearning for an organization is to discharge employees, specifically influential employees such as managers and leaders who remain unable to shed outdated views, attitudes, or procedures. A narrow focus on leadership, again, underestimates how deeply a dysfunctional set of behaviors can be rooted in an organization's culture – in its routine knowledge assets – even after top-management has been exchanged and relevant regulations have been replaced. A slower but more promising form of unlearning is a generational shift of staff.

Adjusting the model

The preceding section identified groups of actors and external pressures which drive the learning spiral and fuel the knowledge conversion process. But the model still suffers three major shortfalls. It seems to assume an evolutionary growth of knowledge; it largely ignores the crucial role of hierarchy, authority, and power; and it does not sufficiently incorporate interrupters.

Incommensurability

The image of a spiral may invoke the impression that the model assumes a cumulative or even evolutionary process of knowledge creation, leading teleologically to an incremental improvement of organizational action towards an optimal behavior. This is not the case, as there is no safe optimum. Organizations which operate in a turbulent environment confront the problem that lessons they have extracted from the past may become useless because the world around them has changed in the interim. Censorship and transmission control of news stories like in the Falklands, Grenada, and Panama, for instance, cannot be an option in an age of live satellite television, mobile phones, blogs, and internet cafés. The lesson of 20 years ago would turn into a grave mistake if applied again. The Pentagon realized this: "The speed with which information passes through the GIE [global information environment] makes censorship of military operations impractical, if not impossible."[67] As a result, the organization had to "tear down obsolete mental maps", as Hedberg put it,[68] and unlearn old routines and outdated procedures. The importance of unlearning and organizational forgetting shows that the model is not assuming an incremental approximation of organizational knowledge assets to the "truth." At two different times in history (and even at one given moment, as will be shown later), the same organization's rules and guidelines can be contradictory. Organizational knowledge is incommensurable as it cannot be judged or measured by the same standard at different times.[69]

This inextricably relates to a second problem. The notion of learning does not imply that organizational performance improved "objectively." Using a neutral and external measurement of improvement to assess performance, as opposed to the intended improvement, would lead to insurmountable problems of standardization and judgment. This raises the question, then, of what learning actually means when used in an organizational context. The criterion must be the decision makers' perception. If the US military produces AARs, battle assessments, and lessons learned which become official doctrine or conventional wisdom in the organization and are then applied in practice, then it has learned. Learning is whatever the relevant actors in the organization believe to be an improvement of past behavior. It is irrelevant whether the insights are "objectively" correct or false, what is relevant is that they are used in decision making. According to this understanding, if an organization learns an appropriate lesson, turns it into systemic knowledge, but does not use it, it has not learned; if it adapts an inappropriate lesson, and acts upon it, it has. Organizational learning can be defined as *the development of insights, knowledge, and associations between past actions, the perceived effectiveness of those actions, and future actions.* As used in this study, learning is a purely formal term.

Hierarchy and power

Scholars of organizational behavior usually distinguish two levels of learning by the *quality* of the learning experience, not by the level of hierarchy on which it occurs. Lower-level learning – not to be confused with a hierarchy's lower levels[70] – takes place within a given set of rules and within a given organizational structure; it involves the incremental improvement of already existing routines and procedures. An alternative term is "single-loop learning."[71] Argyris and Schön illustrate this simple stimulus-response (S/R) type of organizational learning with the metaphor of a thermometer: like a house thermostat, organizations simply react to changes in the environment by adapting a given procedure. A more sophisticated form of change is "double-loop learning," the ability of an organization not to optimize a given procedure within existing frameworks, but to create entirely new procedures, approaches, or strategies. "Higher-level learning"[72] accordingly refers to the readjustment of rules and norms. It involves the development of new frameworks, worldviews, and procedures. Nonaka harshly criticizes this two-tiered view arguing that the distinction assumes both a "mechanistic view of organizations" and the possibility to come up with an objective "right answer." Organizations do not suddenly and surprisingly create a new worldview, he argues, instead they continuously create new knowledge that involves new perspectives and frameworks. Double-loop learning, then, is already "built into" the knowledge-creating model.[73]

In order to reconcile and connect those seemingly contradictory positions, it is helpful to use the organizational hierarchy at which the learning occurs as the distinctive criterion of types of learning, not whether a routine is changed inherently or abandoned entirely. The ideal spiral of knowledge creation spans three hierarchical layers: ground-level employees, middle-management, and top-management.[74] Accordingly three types of learning can be distinguished. Inspired by the spiral model's terminology, I will distinguish between experiential learning, conceptual learning, and systemic learning. This taxonomy incorporates power. While power and authority play no role in experiential learning and only a minor role in conceptual learning, they are vital ingredients for systemic learning.

Experiential learning takes place when routine knowledge assets are changed on the basis of experiential knowledge assets

Experiential learning is an immediate reaction of individuals or teams to everyday problems their unit or department confronts. This type of learning operates on swift and personal feedback loops which may entirely short-circuit documentation and the explicit dimension and thus occur merely tacitly. Experiential learning has a real-time impact on organizational behavior, it is S/R, single-loop, and behavioral, and involves no authorization by middle managers or top leaders. This makes the storage as well as the dissemination of routine knowledge assets created or altered by experiential learning very difficult. It makes it almost impossible to control and manage experiential learning. Externalization, the conversion of tacit knowledge assets into explicit knowledge assets, may not take place at all. Examples are informal After Action Reviews common in the US Army. Such sessions are conducted immediately after training, and they take only a couple of minutes to be completed. Experiential learning does not require authorization by superiors. An AAR is such an effective tool precisely because it deliberately ignores relations of authority during the session. Other examples of experiential learning loops are online forums. Those forums often transgress departmental or even organizational boundaries and can play a major role in experiential learning processes. The internet – or intranet – has long been used as a platform of experiential knowledge exchange in the private sector and is becoming increasingly popular within the US military. A worker or soldier encounters a concrete problem, he posts a question to colleagues sharing his experience by email, and gets a straight answer within a few hours or minutes from a co-worker, possibly sitting in front of her computer screen on another continent. Experiential learning has positive as well as negative aspects. It is superior from a short-term view, in terms of speed, responsiveness, saturation with detail, and efficiency. It is inferior in its long-term implications, outreach, and fallibility.

Conceptual learning takes place when routine knowledge assets are changed on the basis of conceptual knowledge assets

Conceptual learning is facilitated by the immediately higher levels of the organizational hierarchy. It takes place on a unit, department, or branch level. Conceptual learning produces and uses some form of explicit output, such as reports, presentations or articles – what earlier has been called conceptual knowledge assets. This form of learning includes the editing of results, negotiations about

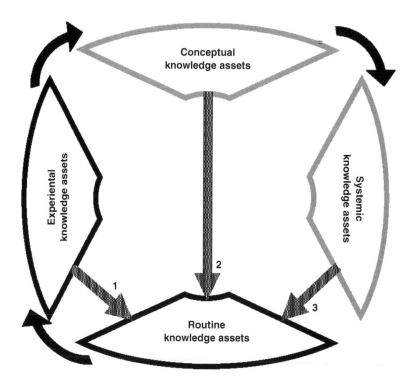

Figure 3 Adjusted cyclical model with three forms of retrieval: experiential learning (1), conceptual learning (2) and systemic learning (3). The first two forms of learning are shortcutting the ideal-type learning cycle depicted in Figure 2.

wording and about what kinds of statements to include. The creation of conceptual knowledge assets involves authorization by middle-managers or heads of departments, but top leadership is not consulted. An example of a conceptual learning cycle is the formal After Action Report the US Army's 3rd Infantry Division (ID) drafted after the invasion phase of Operation Iraqi Freedom. It contained recommendations which contradicted Pentagon guidelines, and was disseminated horizontally among other units using non-official channels. Other examples for conceptual knowledge assets are articles published in military journals. The publication process involves authorization by the journal's editors, for instance by the Army War College in the case of *Parameters*, the school's own periodical. While such articles are part of the doctrinal debate, they do not have the weight of officially sanctioned documents, such as doctrine, directives, or other guidelines. They are voluntary reading for engaged individuals who actively search for new perspectives and pull the information from known repositories, like journals, websites, or colleagues. Self-assembled communities-of-practice are powerful facilitators of conceptual learning, as they help to externalize tacit experiential knowledge and thus prepare it to be disseminated to a broader audience, but they lack the power to lend company-wide significance to the new knowledge. Conceptual knowledge assets cannot be disseminated in the organization with the same authority as systemic knowledge assets. If employees or soldiers operating on an organization's middle and lower levels use and apply conceptual knowledge assets before or without their official authorization, then conceptual learning comes to pass. The systemic level and the authorization by senior leaders is then bypassed and cut out of the learning cycle. Conceptual learning can include the creation of new procedures and the elimination of obsolete ones.

Systemic learning takes place when routine knowledge assets are changed on the basis of systemic knowledge assets

Systemic learning reflects the full learning cycle as introduced above. It involves top-management decisions on the reallocation of resources, the redesign of the organizational structure, a strategic reorientation, or a redefinition of traditional ways of doing or perceiving things by issuing binding guidelines and directives. Systemic knowledge assets by definition have to be authorized by top-management. Once in place, they have repercussions for the entire organization and they need to be communicated to all relevant staff members. Doctrinal publications, directives, and guidelines are systemic documents and required reading for all targeted personnel. This sharply contrasts to the voluntary readings of internal periodicals or blogs. In the case of the Department of Defense, a new directive of the Secretary of Defense is an example of a systemic knowledge asset intended to change routines. A necessary component of double-loop learning is that the top-management of an organization (or sub-organization) authorizes the change. On the other hand, though, double-loop learning is not a necessary feature of systemic learning. If routine knowledge assets are only incrementally changed on the basis of top-level authorized systemic knowledge assets, so that intentionally no significant change of mindset or procedures is involved, systemic learning has nevertheless occurred.

Interrupters

The spiral model does not assume that learning cycles are perfect and not interrupted. Organizational learning processes in practice deviate significantly from the abstract four step cycle. Interrupters have to be accounted for. In reality, the learning cycle is often interrupted at very different stages, with each learning type facing a specific set of problems. The next paragraphs will focus not on the interrupters on the knowledge creation-side (black arrows in Figure 3), which have already been discussed, but on blockers on the retrieval and implementation-side (hatched arrows in Figure 3).

A problem with *experiential learning* is its limited reach. It remains confined to a small and specialized group of individuals who encounter the same problems and share their insights. If the next layer of an organization is not encouraging or at least receptive to articulated new knowledge coming from the lower level, then there will only be experiential learning. A result of its limited reach inside a large organization, and as a result of its lack of explication and documentation, experiential learning suffers a high risk of accidental organizational forgetting.[75] If a small unit which has invented a superior procedure but never disseminated its new knowledge is dissolved, then its knowledge is unintentionally lost. Because experiential learning shortcuts the learning spiral, strategic reorientation (or double-loop learning) cannot occur on this level. Single-loop learning takes place even if the ideal-type learning spiral as introduced above is interrupted in the way that routine knowledge assets are *only* changed on the basis of experiential knowledge assets – although higher organizational levels might not be aware of it.

Conceptual learning faces its own set of difficulties. Three stand out. First, it is highly selective. By definition conceptual knowledge is not, or not yet, authorized by top-management. Its dissemination within the organization therefore happens on a largely voluntary basis. Only engaged and highly motivated individuals may spend their time reading internal periodicals, browse the intranet, write blogs, or discuss and draft suggestions to improve the workflow. Such selectivity can lead to uneven improvements and unforeseen consequences. This relates to the second problem, conceptual learning's high dependency on unofficial distribution platforms. Because conceptual knowledge assets are not authorized, they cannot be distributed on official channels, like directives or emails from the CEO's office. If an organization thus does not offer unofficial channels, such as internal publications, email lists, chat rooms, workshops, and a culture that tolerates criticism, then conceptual knowledge assets will not be disseminated and conceptual learning will not take place. Third, conceptual knowledge is prone to error and emotions. Fresh ideas which come up in presentations or internal publications have usually never been tested in action nor reviewed and authorized by other leaders within the organization. It therefore requires risk-taking and sometimes disobedient sub-units to implement changes that go beyond minor adjustments.

Systemic learning faces problems of sluggishness, vagueness, dissemination, and implementation. A major doctrinal publication, like the *Doctrine on Joint Operations*, is a political document which carries authority and weight, potentially resulting in large volumes of resource reallocations; political stakes can be high. As a result, cumbersome multi-party negotiations about content and formulations are slowing the speed of the doctrinal review process. The revision cycle of a joint doctrinal publication can easily take several years to be completed. If the organizational environment is ephemeral – such as the media and the technological environment in the case of information operations – a crucial disadvantage of systemic knowledge assets is that they are quickly outdated. A second effect of the high significance of systemic knowledge assets is that they tend to lack precision. Both the need to compromise as well as the need to find a general formula applicable to different units and situations result in general statements in which practitioners at the front line of organizational action find little help. Inertia and vagueness, in turn, create a third effect by downgrading the reputation of systemic knowledge assets in the eyes of those who are supposed to use and implement them. And if soldiers and employees do not see much value in reading doctrinal documents or guidelines coming from the Joint Chiefs of Staff or top-management, they most certainly will not read it. All three effects are multiplied in a fast-paced high-stress work environment. This, however, does not necessarily imply that no innovations will happen. They merely get pushed down to a conceptual or even experiential learning level.

Research design and sources

The initial question of this study asked if the embedded media program was the result of a process of organizational learning. The cyclical model as introduced so far will now be reassembled along a time line and applied to the recent history of media management in the US armed forces. The result resembles a learning spiral which captures the change of routine knowledge assets and actual performance (or the lack thereof) on the basis of past experiences. Past experiences can impact routines in the three ways described above: as experiential, conceptual, or systemic learning. A genuine strategy change, however – and this applies to the development of military as well as business strategy – must be authorized by top-commanders or top-management. Decisions and actions by lower-level officers and front-line employees can be tactical or operational, and they may well have a *strategic effect*, but by design, orders from the top are needed to implement an intended strategy. Thus, to qualify as a public affairs *strategy*, the embedded media program has to be the outcome of a systemic learning process. Was this the case?

Looking through the prism of the dynamic theory of organizational knowledge creation, the answer would be affirmative if the innovative program's planning and implementation approximates the spiral pattern as illustrated in Figure 4. In order to visualize the Pentagon's learning process along the temporal dimension, the public affairs policies in the eight major US military operations since Vietnam are grouped into four phases: disastrous public affairs in Vietnam; restricted public affairs in Grenada, Panama, and the Persian Gulf War; experimental public affairs in the wars throughout the 1990s and Afghanistan; and strategic public affairs in the first phase of Operation Iraqi Freedom. The spiral model offers an *idealized* and abstract form of the cyclical process of organizational knowledge creation and only depicts the full systemic learning spiral.

The following part is structured into two layers. First, the DoD's public affairs practice and performance of each military operation since Vietnam (routines) as well as the improvisations and quick-fixes that were invented during those operations (experiential knowledge) are reviewed. The sources were manifold: interviews with officers and journalists involved; articles in military journals published after operations which review and criticize the action; official

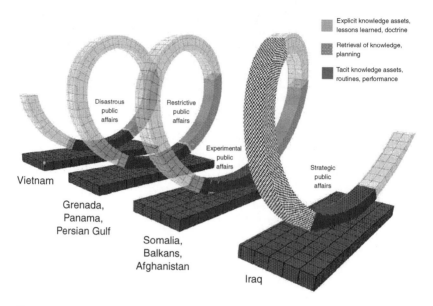

Figure 4 The cyclical model stretched over time into a spiral and applied to the US military's four phases of public affairs.

Note
The spiral pattern does not imply that the organization's performance has steadily improved, but merely that routines were changed (or not sustained) on the basis of past experiences. Each segment of the spiral will be analyzed in detail in the following chapters.

After Action Reports which give a detailed account of the events; graduation papers from war college students; newspaper articles from correspondents who wrote about the military's media management and how it affected their work; memoirs of soldiers and journalists; as well as secondary literature on the subject. The evaluation of the military's public affairs routines focused on anecdotic detail and narratives delivered by personal witnesses rather than on analyses, judgments, conclusions, and arguments derived from the events by analysts and scholars. A major problem of this method has already been mentioned: under conditions of time constraint and ad-hoc improvisation, the documentation of action is of secondary importance to the actors themselves. Routines are difficult to research and quote.

Second, the conclusions which the US armed forces debated after these experiences (conceptual knowledge) and the lessons which were authorized and incorporated into doctrine, directives, guidelines, and ground rules (systemic knowledge) were examined. Each chapter's *lessons learned* subsection draws on explicit primary military sources: official reports and lessons learned documents, articles in military periodicals written by members of the military, studies of military academies, soldiers' memoirs, joint and service doctrinal publications,

Army field manuals, DoD directives, and Public Affairs Guidances. It is not the specific details and particular events of past operations that are the focus of the lessons learned sections, but the general arguments and conclusions which public affairs officers and commanders derived from their observations, mistakes, or successes.

Part II

The history of media operations

We learned a lot in the interim.
(Colonel Jay DeFrank, Director of Press Operations, Department of Defense,
2004, on the question why the media strategy of the 1991 Iraq War was so
different from the one in 2003)

4   Disastrous public affairs
Vietnam

More than any other conflict in US history, the Vietnam War stirred bitter hostility among military officers toward the press. Correspondents and their editors were undermining the American support for the war by putting gruesome images of wounded soldiers and reports of atrocities that were committed by Americans in Vietnam on TV screens, as the military saw it. The media, those officers concluded, lost the war for them. General William Childs Westmoreland, Commander of the US forces in Southeast Asia during the peak of the Vietnam War from 1964 to 1968, was the most prominent uniformed official who argued along this line. But the reasons for the disastrous public affairs in Vietnam lie deeper, in the operational aspects of the war.

In 1955 the first US advisors were sent to Indochina to take over the training of the South Vietnamese Army from the departing French. American involvement incrementally increased over a period of several years. As a reaction to growing Vietcong (VC) pressure in Indochina, the newly elected President John F. Kennedy decided to increase the number of American military advisors from a few hundred in 1961 to 16,000 by 1963. In the summer of the following year, North Vietnamese PT boats and US destroyers clashed in the Gulf of Tonkin. The confrontation escalated the situation. North Vietnamese bases were bombed, Congress passed the Tonkin Gulf Resolution supporting President Lyndon B. Johnson's policy to "prevent further aggression," and soon Hanoi dispatched regular army units to South Vietnam where 23,000 US advisors were now assisting the ally. The Asian country was again descending into outright war. At the end of 1965, as Johnson had initiated negotiations with Hanoi and a bombing halt began, 184,300 US troops had been stationed in Vietnam and 1,636 had lost their lives. During the next two years the administration almost tripled troop levels to 485,000 while the death toll increased tenfold to more than 16,000. Mass anti-war rallies were organized in Washington and New York, and at one point demonstrators even stormed the Pentagon. The following year, 1968, proved decisive. On 30 January 1968, the North Vietnamese carried the war into 108 cities and towns by launching a major attack, the Tet offensive, named after the Vietnamese lunar New Year holiday. In the spring of 1969 the peak strength of US troop levels was attained as more than half a million US soldiers were deployed in Vietnam; General Creighton Abrams commanded

543,400 troops as the US death toll had again doubled to more than 40,000. President Nixon initiated what he called "Vietnamization" of the war: the gradual reduction and retreat of American forces from Indochina. It has often been noted that Vietnam was the first "television war." During the Korean War in the mid-1950s television had only played a minor role, both on the sender's end because it was still difficult to record film material while on the move, and on the recipient's end because television sets were still a rare exception. Vietnam, in contrast, received almost nightly coverage on US networks over a period of several years. Television was the predominant medium of news consumption by the time American military assistance was turning into undeniable military engagement and eventually outright war.

Body-counts

The crucial problem for the media coverage of Vietnam was the nature of the conflict. Other than in the previous campaigns in Korea or in the Second World War, no clear measures of progress existed. The North Vietnamese not only retained their sanctuaries in Laos and Cambodia, the enemy had a superior knowledge of the battlefield terrain and often the civilian population's hidden support. In the guerilla war the Vietcong "owned the initiative," as they controlled the speed of combat and ultimately their own casualties. The fighting mostly took place at remote outposts in inhospitable rural regions. Demarcated front lines did not exist, nor was there a clear distinction between combatants and civilians; US platoons were regularly attacked in ambushes without being able to even see the enemy. The jungle environment with its thicket, paddies, ditches, and boondocks turned into a veritable "green hell" for American GIs. War was utterly confusing and disorienting, for the soldiers who were fighting it, and even more so for the journalists who tried to cover it by making sense of the soldiers' statements after they returned from battle to the rear. The lack of solid proof for progress, in turn, created a problem of justification for the administration. Vast amounts of resources were seemingly wasted in Indochina, American lives in the tens of thousands and dollars in the billions. Because the hard facts on the war's progress were so hard to produce, the military became increasingly involved in the business of justifying and selling the war. The line between reporting the facts militarily and justifying the war politically became steadily more blurred, and the military increasingly began to symbolize a misguided policy. The infamous "body-count" illustrates this.

Internal pressure demanded that a unit's weekly situation report contain some claimed objectives. But it was rare that a valley, a hamlet, or even a town was taken from the enemy. It was equally difficult to measure captured weapons, incidents of enemy defection, villagers relocated, or areas cleared. Neither had the Joint United States Public Affairs Office (JUSPAO) gun camera footage of destroyed tanks or government buildings at its disposal, a measure of success that would only be invented decades later. Any pictures of the adversary the US was facing were rare. CBS's Bernard Kalb once referred to the Vietcong as "the most faceless foe in our history."[1] Consequently, the numbers of bodies of killed enemies became the "grisly yardstick" of success, as Colin Powell noted in his memoirs. He served two tours in Vietnam, the latter during the war's most intense phase, and had experienced the production of the body-count statistics first hand. Powell recounts a random dialogue between a commander and an operator asking for the number of enemy killed: "'How many did your platoon get?' 'I don't know. We saw two for sure.' 'Well, if you saw two, there were probably eight. So let's say ten.'" Numbers were inflated intentionally both to meet quotas of enemy killed and because some officers worked under the assumption that chances of promotion were connected to their unit's body-count. Powell eloquently sums up this logic:

> Counting bodies became a macabre statistical competition. Companies were measured against companies, battalions against battalions, brigades against brigades. Good commanders scored high body-counts. And good commanders got promoted. If your competition was inflating the counts, could you afford not to?
>
> (C.L. Powell and J.E. Persico, *My American Journey*, New York: Random House, 1995, p. 142)

Unintentional inflation by duplication arguably made things worse. Often different units of the various service branches involved in the same battle claimed the dead VC they saw in their own body-counts, thereby counting the same corpses several times. The optimistic and inflated numbers were both reported internally up the chain-of-command and presented to the press at the Saigon briefings. Neither superiors nor reporters could prove the authenticity of those numbers as the retreating Vietcong usually took their dead with them. The directive to deliver body-counts as a measure of effectiveness, however, created a detrimental organizational dynamic with dire consequences for the administration's and the US military's credibility.[2]

An entire cascade of unintended consequences ensued. First, the inflated numbers were reported up the chain-of-command to the department's military and civilian leadership. New communications and computing technology facilitated the local collection of data and their remote analysis in the Pentagon – Secretary of Defense Robert McNamara, a former manager and president of Ford Motor Company, was well known for his near obsessive belief in management practices based on "systems analysis,"[3] and the use of data and quantitative measures of effectiveness to improve processes of production. Applied to a vast military organization fighting a guerilla war in a foreign land, however, those techniques had inadvertent effects.[4] An organizational perception filter was created that turned bad news into not so bad news as the accumulated data reflected success that was just not there. The same situation that looked dismal from the bottom of the hierarchy appeared quite acceptable from the top. This internal bias to see things positively gained additional momentum when official spokespersons met the press. Flawed internal data were used to demonstrate success to the public when spokespersons, themselves relying on inflated body-count statistics and brushed-up reports, added yet another twist to the "official optimism."[5] The government, and with it the military, put its credibility on the line, and lost. That loss is best illustrated by the nickname the Saigon correspondents came up with for the official briefings.

The five o'clock follies

Official briefings in Saigon were an important source of information for many of the correspondents working in Vietnam. And there were many: 419 international news media representatives were accredited by the Military Assistance Command, Vietnam (MACV) in 1966, including support staff. In 1968, during the Tet offensive, the number had climbed to 637 accredited correspondents. After the lunar New Year offensive and the belated coverage of the My Lai massacre it declined: in 1969 there were 467 accredited correspondents; in 1970, 392; in 1971, 355; in 1972, 295; by 1974 the number of correspondents had dwindled to five.[6] Those large quantities of press representatives nevertheless may give a wrong impression. Few saw combat. The number of journalists who accompanied troops and witnessed actual hostilities and bloodshed was usually low: "No more than forty reporters were where bullets were flying," recounts the *Washington Post*'s Henry Allen, himself both veteran and journalist. During the Tet offensive probably 70 to 80 reporters saw combat.[7]

Reporters enjoyed remarkable advantages in Vietnam. The military had installed press camps throughout the country to provide "rudimentary amenities" to the newsmen when they visited combat units in the field.[8] Back from their sojourns, the correspondents had access to the comforts enjoyed by the officers in the rear echelon. Later in the war helicopters were assigned exclusively to fly reporters to units in the field. With some luck the newsmen were able to shoot some good film or produce a story at an outpost, catch a ride back to Saigon the same evening, get the product on its way to the US, and have a French dinner downtown. "You could first take a hot shower in your hotel and then go to the five o'clock follies," remembered Ron Nessen, who covered the war first as a journalist but later changed sides and worked as President Ford's White House spokesman. The information and the body-count the military briefers presented at the briefings directly contradicted the impressions the reporters were able to make first-hand: "It didn't match up," Nessen said, "what they said at the five o'clock follies and what you saw with your own eyes didn't match up."[9] The Pentagon and the State Department evidently were unhappy about being ridiculed by the reporters' phrase "five o'clock follies." Determined to end the unbearable situation the embassy decided to move the sessions to 1645.[10]

This presumably had little effect on the widening "credibility gap" which was the result of a contradiction between two perspectives.[11] It was easy for media representatives to get access to the battlefield. Freelancers only needed confirmations from three media organizations confirming their interest in using the reporter's work. They were then eligible to obtain a press card that entitled the journalists to free military ground and air transportation, interviews with field commanders, as well as meals and shelter.[12] Even communication facilities were provided by the military. Correspondents like Peter Arnett or Joseph Galloway were still in their twenties when they ventured out and not only saw combat but were sometimes involved in it, and carried and used personal weapons. For them the Saigon briefings were particularly distressing. Other than US embassy officials or top military leadership in Saigon they had seen the war in the boondocks. Henry Gole, a teacher at the Army War College in the 1980s and himself a Vietnam veteran, describes the problem:

> Energetic young journalists went on combat operations with the advisers they admired, made their observations, and then heard accounts of those operations from Saigon warriors [spokespersons] whose information had been sanitized to make good news of bad news as it was passed up the chain-of-command.
>
> (H.G. Gole, "Don't Kill the Messenger: Vietnam War Reporting in Context," *Parameters*, 1996, Winter, p. 150)

The briefings delivered by the JUSPAO were based on "hasty, fragmentary, inevitably inaccurate field reports," points out Peter Braestrup, author of one of the most widely received studies on the Vietnam War's coverage and the *Washington Post*'s former bureau chief in Saigon. Evidence of seemingly random small unit engagements dominated the briefings. Official communiqués were designed to deliver some hard facts to the wire services and to demonstrate that progress was made. As a consequence of those "years of official optimism," which then proved unfounded, the press representatives attending the meetings were dismissing all positive statements, even if they were reported dutifully and truthfully, as Braestrup observed.[13] Official and military spokespersons had lost their organization's most important public affairs asset: credibility. The American public's and the US government's psychological and geographical detachment from the grisly realities of guerilla warfare in the rice paddies and rain forests found its cynical analogue in the detachment of official language. Colonel Harry Summers, also from the Army War College and an outspoken critic of Vietnam, later wrote about the use of language during that campaign:

> In order to smooth our relations with the American people we began to use euphemisms to hide the horror of war. We became the Department of the Army (not the War Department) and our own terminology avoided mention of the battlefield. We did not kill the enemy, we inflicted casualties, we did not destroy things, we neutralized targets. These evasions allowed the notion to grow that we could apply military force in a sanitary and surgical manner. In doing so we unwittingly prepared the way for the reaction that was to follow.
>
> (H.G. Summers, *On Strategy: A Critical Analysis of the Vietnam War*, Novato: Presidio, 1982, pp. 63–4)

That reaction of the American public was protest against the war, and loss of trust in the government as well as the military. And the most intense expression of this public disappointment was triggered by the press coverage of one of the most decisive events in the entire war. Decisive precisely because of the reportage it received, not because of its military significance. On 30 January 1968, the Vietnamese lunar New Year celebration, North Vietnamese forces launched a coordinated assault.

Tet

Westmoreland declared in a speech in November 1967 in the National Press Club that the enemy could no longer conduct major operations near South Vietnam's cities. "Success lies within our grasp," he had declared somewhat optimistically.[14] Less than three months later the Vietcong, supported by the North Vietnamese Army, attacked with an estimated strength of 67,000 troops. For a brief but chaotic moment the onslaught turned Saigon into a war zone, and a small group of enemy troops even penetrated the US embassy in Saigon. Although approximately 14,000 South Vietnamese and 4,000 American soldiers were killed, the attack was a massive defeat for the North. After a few weeks the North's units were driven out of every city they attacked, and their military infrastructure and equipment was destroyed. The attackers suffered horrendous human losses, probably between 45,000 and 84,000 men.

On the morning of 1 February 1968, in Fort Leavenworth, a young officer named Powell, who later would become the chairman of the Joint Chiefs of Staff, came out of his bedroom, put on the coffeepot, turned on the TV news, and was shocked – as were many of his compatriots. The screen showed US marines as they were fighting in the American embassy in Saigon, and Vietnamese forces battling in front of the presidential palace in the heart of the ally's capital. The attack on the embassy received intense TV coverage and it was probably the first battle in Vietnam that made sense to many Americans. Eventually they could see the adversary. "The images beamed into American living rooms of a once faceless enemy suddenly popping up in the middle of South Vietnam's capital had a profound effect on public opinion," Powell remarked later, and he added, with respect to the consequences of the newscasts: "Tet marked a turning point, raising doubts in the minds of moderate Americans, not just hippies and campus radicals, about the worth of this conflict, and the antiwar movement intensified."[15] Probably more than anyone else Walter Cronkite spoke for moderate, ordinary Americans. He was host of *CBS Evening News*, the first consistently popular half-hour news show; President John F. Kennedy himself had inaugurated the first edition. Cronkite was equally shocked by the events in Vietnam of that early February. The anchorman remembers reading the news agency tapes in the newsroom in New York after the reports were coming in: "What the hell is going on? I thought we were winning the war?"[16] Cronkite, a veteran correspondent of the Second World War, decided to travel to Vietnam to inspect the situation. He toured the country and met with senior officers, even with Creighton Abrams, Westmoreland's successor, whom he knew as a colonel from the battle of the Bulge. He was still shocked by what he saw in Vietnam and became convinced that the war was lost. When Cronkite returned from the trip, he commented in heavy and memorable words on Tet in a CBS News Special, *Report from Vietnam by Walter Cronkite*: "The only national way out then will be to negotiate, not as victors, but as an honorable people who lived up to their pledge to defend democracy, and did the best they could."[17] This was Walter Cronkite calling to accept defeat in Vietnam. After his remarks – the impact of which cannot be underestimated[18] – President Lyndon B. Johnson reportedly concluded: "If I've lost Cronkite, I've lost Middle America."[19] A few weeks later the incumbent announced that he would not run for the presidency a second time.

The television images usually did not graphically show the dead and wounded. Action was unpredictable in Vietnam. Accordingly bureau chiefs were reluctant to station their expensive TV crews at some distant outpost, where chances were high that nothing might happen at all. But military operations – with few exceptions like the 1968 Tet offensive and the 1972 Easter offensive – only took place at remote outposts. This had an effect on the coverage that arrived in America's living rooms. From 1965 to 1970 only 3 per cent of all evening visual news reports from Vietnam showed "heavy battle" scenes, including Tet. But if there was a lack of graphic imagery, the year 1968 solved that problem. In retrospect, two images stand out as powerful icons that have entered the collective memory, perhaps not only in the US but world-wide, to represent the American defeat in Southeast Asia. The first one shows the Saigon police chief General Nguyen Ngoc Loan holding a gun to the head of a captured Vietcong, who was believed to have killed a major and his family. The executed officer had his hands tied behind his back. Associated Press photographer Eddie Adams took the photo during the Tet offensive, and won a Pulitzer Prize. The image captured the horrors and injustices of the war, and it raises doubts about the morality of the people American soldiers were being sacrificed for.[20] The second image was taken several years later, on 8 June 1972, also by an AP reporter, Huynh Cong "Nick" Ut. It shows a naked nine-year-old girl, Phan Thi Kim Phuc, screaming in pain as she is running along a deserted road near Trang Bang toward the photographer, her skin heavily burned by a napalm bomb, a massive explosion rising into the skies in the background. The picture became a powerful symbol for the sufferings of innocent civilians in Vietnam. Both images had a tremendous impact in the United States. The effect of those and comparable stories and images are analogous to that of a magnifying glass in the sun. The media limelight was bundled and concentrated on isolated operations, such as the Tet offensive, or even the bombardment of a single hamlet. From a professional soldier's perspective, the US armed forces won every major battle of the war.[21] From the public's perspective, however, the government, and with it the military, did not live up to its official optimism and promises.

Those were the two ingredients of the cocktail that poisoned the military–media relationship for decades to come: the gruesome images of executions or massacres in a war that is being lost strategically, as well as, from the military's perspective, the sum of tactical victories. The war, as soldiers saw it, was not really lost in the boondocks, it was lost somewhere on the way the reports took from Vietnam's rice paddies to America's mid-west. Only decades later, after an entire new school of thought on information operations had been developed during the 1990s, did official doctrine grasp the problem more adequately – and thus shift the burden of responsibility away from the media onto the US military's shoulders:

> US forces defeated the North Vietnamese on the battlefield during the Tet offensive of 1968, but the information battle was the strategic battle that the US forces most needed to win, both within South Vietnam and at home. By ignoring the information battle, the overwhelming US tactical victory was a strategic defeat.[22]

Such sober discussion and analysis of the new dynamics on the battlefield was difficult, if not impossible, in the emotionally charged atmosphere in the post-Vietnam American military.

Lessons learned

The media lost the war for the military – this was the major lesson the US military drew from the Vietnam War: "America's professional soldiers blamed the media for stressing the enemy's Tet successes while overlooking the loss of infrastructure that had taken generations to build. Ergo, bad media, true to form, undermined the noble efforts of American soldiers and Marines."[23] Another commentator, in the same journal, casts a critical eye on the Army's heritage of its defeat in Indochina: "Unfortunately, one of the erroneous legacies of the Vietnam War has been the belief, which is especially prevalent in the military, that it was the media that lost the conflict," an article in *Military Review* said in 1992.[24] This lesson was not analytically developed in formal After Action Reports, and the legacy was not rationally passed down to the next generation of officers in doctrinal publications. The lesson was learned tacitly, and conserved in narratives and anecdotes, often blunt and emotional.

The effect was a hostile attitude toward the press. It permeated the entire organization, from its top-management down to the captains, lieutenants, corporals, and sergeants. The former commanding general, Westmoreland, expressed what many believed but did not dare to say publicly: "Most South Vietnamese units fought well, but it was not the 'in thing' in media circles to say anything good about the South Vietnamese," he opined in an article. "The media misled the American people by their reporting of 'Tet,' and even a number of officials in Washington were taken in." And the general makes clear how, in his opinion, the unfavorable and unfair media coverage penetrated the decision loop in Washington, finally making his job impossible: "The mood of the Congress, a reflection of public attitudes, in turn influenced profoundly by the media –

particularly by daily television reports – grew further away from the policy of the executive branch."[25] Westmoreland was by no means an exception. Douglas Kinnard, himself a retired general, surveyed more than 100 top officers who served in command positions in Vietnam. Thirty-nine percent of the generals said that television coverage was "probably not a good thing" because of the lack of context, and 52 percent thought TV to be "not a good thing" and believed the media were "counterproductive" to the war effort. Only four generals said that the coverage was "good for the American people."[26]

Not only the top brass, however, was biased and prejudiced against the "scribblers" or "newsies," as military venom had it. Braestrup points out that "there is no question that televised coverage of Vietnam lingers large in the minds of senior military officers," but he also emphasizes that the interpretations of senior officers were winding their way down the ranks: the biased perceptions of the press, particularly television, have been "transmitted down the line to junior officers."[27] Even those younger officers who gained no personal experience on Vietnam's battlefields accepted the organizational wisdom. Routine knowledge assets were acquired through socialization, rather than through reading explicit textbooks – no official document articulated let alone demanded an emotional bias against the fourth estate, that bias was deeply entrenched in military culture. Bernard Trainor wrote as late as 1990: "Today's officer corps carries as part of its cultural baggage a loathing for the press. ... Like racism, anti-Semitism, and all forms of bigotry, it is irrational but nonetheless real."[28] Henry Gole experienced this reality in the courses he gave in the Army War College. The colonel had served two tours in Vietnam with the 5th Special Forces Group and later became faculty member. As a veteran he closely observed the college's students at the beginning of the 1980s. Those students, he remarked, knew that they were the first generation of American officers to lose a war. This resulted in demoralization. Gole describes the officers in their mid-forties, with around 20 years' experience in uniform, having served in Vietnam once or twice, and still in competition for stars. "And they were angry," he wrote about the young military elite which would later command American forces in theater. "They almost unanimously despised journalists and made no effort to conceal their attitude." Those young officers held Congress and the civilian leadership in low regard, and they felt bitter about the public's apathy and the anti-war movement's ignorance about national security. "But they reserved a special venomous attitude for 'the media,' a term more sneered than spoken," Gole writes.[29] Some of these officers made little effort to conceal their disrespect of the press; one Marine Colonel wrote in the Navy periodical *Proceedings*:

> Members of the news media seemed convinced that they alone had discovered that war is ugly and felt compelled to share their discovery with every American citizen. While U.S. servicemen battled the Viet Cong and North Vietnamese, the countless networks and syndicated and freelance reporters roaming Southeast Asia battled each other for one-upmanship. ...

Antiwar activist and the news media eventually began to feed on the fruits of each other's labor.

(R.L. Upchurch, "Wanted: A Fair Press," *Proceedings*, 1984, July, p. 70)

Upchurch, like many of his contemporaries in the armed services, accused the media of refusing to accept any responsibility for the Vietnam debacle. The Army's elite college at Carlisle, Pennsylvania made considerable efforts to counter this trend, which was considered dangerous. Instructors attempted to teach their students the importance of a free media, an informed electorate in a democracy, or the competitive logic of the journalistic profession. Outstanding journalists were invited to annual "media days" where they engaged in discussions with students. Most of these efforts, recalls Gole, barely bore fruit: "Some 20 years after their experience in Vietnam, student attitudes toward the media were overwhelmingly negative and seemingly permanent, at least in that generation of embittered officers."[30] Colonel John M. Shotwell was the head of the media branch at headquarters of the Marine Corps during the late 1980s. Like Gole in Carlisle, he was responsible for setting up media-military seminars at the Command and Staff College and the Amphibious Warfare School. Shotwell later reported that he never ceased to be amazed by the "fingerpointing antipathy" and the "depth of suspicion" that became apparent during the discussions in the seminars: "Officers who'd never once had to confront either a reporter or an armed opponent blamed the media for losing the war for us in Vietnam, impugned their morals, and maligned their loyalties."[31] The bias against the media proved remarkably deep-rooted and persistent. As recently as 1999 Captain Scott Stearns pointed to the enduring legacy of Vietnam in an article in *Military Review*: "The idea that the media 'caused us to lose' the Vietnam War by poisoning public opinion and eroding public support is now a part of our national military lore and is accepted as the leading cause of our defeat."[32] True, numerous studies in history and political sciences have been produced that should have eliminated that myth. This, of course, was clear to Stearns: "Of course," the public affairs officer hastens to add, "as military historians and political scientists can attest, the cause of our loss in Vietnam ran deeper than bad public relations, but the 'antimedia' stigmatism remains."[33]

The anti-media bias had soaked deep into the military's cultural tissue. It became common organizational wisdom, conserved in rumor, tales, narratives, jokes, or films. Routine knowledge assets, in the model's language, were changed on the basis of experiential knowledge assets. The perception that the press lost the war for the military was rarely elaborated and spelled out as conceptual knowledge (the majority of articles in military periodicals, like Stearns's, in fact were critical of that simplistic view), nor was it authorized by leadership and disseminated through official doctrine or directives as systemic knowledge. Despite the lesson being shortsighted, wrong, and counterproductive, as became clear later, it was "learned" experientially from Vietnam. And despite this lesson being learned unintentionally, it was robust. So robust that it became a defining feature of the US military's public affairs policy for the next quarter century. The lesson, translated into practical advice for future operations, was that the press needed to be treated like an adversary and that media access to the battlefield should be strictly denied: "The overwhelming lesson from Vietnam seemed to have been, 'Keep the press out!' a study of the Army War College found in 2001."[34] Eliminating the media's access to the battlefield, it was reasoned, would eliminate the problems created by having the media on the battlefield.

5 Restrictive public affairs
Grenada, Panama, and the Persian Gulf

The Pentagon's media management in the three larger subesquent military campaigns following the American defeat in Southeast Asia was Vietnam-driven. In Grenada, 1983, the press was entirely shut out during the operation's hot phase. Following intense criticism by bureau chiefs and journalists, a new pool system was installed to guarantee media access in subsequent operations in an institutionalized fashion. But in Panama, in 1989, the newly created DoD National Media Pool was misused by the Pentagon to restrict media access instead of facilitating it. In the Persian Gulf War in 1991, media pools were again primarily used to relay and curb a free information flow, albeit with more preparation and sophistication than in Grenada and Panama. The period from the mid-1970s to the early 1990s can aptly be described as an era of restrictive public affairs.

Grenada

President Ronald Reagan made the first public announcement on Operation Urgent Fury on the morning of 25 October 1983, after military action in Grenada had already started. The operation's objective, the President said in his press statement, was to "protect our own citizens, to facilitate the evacuation of those who want to leave, and to help in the restoration of democratic institutions in Grenada."[1] Memories of the Iranian hostage crisis and an aborted rescue attempt, Desert One, were fresh, and a comparable disaster with the medical students trapped on Grenada was a frightening scenario for many in Washington. But the more relevant motive of the President to intervene in Grenada was somewhat concealed in the last part of that statement, the restoration of democratic order. In the Cold War days of the early 1980s the Reagan administration was on alert to counter the demon of communism wherever it threatened to raise its head. Reagan and his advisors feared a growing influence by a new Marxist military regime that had toppled and killed Prime Minister Maurice Bishop on the tiny Caribbean island of Grenada, a member of the British Commonwealth with a geo-strategically relevant location. The island was home for an estimated 110,000 people and had a size only twice that of the District of Columbia. Only nine years prior to the crisis, in 1974, Grenada had gained independence from Britain. Governor-General Paul Scoon and a group of neighboring Caribbean governments had requested American help to turn down the military coup. Six days after the new regime had seized power, on 25 October 1983, at dawn, US Marines, Army Rangers, Navy Seals, and parts of the 82nd Airborne Division entered the island with the objective to unseat it again.

H-Hour was originally scheduled at 0200, it was then moved to 0400 and later it was again pushed back one hour. (Only two days prior the launch of Operation Urgent Fury in the Caribbean, on 23 October, and on the other side of the globe in Beirut, Lebanese terrorists killed 241 Marines in a devastating car bomb attack.) The small Grenadian army was assisted by Cuban soldiers and workers. After several days of fighting, their resistance was broken by a relatively small number of American forces. Urgent Fury was led by Vice Admiral Joseph Metcalf III, commander of the US Second Fleet. The command post of Task Force 120 was on the helicopter carrier *Guam*, and the entire invasion involved little more than a battalion sized force. Compared to Vietnam or the Iraq War it was a minuscule operation. Two Marine rifle companies, about 400 men, were shuttled from the *Guam* to a field close to Pearls Airport; 700 Rangers from the 1st and 2nd battalions, 75th Infantry Regiment, parachuted onto a runway near Point Salines, in Grenada's south; and several teams of Navy Seals went into the capital city of St George's. The operation involved all four services and a complicated and ill-conceived command and control system, but US forces encountered relatively little resistance. Most American troops had left the island by mid-December 1983.

Improvisation

The President had set three objectives for the commanding admiral: first, to find and rescue the American medical students believed to be at True Blue campus near Point Salines; second, to rescue Governor General Paul Scoon; and finally to neutralize the People's Revolutionary Army (PRA) and secure the island.[2] Urgent Fury differed from other wars not only in magnitude, the number of deployed troops, and a brief duration of the entire operation; the time that went into planning and preparation was equally short. Military planning for the operation was secretive, hectic, and improvised. Admiral Metcalf was notified that he would be the commanding officer less than two days prior to first US troops entering the island. Metcalf and his Army deputy and advisor General Norman H. Schwarzkopf arrived on the command ship only 11 hours before the marine assault was scheduled to begin. Media planning played virtually no role. Metcalf recalls:

> From the time I was notified that I was to lead the Grenada operation until the first troops landed only 39 hours elapsed. In this brief period before combat, the only consideration that I gave to the media occurred about six hours into the 39. A lieutenant commander, an Atlantic Command public affairs officer, came to me and said: "There will be no press. Do you have any problems with this?" I said I did not.
>
> (J. Metcalf, III, "The Mother of the Mother," *Proceedings*, 1991, vol. 118, 8, p. 56)

Schwarzkopf was notified even later. The general was briefed on the plan at Atlantic Command only 19 hours before the invasion was launched. At the end of this last planning meeting, the question of media access was raised: "As the meeting closed, somebody raised the question of the press. We agreed that we would open Grenada to reporters at five o'clock the next afternoon, because by then Grenada would be ours."[3] The operation was planned as a so-called *coup de main*, a rapid one-punch knockout. From a military standpoint, as Reagan noted later, the rescue operation in Grenada was a "textbook success."[4] This, however, does not apply to its public affairs handling.

Information on the planned invasion of the island was vigilantly guarded in the White House and the Pentagon. The president made his first announcement only after the operation had started. On 24 October, only a couple of hours before H-Hour, Reagan scheduled an evening White House meeting with leading members of Congress. The President had told them that the meeting was, in his own words, "so secret that they should not even mention to their wives that they were going to the White House."[5] So tight was Reagan's grip on mission-relevant information that even the official spokespersons of the White House and the Pentagon were not filled in about the political and military planning under way. The White House spokesman, Larry Speakes, and his staff were excluded from the National Security Council (NSC) planning sessions and learned of the invasion only after it was launched. The Pentagon's speaker, Michael Burch, was not informed until the night before D-Day. The close-hold was based on the assumption that those officials dealing with the press on a permanent basis would be better off not knowing and hence not (knowingly) lying to the reporters in order to preserve the secret. The White House's chief-of-staff at the time was James Baker, a former Marine and later Secretary of State. He decided to inform neither Speakes nor David Gergen, the President's communications director, because, as he maintained later, "the element of surprise was critical and American lives could have been lost."[6] In the Pentagon the Chairman of the Joint Chiefs, General John W. Vessey Jr, took a similar decision. Three days before D-Day, Secretary of Defense Caspar Weinberger had inserted the chairman into the operational chain-of-command. The general was on high alert for communications security and imposed special category (SPECAT) restrictions on all planning message traffic, which limited planning information to a few selected members of the intelligence (J2) and operations (J3) directorates.[7] Officers performing a public affairs function were left outside the decision and information loop.

Denial of access

Despite those efforts to guard the secret, rumors and early reports about a looming military operation already had appeared in the news. Three days before the presidential statement, on 22 October, Edward Cody, a *Washington Post* correspondent, reported from Port of Spain that Eastern Caribbean leaders were considering sanctions against the new military regime in Grenada that would range from a trade embargo to the endorsement of a possible US intervention. The *Washington Post* and others carried the report. A Pentagon spokesman had acknowledged that a Navy task force originally bound for Lebanon was on station in the Caribbean on 24 October, one day before Reagan officially announced the invasion. The White House denied that American citizens on Grenada were in any danger but put out word that the "situation remains unstable" on the island. Shortly before the presidential announcement on 25 October, ABC News reported from the neighboring island of Barbados that Marines were landing at a Grenada airport. Such reports alerted news organizations to deploy their correspondents to the region.

On Monday, 24 October – before a large number of media representatives and a small number of public affairs officers arrived on Barbados, and before the commanders arrived on the *Guam* – a group of seven adventuresome reporters with tactical foresight had hired a fishing boat. After a rather painstaking trip they had managed to reach Grenada and St George's, the capital, six hours after H-Hour only to be restricted by Grenada's military forces, the People's Revolutionary Army (PRA). The most prominent reporters among them were the *Washington Post*'s Edward Cody and Bernard Diederich from *Time Magazine*. While Diederich stayed on Grenada, Cody and three other reporters headed on a helicopter to the *Guam*, which was anchoring close to the island, hoping they could file their stories from the command vessel.[8] The vessel's staff was confused that a reporter demanded to file his stories from the ship. The newsmen were held incommunicado on the boat for three days.[9] When the presence of news media on the ship was reported up the chain-of-command to the Pentagon the "no press policy" was reaffirmed. Admiral Metcalf noted later that he was "admonished for having allowed the reporter on board."[10] The incident would become known as the "Ed Cody affair," and it would trigger harsh criticism and condemning of op-eds on the Navy's tough handling of the press.

Cody's boat, however, was the first and only one to get through to Grenada. As soon as the military operation began, Admiral Metcalf aggressively banned all transportation to the island. A couple of days later another group of reporters persuaded a local charter service in Barbados to ship them the 120 miles to Grenada. They departed Wednesday afternoon, one day after D-Day, on the same route that Cody and his fellow reporters had used. The Navy was alert and determined. The commanding admiral remarked later: "I had also learned that a number of more adventuresome members of the fourth estate, determined to open up their second front on Grenada, were on the way by speedboat. My response was to quarantine the island. I established an exclusion zone around Grenada, enforced by destroyers and aircraft."[11] An A-6 Intruder aircraft spotted them and dropped a canister in the boat's path as a warning, which persuaded its captain to turn around.

The military rationale for such an aggressive denial of access policy was twofold. Concern for operational security blended into the strategic imperative to maintain the element of surprise. The commander-in-chief of Atlantic Command was Admiral Wesley McDonald. His "Urgent Fury Report" was released on 6 February 1984. It stresses the significance of the element of surprise:

> The absolute need to maintain the greatest element of surprise in executing the mission to ensure minimum danger to US hostages on the island and to the servicemen involved in the initial assault dictated that the press be restricted until the initial objectives had been secured.[12]

This view is echoed by the admiral he ordered to command the task force. Metcalf, as many of his uniformed contemporaries, was intimidated by television. CNN had a civilian C-130 transportation airplane loaded with equipment for satellite broadcasts on standby at the airfield in Barbados. The network's plan was to broadcast directly from Grenada. But "live or almost live battlefield broadcasts," Metcalf feared, posed a security problem. He established the rules for media presence only during the combat phase of the operation; the prime rule was that the media must not interfere with the safety of personnel and the security of the operation.[13]

The military's concern and restrictive handling of the press only increased the news-value of the Grenada story. Hundreds of journalists were flocking to Barbados, eager to report on combat and military action. The chief public affairs officer for CINCLANT, commander-in-chief Atlantic Fleet in Norfolk, Virginia, was Captain Owen Resweber. He did not receive order to develop a public affairs plan for an information office in the region until 26 October, more than one day after the operation had started.[14] After the Pentagon's public affairs officials got permission by Weinberger and Vessey, they tasked Resweber to put together an interservice public affairs team. Admiral McDonald gave his final approval of the team that was about to set up an information office on Barbados only late on Wednesday, 26 October. Commander Ronald Wildermuth, US Navy, along with five aides, was sent to Barbados where he arrived in Bridgetown at 1000 on 27 October. Hastily the team set up a Joint Information Bureau (JIB) in a building at the Grantley Adams airport where the US Air Force had installed base detachment to control the US shuttle aircraft to and from the battered island. A large crowd of reporters was awaiting the officer and his small staff. The bureau registered 369 American and international reporters at its first day. Although a large part of them were technicians accompanying the TV crews, this number of journalists was considerably larger than the number of press accredited at the Military Assistance Command in Saigon during the Tet offensive on 1 March 1968. The small operation in Grenada had an extraordinarily high news value. On the next day, a Friday, the JIB sent a spontaneously assembled pool of 24 reporters into Grenada on a guided tour, with advice on selection from the US embassy and the Pentagon. The reporters on the first pool saw little more than warehouses and the airport, and they were allowed to interview the rescued medical students. A pool of 47 was sent to Grenada on Saturday, including Thomas Ricks of the *Wall Street Journal*, and another 182 journalists on Sunday. By then, the Rangers had already left the island and the Marines were departing to Lebanon.

Lessons learned

In an article in *Military Review*, almost ten years after Grenada, a young officer wrote about the media–military relationship during that conflict: "The reaction of the Pentagon and the Reagan administration to the ingrained belief that it was the media that led to the defeat in Vietnam was to exclude the media from covering the invasion in Grenada."[15] Given the extremely compressed planning phase and the absence of explicit public affairs guidance, the deep distrust of the media resulted in the military's knee-jerk reaction: deny access. Although rigid communications security during the operation's planning is partly justified by the imperative to maintain the element of surprise, operational considerations cannot explain nor justify the entire absence of any public affairs planning and guidance. In hindsight, the task force Commander was very critical of the public affairs performance in Operation Urgent Fury. In Metcalf's words:

> Looking back, how was media policy for Urgent Fury formulated in the Joint Chiefs of Staff and Department of Defense? In my opinion it probably "just happened." The policy of "no-media" likely became a logical extension of the tight security that covered the early planning and the diversion of the amphibious force and carrier battle group to the Caribbean. It is also likely that few in the Pentagon, if they had been consulted, would have objected strongly. Prior to my acquiescence to the no-press policy, I was not consulted. I had no voice in media matters.
>
> (J. Metcalf, III, "The Mother of the Mother," *Proceedings*, 1991, vol. 118, 8, p. 58.)

Two themes dominated the military's culture in dealing with the media on the battlefield after Grenada. First, the organization was emotionally strongly biased against the media. After Grenada, Brent Baker, a Navy captain with more than 20 years of experience as a Navy public affairs officer (PAO), a member of the government's official review commission, and later, as an admiral, chief of information for the Navy in the Persian Gulf War, lamented the decline of quality journalism in the naval periodical *Proceedings*: "I am concerned with the erosion of 'objective' journalism today," he wrote. The majority of journalists had no military experience or in-depth knowledge about military affairs. Captain Baker pointed out that these journalists fail to distinguish between the tactical battlefield environment and the decision making in Washington, DC: "They seek to link directly each isolated combat action with some policy decision in Washington."[16] Upchurch, a graduate of the Naval War College, joins this critique: "Many newscasts, commentaries, and newspaper stories were so openly antiadministration and antimilitary that they lacked credibility." Reporters, he argues, were obviously disappointed when returning medical students continued to express relief and gratitude for their rescue, "despite the reporters' repeated attempts to ferret out doubt or displeasure." Upchurch describes a common view in the US armed forces of the 1980s when he writes that "there is a standard of journalism today that disregards privacy, national security, and dignity."[17] The absence of a thorough public affairs plan paved the way for emotional reactions. Second, operational security concerns were at their peak, as has already been shown. In a rare appeal to the news media, Pentagon spokesman Burch issued a statement on 2 March 1984. News media dispatches, it said, revealed the specific location of Marine observers in the hills of Lebanon; the "attendant publicity put the observers in danger." Following the news reports, one of the American troops was allegedly wounded by incoming fire.[18] It remains unclear whether this charge was justified.

Many correspondents were equally distrustful of the military which did not come back from Vietnam with a particularly good reputation for accurate public statements. To improve the sour relationship between the two institutions, the government tried to institutionalize cooperation between them. With this aim in mind, the chairman of the Joint Chiefs at the time, Vessey, appointed an expert commission to recommend a policy to improve relations between the military and the media. Major General Winant Sidle was chosen to head the panel which subsequently became known as the Sidle Commission. In its final report, the group recommended the creation of a press pool in Washington on permanent standby:

> When it becomes apparent during military operational planning that news media pooling provides the only feasible means of furnishing the media with early access to an operation, planning should support the largest possible press pool that is practical and minimize the length of time the pool will be necessary.
>
> (W. Sidle, *Report of the CJCS Media–Military Relations Panel*, Washington: Department of Defense, 1984, p. 1)

The DoD national media pool was formed by order of the Secretary of Defense in April 1985. It consisted of up to 16 media representatives and three escort officers.

In sum, after Grenada there was little improvement of the media–military relationship and virtually no attempt by the US armed forces to incorporate public affairs into strategic thinking. Very slowly, the idea that media coverage could actually have a positive effect was inching forward in the public affairs debate. Two years later, in 1987, Captain Harry F. Noyes argued that an open media policy could work for the military advantage. Only with the help of the media in Grenada, he maintained, had it been possible to turn a tactical victory into a strategic and political success. The Air Force public affairs officer and distinguished graduate of DINFOS referred to the images of joyous Grenadians welcoming and helping US forces as well as to the much publicized image of an American medical student kissing American soil upon arrival.[19] The scene reportedly touched the President who entered into his diary that "it was heart-warming, indeed thrilling to see these young people clasp these men in uniforms to their hearts."[20] A group of progressively thinking public affairs officers started to break with the traditional wisdom distilled from Vietnam and realized very slowly that media coverage could have a positive effect for the military after all; a thought that did not occur to the planners of Operation Just Cause in Panama.

Panama

Six years after Grenada, the United States engaged in another small, brief, and politically as well as militarily successful invasion in its southern sphere of influence. And again the US military's public affairs performance was dismal. The invasion of Panama was predated by a significant reform of the chain-of-command in the Department of Defense, the Goldwater-Nichols Defense Reorganization Act of 1986. The commanders-in-chief of the unified regional commands – for instance Atlantic Command, Pacific Command, or Central Command – were given full combatant command authority in the case of war. The reform act allowed the President, other than in Grenada, to use the chairman of the Joint Chiefs of Staff as the communication interface between the national command authorities and the relevant commander-in-chief, or combatant com-mander, CINC in military idiom (pronounced "sink"), who would have full command authority over his service components and the employment of these forces. The chairman, in turn, was now the principal military advisor and no longer limited to a messenger who had to convey the compromise the service chiefs had reached to the Secretary and the President. Just Cause in Panama would test this new system.

In 1988 relations with Panama began to deteriorate when federal grand juries in Miami and Tampa in Florida indicted Manuel Antonio Noriega, the dictator of Panama and a former intelligence officer, for drug trafficking. The following year Noriega overturned the result of the May elections. In mid-1989 President George H.W. Bush installed the Army General Maxwell R. Thurman as the commander of Southern Command (SOUTHCOM), the regional command that had Panama in its area of responsibility. The general had a more aggressive approach than his predecessor and accelerated the build up of American forces in Panama. In late 1989 the relation between the US and Panama turned sour. On 15 December 1989, the National Assembly in Panama City declared a state of war against the United States; Noriega named himself maximum leader. After an American soldier got killed at a roadblock of the Panama Defense Forces (PDF), and another soldier and his wife were jailed and physically assaulted in detention, Bush and his advisors contemplated an intervention and decided to act on 17 December 1989. H-Hour was scheduled three days later, at 0100 on 20 December.

The objective of operation Just Cause was not only to remove and capture Noriega and to install the elected Endara government, it was to eliminate the Panamanian Defense Forces. Lieutenant General Carl W. Stiner, selected by Thurman under Goldwater-Nichols, commanded the joint task force. Its strategy was to strike every major unit of the adversarial army. Army Rangers para-chuted onto the main barracks of the PDF at Río Hato while the Air Force supported them with F-117A stealth bombers. The 82nd Airborne Division flew in from Fort Bragg and seized objectives east of Panama City. More infantry units from the Army's 7th Infantry Division in California were used to gain control of the country and restore law and order while the American forces already stationed in Panama took the *Commandancia*, Noriega's headquarters. Navy Seals captured the airfield where the dictator kept his plane, and Special Forces searched for him. All in all, 14,000 troops invaded and joined 12,700 troops that were already stationed in Panama to guard the channel. On 3 January 1990 Noriega surrendered to US forces. Initial lawlessness and looting in Panama City was soon brought under control. By the end of January the situation was stable, Operation Just Cause ended successfully, and US forces were withdrawn.

Pool restrictions

The public affairs management and the deployment of the DoD National Media Pool in Panama was a failure. Bush had approved the use of the pool but did not specify whether it should be comprised of reporters already in Panama or of journalists who were still in Washington. The journalists on standby for the official DoD pool were scattered all across the DC area. Out of security considerations, Lieutenant General Thomas Kelly, the Joint Staff's Director of Operations and one of the Pentagon's briefers later in the Persian Gulf War, preferred to work with the reporters already in Panama. But Cheney overruled him. A final order to deploy the pool was given only at 1700 on 19 December by Assistant Secretary of Defense for Public Affairs (ASD/PA) Pete Williams to his staff and the responsible officer of the Southern Command. Cheney then further postponed the pool's callout until after the evening news, out of fear that the Panama Defense Forces "might be waiting for us," the Secretary said later. "We basically decided to notify the pool after the evening news on Tuesday to minimize the possibility of leaks."[21] For Cheney operational security and media coverage remained incompatible: "I really felt it was a direct trade off between maintaining security of the operation and protecting lives ... versus accommodating the press. Protecting the security of the troops was my first priority."[22] Kelly, speaking for the joint staff, said that "we didn't play any role" in framing Cheney's and Williams's decision.

After the news, at 1930, the pool was eventually alerted, only five-and-a-half hours before H-hour. Colonel Alexandrakos, the head of the Pentagon's Public Affairs Plans division, began to notify reporters by phone. These journalists had two hours, until 2130, to report to Andrews Air Force Base where their departure to Panama was scheduled at 2300. But unexpected difficulties caused some delay. It was 20 December, and most reporters were occupied with Christmas festivities, so the call for combat coverage came as a surprise. Dick Thomson, a *Time Magazine* correspondent, had to rush from a Christmas party and did not find the time to change clothes or pack anything. He left to tropical Panama with a winter suit. The pool departed from the base at 2326. The reporters were not informed about their destination before they entered the plane and took off. Most, of course, suspected that the spontaneous trip was headed to Panama. The pool consisted of 14 reporters, two technicians, and three escorting public affairs officers.[23]

OPLAN 90–2, the invasion plan, contained a public affairs annex. It identified the Joint Information Office (JIO) of Southern Command as the coordinator and only release-authority for operational news. The public affairs officer of the Joint Task Force would support the information office by denying the release of information concerning future operations, the order of battle, or the effectiveness of enemy tactics. The basic rationale the commanding officers were applying was to restrict the information flow. The pool, outflow of a decision taken in Washington, was not part of the operational plan at all. When the operation began, more than 800 journalists were streaming to Panama to cover the action. Southern Command had, as planned, set up a Joint Information Bureau at Quarry Heights Officer's Club to deal with media requests. But as in Grenada, the media handling was largely improvised and lacked planning. The public affairs officers of the relevant outfits were not part of the secretive communication channels that were used for operational planning. As a result, the press officers of Southern Command, of the XVIII Airborne Corps, and of the Army's Special Operations Command were not informed that the operation would occur until 17 December. Once they were informed, they were given instructions not to discuss it with their staff. These security restrictions, Colonel Ronald Sconyers said, a SOUTHCOM officer stationed in Panama, barred him from starting preparations.[24] The 82nd Airborne Division's PAO did not learn of the operation until 18 December, and the 7th Infantry Division's responsible officer not before 19 December. The army chief of public affairs was informed even after the pool reporters had been called, one hour before H-hour.[25] The fear of security leaks precluded the joint coordination of public affairs in Panama, and, as a result, the office at Quarry Heights was again ill-equipped to deal with the incoming quantities of journalists.

The pool arrived in Panama more than four hours after H-Hour, only to be held at Howard Air Force base for another five hours. While waiting there, the reporters themselves were watching the war's CNN coverage: "We actually watched a Bush news conference," said *Dallas Morning News* reporter Kevin Merida. "We were right there with the viewer watching CNN."[26] When a briefer finally arrived, it was an official from the American embassy who knew little about the military operation under way. He lectured the reporters about the history of Panama, beginning with its founding in 1903. When the pool was finally deployed, its military escorts were hindered by restrictions and logistic difficulties. Steve Komarow, working for AP at the time, remembers similar scenes:

> After the operation started, we were called out to Washington and then sent down to Panama. They didn't know what to do with us down there once we got there. We were taken to the Army headquarters at Quarry Heights.

> We were kept basically locked in a room at Army headquarters, while they allegedly were trying to get us a helicopter to watch the fight.[27]

Navy Commander Dave Thomas, Deputy Director of Plans in the spokesman's office in the Pentagon, was one of the escorts of the pool. In hindsight, he attributes the problems the pool faced in Panama to the dominant attitudes of the officers in the field: "The culture in the field hadn't changed as far as people in Washington would have expected it to change."[28] Thomas illustrates his statement with the example of a group of Army soldiers that the journalists he escorted wanted to interview. The soldiers plainly refused to talk to the journalists. Upon being asked for the reason for their refusal, they said they had received orders from the Army's PAO escort responsible for the pool not to talk to the media. Thomas objected. But in a combat situation, the soldiers were not prepared to be overruled by a Pentagon official, despite the fact that he was higher in rank than the PAO they received orders from and showed a letter of authorization signed by Secretary Cheney. The pool escorts from Washington were not part of the formal chain-of-command, and hence powerless: "There was nothing I could do to convince him to talk to the reporters," Thomas remembered.

Problems with logistics, the result of insufficient planning, made things even worse: "A lack of helicopters – which could have been avoided by proper planning – prevented the pool from reporting much of what was left of the action by the time the pool reached Panama."[29] NBC's Fred Francis, the only Pentagon correspondent on the pool, remembers the trouble that beset the pool in Panama:

> Less than two miles away, the pool could clearly see the area around Noriega's headquarters in full blaze. Loudspeakers were blaring at Noriega loyalists to surrender. A tank was pounding away. We told our escorts that that was where we needed to be. We were told, "it's too dangerous."[30]

Out of sheer frustration the pool coined two mottos: the press printed T-shirts with "semper tardus" on the front, ridiculing the Marine's motto *semper fidelis*, as well as shirts that read "if it's news today, it's news to us."[31]

The Marriott incident

Other journalists were better suited to cover the war. Spanish speaking Peter Copeland was one of Scripps Howard's regional correspondents at the time. His news organization had tried to fly him into Panama but the Southern Command's commander, Thurman, threatened to shoot down any airplane trying to enter Panama airspace. Undeterred, Copeland flew to Costa Rica and paid a bus-driver to get him into Panama.[32] When fighting swept across town, he ended up being one of several reporters who were trapped in the Marriott hotel in Panama City. Noriega's so-called dignity battalions came into the Marriott to search for foreigners: "There was fighting. They came into the hotel," he remembered. The soldiers dragged several people out of the hotel and beat them up with pipes, according to Copeland: "Right below my window, that's how close the war was."

Unlike the pool reporters, the journalists in the hotel were able to use modern communication facilities to file their stories: "What made the reporting possible in Panama was [that] we had independent means of communications. It was an urban conflict in a moderately developed country. So I honestly filed my stories in the Marriott."[33] Copeland remembers being on the phone with his editors in Washington while some of his colleagues were beat up below his window. Through their instant reporting, the journalists trapped in the Marriott thereby built up significant political pressure in Washington. All three major news networks, ABC, CNN, and NBC, were broadcasting live from the Marriott[34] and offered an isolated view – what would later be called "soda-straw" view – from a single hotel in Panama City with little operational relevance for the overall military situation on the ground. But that isolated event's significance was magnified by the reporters' live coverage.

Brent Scowcroft, Bush's National Security Advisor, called the JCS chairman in the Pentagon to pressure him to send troops to rescue around 30 American citizens believed to be hiding in the Marriott. Powell hesitated to take action and said that the journalists were in no danger, that the fighting would "soon sweep right pass them."[35] The sporadic engagements around the Marriott were, from an operational view, insignificant. But the political pressure created by the media's bureau chiefs and network executives was growing. Scowcroft finally jumped one level up the chain-of-command and involved Cheney. The Secretary then called Powell and ordered the military commanders against their strong reluctance to rescue the reporters. Eventually the 82nd Airborne stormed the Marriott, but ran into a stiff firefight. In the process three soldiers were seriously wounded and one Spanish journalist was killed by American fire while covering the rescue.

"This was a new, tough age for the military, fighting a war as it was being reported," Powell remarked later. "We could not, in a country pledged to free expression, simply turn off the press."[36] The Marriott incident is an early demonstration of how live media coverage gives strategic relevance to a largely irrelevant tactical situation, a problem that would become virulent in succeeding military operations when the modern communication equipment at the hands of the press radically changed the nature of war reporting. The incident also illustrates how the changing media environment affected military operations. In 1989, NBC's satellite uplink dish, together with the associated technical equipment, still weighed more than a ton. But technological change was rapidly eliminating the logistic difficulties for journalists created by such cumbersome equipment.

Lessons learned

On 20 March 1990 Fred Hoffman submitted a report that reviewed the entire public affairs performance during the Panama invasion to the Assistant Secretary of Defense for Public Affairs, who had commissioned the review.[37] Hoffman knew both sides, he had worked as an AP Pentagon correspondent for 22 years, and he held the government post of deputy ASD/PA from 1987 to 1989. The Hoffman Report, as the document would become known, contained 17 recommendations. At its core were two issues, planning and internal communication. First, public affairs personnel and planning for the pool deployment should be brought into the operational planning process as early as possible, and not be excluded to protect sensitive information. All war plans, the report demanded, should contain a public affairs annex. Second, communication about those public affairs activities up and down the chain-of-command should be improved, with DoD leadership urging all commanders to support the pool logistically in the future. Public affairs branches, in turn, should brief and inform the highest levels of military command on their plans. To reach those goals, Hoffman recommended to the Secretary that he issue a directive stating his official sponsorship of the media pool, and to the JCS chairman to send a message to all commanders, ordering them to give full cooperation to the media pool and escorts.

As demanded, the recommendations were communicated internally. In a message to all regional combatant commands, Powell criticized the evident and complete lack of public affairs planning in Panama: "Media coverage and pool support requirements must be planned simultaneously with operational plans and should address all aspects of operational activity," his message stated.[38] He knew that public affairs ranged at the very bottom of the priority list for many commanders, particularly when they were planning an operation. Reporters were perceived as swarms of "newsies," as Powell privately referred to journalists, akin to gadflies descending on a military operation, but not as something that had to be dealt with when there were far more important things to plan and organize prior to deployment. Consequently, to stress the media's importance, Powell and his staff tried to link successful public affairs to operational success – a conceptual link that would later be used extensively during the planning process for the 2003 Iraq War, just far more persuasively and skillfully. In 1990, however, many commanders did not appreciate or even understand the argument's consequences, which was not spelled out in the same in depth and detail in Powell's message as it would be in two similar communiqués prior to the Iraq War: "Commanders are reminded that military actions in Grenada and Panama demonstrated that otherwise successful operations are not total successes unless the media aspects are properly handled."[39] The next bullet point states somewhat repetitively and without much emphasis: "Commanders are reminded that the media aspects of military operations are important, will get national and international attention, and warrant your personal attention." The media's importance was not justified in operational terms or framed strategically. It was left somewhat unclear how exactly operational success is linked to successful PA. References that the media can be used as force multiplier, for counterpropaganda purposes, or as a tool of information warfare, are entirely absent. The idea, however, to incorporate reporters into military units, what would later be christened embedding, was already dormant in the message Powell disseminated several months prior to the Persian Gulf War: "Essentially, the goal should be to treat reporters as members of the units, allowing them to move with the units."

The Panama incident shows that despite the creation of conceptual and systemic knowledge assets (the Sidle Commission's report after Grenada and the adoption of its recommendations by DoD), a change of routines did not occur. The Vietnam lesson to keep the press out was too well established in the culture and the routines of the military. The media management in Panama instead illustrates "doctrinal dissonance," the unsuccessful attempt to change routines and procedures on the basis of abstract directions and guidelines – systemic knowledge assets. America's first war against Iraq would prove that doctrinal dissonance in public affairs would persist, and that Powell's goal of an improved cooperation between the media and the Army would not be reached very soon.

The Persian Gulf

On 2 August 1990, Saddam Hussein invaded Kuwait and incorporated the country as the 19th province into Iraq: America's reaction to the rare case of aggression of one state against another state was intense crisis diplomacy, and finally the liberation of Kuwait by means of force. The military operation fell into three parts. On 12 August 1990, President George W.H. Bush ordered US forces to Saudi Arabia, only seven months after US troops had left Panama. The first phase of the deployment at the Persian Gulf, Operation Desert Shield, was designed to protect oil-rich Saudi Arabia, an ally of the United States, against its aggressive neighbor. The second phase, Operation Desert Storm, was launched on 17 January 1991. Other than the small operations in the decade prior, Desert Storm was a full blown war with all implications. The short but intense ground war can be regarded as a third phase of the war. It lasted only 100 hours.

On the same day that Bush launched Operation Desert Shield, the Pentagon activated the National News Media Pool in Washington and the largest public affairs operation to date in an American-led war unfolded.[40] The Pentagon's public affairs policy in the Gulf War was characterized by four main features: first, military briefings dominated by gun-camera footage; second, a large-scale test of the pool system with its security review process; third, a strong imbalance in media aptitude between the Army and the Marines; and finally the adversary's rather successful information campaign. But more than anything else, it was the size of the media operation in 1991 that was remarkable. The sheer number of journalists trying to cover the war against Iraq in 1991 was unprecedented. More than 160 pool journalists would accompany US units into the Gulf War, approximately 2,000 journalists registered with the Joint Information Bureau in Dhahran, Saudi Arabia.[41] Entirely new dynamics in media–military relations ensued. For the first time since Vietnam, significant numbers of troops came in contact with significant numbers of news media representatives for an extended period of time. And sometimes cultures clashed. In Grenada and Panama, by contrast, reporters were excluded from action and mostly had contact only with a handful of public affairs officers.

Briefings

Briefings were the major conduit of the Persian Gulf War's information policy. The focus on the briefings was largely the corollary of the old emotional distrust of news-people nurtured by many in the military, dealing with the press in a briefing room was surely better than having them in theater. That irrational distrust was underpinned by a rational argument. Military commanders operated under the assumption that the enemy was using the media as a source of intelligence. The adversary is watching, reading, or listening to what you are saying in the media, and you better not give away information of military value when asked for details by reporters, the argument ran: "In Desert Shield/Storm, it was clear that the Iraqis were watching CNN," said the US Navy's chief of information, Rear Admiral Brent Baker, after the war. "Peacetime media 'business as usual' (open access) is *not* possible in modern warfare, where the enemy is watching 24-hour television, and we are involved in a fast-paced campaign," the admiral wrote.[42] While military briefers were often uncertain about how to react to questions facing a hoard of reporters, they were never uncertain about the fact that operational security was at risk in those situations. Blending distrust with security concerns, General Schwarzkopf went into his first press conference in Saudi Arabia, in the Dhahran International Hotel. It was early September 1990, long before the bombardment of Baghdad would begin, and about 200 reporters and half-a-dozen TV cameras were awaiting him. Schwarzkopf had prepared to be more open to the press than in his previous role as a commander at war: "I felt it was crucial not to repeat the mistake we'd made in Grenada, where the military had stonewalled," he wrote in his memoirs.[43] In order to cope with the media, he had set up several personal rules for himself. One of those rules was never to answer any question that would help the enemy. A US reporter asked point-blank in that briefing whether it was true that the US would still be weeks away from being able to defend the Saudi kingdom against an Iraqi attack. The question was right on target. It was true, the US presence in the region was still weak, but the general of course could not publicly confirm that. His answer was that if the Iraqis would be "dumb enough" to attack, they would "pay a terrible price."[44]

Later Schwarzkopf reflected on the intentions of his statements during that press conference: "With those cameras grinding away, I knew I wasn't talking just to friendly audiences, but that Saddam and his bully boys were watching me on CNN in their headquarters. I wanted to make sure they got that message."[45] As soon as the ground war began, however, Central Command was not so much concerned in making sure the enemy would get a particular message, but rather in making sure he would *not* intercept information that could be of military value: "To complicate matters, we now had to contend with more than 1,300 reporters in the war zone; there were always 180 of them out in pools on the front lines," Schwarzkopf remarked with concern. From his perspective, the troops were hosting 180 potential leaks that could endanger the operation's success and the lives of American soldiers:

One night early in February, we'd turned on CNN to watch a White House press conference. A live report from a pool correspondent with the troops preceded it. She said breathlessly, "There has just been a major artillery duel in my location between the 82nd Airborne and the Iraqis."

This was the kind of mission-critical information the general did not want to see broadcast on CNN to the rest of the world, particularly not to the adversary. During the planning phase he was extremely reluctant to grant more access to representatives of the news media: "Son of a bitch," Schwarzkopf exclaimed, feared for his aggressive style as a commander. The 82nd Airborne was the division farthest to the west. Any "halfway competent Iraqi intelligence officer watching CNN," he fumed, could easily note the time of the broadcast and determine the precise location where the exchange of fire had taken place.[46] The Iraqis could then find out that the division was vulnerable to a flanking attack, the general reasoned. Captain Ron Wildermuth, the public affairs chief of Central Command, was ordered to chew up the 82nd Airborne's PAO. There were several similar incidents. A few days later *Newsweek* carried a story on the operation. "This stinks!" Schwarzkopf complained on the phone to Powell. "*Newsweek* just printed our entire battle plan. Now the Iraqis could put chemical weapons in that area and completely reorient their defenses."[47]

The chairman himself, who often briefed in the Pentagon, had a view not unlike Schwarzkopf's. For him it was equally clear that in an age of global media it was impossible to neatly distinguish between the various target audiences and talk to them on separate channels: "By the time [Dick] Cheney, Norm [Schwarzkopf] and I went on television, we understood the dynamics," Powell noted:

> We were not only talking to the press assembled in front of us; we were talking to four other audiences – the American people, foreign nations, the enemy, and our troops. I would never, for example, say anything for domestic consumption and ignore its impact on Iraq, or vice versa.[48]

Already during the Panama crisis Powell had demonstrated that he was committed to working with the press. The chairman had no intention of using the media and taking strategic advantage of the reporters' coverage, he merely felt the democratic responsibility to accommodate the fourth estate and to inform the American public. "Sure, you want to see if you can get the press to support the goals [of the military effort], but that's not why you work with the press. You work with the press because it is your obligation."[49]

In hindsight, the Gulf War briefings are best remembered for their most innovative and distinguishable feature – views through the cross-haired video-eye in the cones of precision-guided bombs diving precisely into their targets, often invoking comparison to a video-game. The idea to use those images in televised briefings was remarkable. So-called "smart bombs" are guided by a laser beam into their target. The pilot of the plane dropping the bomb pegs a laser marker onto a particular structure, like a rollway or a bunker, a computer in the projectile then uses that laser dot as a point of orientation and, ideally, navigates the bomb precisely into its designated target. The videos, originally, are used for internal targeting statistics purposes, for "bomb damage assessment," or BDA, as it is called in the military. But gun-camera footage quickly turned into a useful public affairs tool. The images produced for the internal assessment of a single bomb's precision were ideally suited for the external demonstration of the entire air campaign's precision. During the first five nights of combat, F-117s dropped 167 laser-guided bombs. Seventy-six missed their target because of pilot error, technical malfunctions, or weather conditions. The impression conveyed in the briefings by selectively showing the gun-camera videos of successful hits exaggerated the accuracy of the munitions by far.[50] One effect of this selective demonstration was that the public got the faulty impression of a bloodless war with not only low numbers of civilian victims but also few military casualties. The metaphor of "surgical strikes" was brought up by briefers and critics alike. Contrary to what the persuasive images were insinuating, the majority of ordnance dropped over Iraq were dumb bombs. It was the absence of an adequate coverage from the ground that distorted the public's view of the war.

Pools in the desert

The main reason for this distorted perspective is that the pool system, the second major feature of the Gulf War's public affairs effort, did not work sufficiently well. An example of the Army's 1st Infantry Division illustrates how the system worked. At a given day during Desert Shield, at daybreak, a selected group (pool) of reporters would be taken with a bus to cover an event or a unit. Escorted and always on the record, the journalists were brought to specific sights and allowed to interview soldiers. After the reporters had later produced their stories, they would meet again with their escorts and hand the reports to the division's public affairs officer. Major Bill McCormick would then review the copy according to the ground rules, which were designed to protect the operation's security. If he found that the report violated these rules, three escalating steps to resolve the issue were possible. First, Major McCormick would ask the journalists to alter the text. If they would not agree, the issue was pushed up one level. The PAO was not authorized to alter the story. He would "flag" the questionable section in the text at the margin, mark it with the number of the violated rule, and send it to the Joint Information Bureau (JIB).

Most reports were reviewed and distributed in the JIB. A so-called Joint Information Bureau was established in the Dhahran International Hotel at the King Abdul Aziz Air Force base. A section of the hotel's banquet room was appropriated and computers, fax machines, telephones, copy machines, and other facilities were installed. During the first months of the operation, 34 military personnel were assigned to the bureau, 17 of which were escort officers. The total staff was later upgraded to more than 42 public affairs officers. The bureau was cooperating with the Saudi Ministry of Information in issuing visas to journalists and accrediting them. In the bureau a joint public affairs officer would discuss the questionable paragraph with media pool representatives. If still no agreement could be reached, the issue would be pushed up yet another level to Pete Williams's office in the Pentagon for final resolution with editors in Washington. For the entire duration of operations Desert Shield and Desert Storm, among 1,300 reports filed only five disputes between PAOs and reporters had to be resolved in Washington, only one report was changed.[51]

"All of the stories and pictures – still and electronic – were subjected to security review. It is to the credit of the escort officers that few violations occurred," Captain Mike Sherman pointed out, somewhat distrustful of journalists emphasizing the importance of escort officers.[52] The Navy captain, who was the chief of the Joint Information Bureau during Desert Shield, pointed out that the journalists were "responsible and patriotic" but sometimes accidentally released information due to the "ignorance of the reporter of things military."[53] Many of the soldiers running the JIB or the pool escorts had the same operational security concerns as Schwarzkopf and Powell, equally coupled with distrust: "Those who faced the prospect of dealing with thousands of media representatives under unilateral conditions in an age of instantaneous news and audience gratification know full well the nightmarish scenario that might have unfolded," Sherman feared.

Instead of vetting articles, military minders applied two far more effective techniques: denying access and delaying transmission. Peter Copeland was a reporter who was on the initial pool made up of 17 reporters during the Desert Shield phase: "There was censorship and review," he remembered, "but the main way they controlled us was they limited our access. We could write and say anything about what they allowed us to see. So that is the key part. They controlled what we could see."[54] Copeland, who had an impression of urban warfare from his experiences in Panama one year earlier, thinks that Saudi Arabia's desert environment enabled the military's tight grip on press access in Kuwait and Iraq: "It made it so impossible for us to get around; you couldn't just drive out in the desert and find the troops. If it had been in an urban area, it probably would have been different. It made it easier for them."[55] Other reporters echoed this judgment: "Military censorship, in the literal sense of the word, was not the problem," concedes John Fialka, who tried to cover the war for the *Wall Street Journal*.[56] In retrospect, that analysis is shared by those on the other side.

Reflecting on the coverage of the Gulf War, the General Andrew Davis, former Marine's chief of public affairs, concedes that "the way the press was controlled was access to the battlefield was controlled." But he adds another means of news management. Not only denial of access was used, the denial of transmission created another obstruction for reporters to cover the war: "The ability to get stories back was controlled," Davis said.[57] Only 21 percent of the pool reports arrived in Dhahran at the JIB in less than 12 hours. The reports then still needed to be sent to Washington, or elsewhere, for further processing and publication. The majority of all articles, 69 percent, arrived in less than two days, and every tenth story was on its way for more than three days, some took more than six days. Tremendous delays diminished the newsworthiness of numerous reports, rendering them worthless in many cases. The reasons for setting up this cumbersome system were not technical, but cultural. A comparison of the Marine Corps and the Army in the Persian Gulf War illustrates this.

Marine Corps v Army

The third major feature of the Gulf War's media operation is the cultural difference within the US military: "Let me say up front that I don't like the press," a senior Air Force officer began a press briefing in January. "Your presence here can't possibly do me any good, and it can hurt me and my people. That's just so we know where we stand with each other."[58] This statement sums up the dominant attitude in US military culture at the onset of the Gulf War. Most senior commanders saw journalists as something they needed but did not want to deal with. And they controlled the public affairs assets. Vehicles, helicopters, public affairs officers, lines of communications, and access to the troops were in control of military commanders in the field, and ultimately Norman Schwarzkopf. It was not, as one might expect, the JIB in Dhahran that was responsible; its director when the war started, Colonel William Mulvey, was not part of the decision loop. One time the JIB released a video of a naval missile launch to CNN. Mulvey afterward almost got fired by an enraged Schwarzkopf who did not approve of the video being released without his consent. Technically the CINC was his boss, although the director of the JIB had been appointed by DoD spokesman Pete Williams. The unclear power distribution in the public affairs realm is where culture, in particular service culture, comes into play. During the short ground war the cultural differences between the ground components, the Army on the one hand and the Marines on the other hand, became all too obvious: "The differences between the two services' skills in handling public affairs were so vast," John Fialka pointed out, "that reporters sometimes wondered whether they represented different countries."[59]

The Army was closed-minded and gave news coverage a low priority. A good example is its main mechanized advance into Iraq, known as the "left hook." Four army divisions of the VII Corps, the 1st and 3rd Armored Divisions, the 1st Infantry Division, and the 1st Cavalry Division, led the main flanking attack, a maneuver designed to encircle the Iraqi units from the west. The objective of the Army's famous left hook was to outflank and destroy the Republican Guard with its units and to block the Iraqi army's getaway routes. The attack included more than 100,000 US troops confronting tank-heavy armored Iraqi divisions. What ensued was one of the largest tank battles in military history, and a unique success for the US Army. But the 32 reporters who were carried into battle with the VII Corps were effectively prevented from reporting it. Each division had two couriers and two four-wheel-drive vehicles for the entire war. They drove copies of news articles to the corps's rear base, where the material was turned over to other couriers who again drove the news product to King Khalid Military City, and from there a C-130 airplane was supposed to fly the quickly perishable freight to Dhahran once a day. The entire logistical enterprise took 72 hours at best, according to Lieutenant Colonel James W. Gleisberg, the chief PAO of the corps.[60] Attempts to improvise and set up a more efficient system – using a fax machine or the electronic mail system, for instance – were rejected because "the news was low priority," according to the official in charge of running the system.[61] Additionally, reporters were often harassed and treated as if to show them that they were at the very bottom of the pecking order. The frustrated journalists, again resorting to cynicism, dubbed the Army's system to get the news out the "pony express."

The Marines, in extreme contrast, were open-minded and treated the media as a high priority issue. Lieutenant General Walter E. Boomer commanded the 1st Marine Expeditionary Force in the war and directly reported to Schwarzkopf. The Marine commander was adept and knowledgeable about public affairs. Before he received his third star, Boomer had been the Marines' chief public affairs officer, a career path unthinkable in the Army. But the Marines historically have a very different attitude towards the American people. In the past, when money was short, the added value and the existence of the entire Corps was regularly called into question by Congress. Marines had to make sure that the United States really committed itself to a light amphibious force, despite the three powerful service branches that could do the job of the Marines just as well: "The continuous struggle for a viable existence," one of their generals put it, "fixed clearly one of the distinguishing characteristics of the Corps – a sensitive paranoia, sometimes justified, sometimes not."[62] The Corps, its officers are taught, exists not because America truly needs it, but because the American people want it.[63] As a result, the smallest of the US military services traditionally regards public affairs as existential. This culture breeds an open and distinctly pragmatic attitude towards working with the media. Every Marine is a public affairs officer, a common adage goes. Prior to the Persian Gulf War, an agreement with the Pentagon had foreseen 18 pool reporters for the Marines as well as for the Army. By the time the war started, however, the Marines had managed to drive up the number to 53. Molly Moore was one of the few selected journalists who were personally invited by General Boomer to join him in his mobile command post during the ground war. Marines were willing to improvise in troublesome situations and offer technical support to journalists, and this supportive attitude extended beyond the specialized group of public affairs officers. Moore describes the way she was assisted in getting her stories out.

The Marines, unlike the Army, had indeed advanced since the Civil War. Now, I could sit in my tent, run an extension cord to an electrical line that snaked through the tent, and tap out my story on a laptop computer. I could then take the floppy disk to the camp communications tent, where a computer-whiz sergeant would insert it into his computer, punch in a few code letters, and zap the story by electronic mail to a base at Jubail. There, a public affairs officer would make a printout of the story and fax it to Dhahran, where it would be copied and passed out to waiting reporters.

(M. Moore, *A Woman at War*, New York: Scribner's, 1993, p. 142)

In order to get video and film back to the rear, the Marines devised a system that exploited existing logistical channels. About a dozen people were placed as couriers who piggybacked aboard medevacs, fuel trucks, or ammunition wagons returning to the rear areas from the battlefield. There other marines would be waiting to pick up the material and rush it to Jubail or Dhahran.[64] Chief Warrant Officer Eric R. Carlson had devised a way of getting the news from the 1st Division to the rear in minutes. He explains the rationale behind this aggressive media support: "We didn't view the news media as a group of people we were supposed to schmooze," he somewhat defensively said. "We regarded them as an environmental feature of the battlefield, kind of like the rain. If it rains you operate wet."[65] And the smallest of the US military services with its specialization in amphibious operations excelled in this kind of "wet" environment.

The Iraqi information campaign

While some in the US military tried to starve the information-hungry reporters on the ground, the Iraqis tried to feed them systematically. American strategists in Washington or in Central Command's temporary headquarters in Saudi Arabia realized that they could use the media for their purposes only very slowly and reluctantly. Iraqi military thinkers, in contrast, seemed more adept and a step ahead. At least temporarily the regime in Baghdad was able to gain the "information initiative," as US information operations doctrine would call it several years later. The Iraqi regime had its own "JIB" in the al-Rashid Hotel in Baghdad, where Saddam's aides briefed the reporters assembled there. Peter Arnett, Bernard Shaw, and John Holliman were able to provide live coverage from the hotel's rooftop when the US bombardment began. It was one of journalism's historic moments when Peter Arnett stood on the al-Rashid Hotel's ninth floor, the sky above Baghdad ablaze with explosions from cruise missiles behind his crew, the Iraqi air defense's tracers raining upward into the night – all live on CNN. From the hotel's rooftop, the reporters had opined that coalition bombs seemed to hit designated government targets in downtown Baghdad with precision. The next day, Bush quoted CNN with this remark in a press conference to underline the attack's life-saving accuracy to an American public who had, it was assumed, a low tolerance for civilian casualties.

Iraqi officials soon prohibited that CNN go live from the al-Rashid's rooftop. On the third day of the war most western news organizations were ordered by the ministry of information to leave Iraq. The only large news organization the Iraqis had allowed and in fact asked to stay in Baghdad was CNN. Most western reporters, including the network's technicians, had already left Baghdad at that point in time. Arnett was one of the few western journalists who were still allowed in town and able to report. The experienced war correspondent had his cumbersome satellite phone installed in the hotel, and knew how to use it. The Iraqi military, in turn, knew how to use CNN. Not unlike the bus tours the American JIB in Dhahran was conducting, Iraqi "public affairs officers" drove the remaining western reporters with buses to cover stories of their offering – in both cases a government organization decided whether a particular event was newsworthy or whether it was not. An example was the offer by Iraqi minders to interview American prisoners of war. One of Arnett's Iraqi escorts, Sadoun, was unambiguous on the question of why the news organization's front man was asked to stay in Baghdad. In his memoirs the reporter wrote that his minder was "not a subtle man" and explains: "He made it clear to me that the only reason CNN was asked to stay was because our reports would be valuable for the Iraqi cause."[66] The interests of the Iraqi regime and those of the Atlanta-based news network were compatible, Arnett reasoned, apparently working under the assumption that he would uncover any attempt to use him as a propaganda tool by faking a story. The reporter believed that only an untrue story with factually false information could be propaganda: if US bombs went astray and killed civilians, and he would report on their plight, that would not be propaganda but factual reporting.

On 23 January 1991 American bombers attacked a compound in Baghdad which was designated as a biological weapons facility on the pilots' target lists. Iraqi officers swiftly herded a couple of reporters into the suburban Abu Ghraib area, where the compound was located. When the group visited the site of the destroyed biological weapons facility, some journalists came to believe that the complex was a factory for infant formula. At 2030 Arnett sent a news story about the destroyed factory to Atlanta, from where it was broadcast on CNN International. He quoted Iraqi officials saying the site was a civilian facility, and emphasized that he could not find any hint that the compound was being used for military purposes. The Iraqis had conveniently printed signs and logos on the worker's jackets in English, to support the milk-factory story line. Arnett actually noted in his report that "the intact signboard at the entrance to the factory read 'Baby Milk Plant' in English and in Arabic."[67] Government spokespersons denied the claim and maintained that their bombs had destroyed a biological weapons factory. The network's coverage of the event prompted a critique by the White House Press Secretary Marlin Fitzwater on Wednesday, 23 January, calling the channel a "conduit for Iraqi disinformation."[68] Presumably inspired by President Bush's characterization of Saddam as Hitler, the CNN correspondent was attacked by one senator in Congress as the Josef Göbbels of Iraq's dictator. The authors of the government sponsored *Gulf War Air Power Survey*, published two years after the war, were not impressed with the quality of Iraqi psychological operations. They regarded the attempt to exploit the incident as an example of the "poor use of western television" by the Iraqi regime, but admit that it had some effect.[69]

A similar event occurred on 13 February, ten days before the ground war started, when a US Air Force F-117 attacked and destroyed a bunker in the al-Firdos neighborhood of Baghdad with two large bombs. The CIA and the

Defense Intelligence Agency (DIA) repeatedly had validated the target as a command and control bunker.[70] At the time the al-Firdos complex was struck, at 0400, it was used as a civilian air-raid shelter. While this was not known to the pilot or the target planners before the attack, it was quickly known to TV watchers and news consumers all over the world after the attack. Iraqi sources accurately said that 200–300 civilians, including over 100 children, had died in the bunker.[71] That morning, Arnett's breakfast in the Rashid Hotel was interrupted by his agitated minder, who had immediately organized a bus to ferry the international press corps to the site. Reporters and their camera crews were there to witness and broadcast images of burned corpses and injured civilians, and the hectic first aid effort under way.[72] CNN interviewed the caretaker of the bunker, saying that hundreds of people, mainly children and women, had been killed by American precision bombs. Meanwhile the Cable News Network's reporting grew increasingly unpopular in official Washington and the political pressure to limit strikes was growing: "The perceived pressure created by the Iraqi's prompt exploitation of the western media," an official Air Force survey pointed out after the war, "produced a sharp reduction in Coalition airstrikes against L[eadership] targets over the next week."[73] General Schwarzkopf felt compelled to review personally all targets selected for air strikes in downtown Baghdad.

Lessons learned

The *Gulf War Air Power Survey*, a five volume study commissioned by the Air Force, concludes that "operations Desert Shield/Desert Storm demonstrated that press coverage is an unavoidable yet important part of military operations."[74] The lesson falls into four components. First, the pool system was not working properly. While the American people were satisfied with the press coverage of the war, journalists and bureau chiefs were not. Their fierce criticism of the pool system dominated the immediate reflections and discussions on the public affairs performance during the war, and soured the military's relationship to the mainstream media. After eight months of discussion with bureau chiefs the Pentagon issued a directive adopting nine principles of war coverage. The most important ones were that open and independent reporting was declared the principal means of covering a conflict; pools were not to serve as a standard and should be disbanded as soon as possible; journalists should abide by a set of ground rules; and the military would take care of adequate transportation and transmission facilities.[75] The primary objective of this process was to reconcile angry journalists and, eventually, to improve the existing pool system for future contingencies. In progressive military circles it was increasingly becoming clear, however, that the pool was a flawed concept and not just badly executed.

Second, censorship would be far more difficult in future wars. The technological trend towards ever more mobile sophisticated equipment and more powerful commercially available communication gadgets was evident: "Technology is not going to make matters easier," the Navy journal *Proceedings* noted in an article after the war. "As it becomes more portable and more miniaturized, television coverage will become more intrusive."[76] Not only was technology becoming more global and intrusive, news networks were establishing themselves as a permanent part of the environment of most future battlefields. Jamie McIntyre, the Pentagon correspondent of the network that rose to global fame in the Gulf War, commented: "Wherever commanders go, they should plan for CNN. Like the weather, we'll always be there – just another feature on the battlefield terrain."[77] And this new element of the operational environment could not be controlled any more by traditional means of censorship.

Third, the Marine's success in their public affairs work was painful for the Army. The VII corps fought a tank battle of historic dimension but not a single picture of it exists. Not even Combat Camera units had produced documentation of the battle.[78] Worse, no reporter delivered a vivid history of the Army's gigantic battle comparable to the compelling stories that exist of the Marine Corps breaking the berm, an attack merely designed to support the far larger effort of the VII Corps. In an article in the *Marine Corps Gazette*, Colonel Shotwell, the Marine commander's public affairs officer, later outlined his and Boomer's rationale in working with the media. The text was entitled *The Fourth Estate as a Force Multiplier*. Marines were more adept at providing logistical support for the media because they knew that "by telling the Marine Corps story to an audience voracious for news from the front they helped build and maintain the support of the American public."[79] The article can be regarded as a snapshot of the most sophisticated attitude on public affairs in the entire US military at the time. Yet, Shotwell does not mention that the media could help to counter adversarial distortions or disinformation, nor does he conceive of the media as a channel to put psychological pressure on the adversary. In this respect, the Iraqi regime was ahead of the American government and military.

Fourth, future adversaries were likely to become more sophisticated in orchestrating their own information campaign, targeted at public support in the US or at the coherence of an alliance. This was the second important trend recognized by military thinkers. Air Force Colonel DeFrank, director of press operations in the Pentagon, pointed to the Persian Gulf War and its first "blatant attempts of disinformation, propaganda, and exploitation – milk factories and all those other things."[80] The planners at the Potomac henceforth would assume that future adversaries would try similar techniques. The Persian Gulf War made clear that the US military needed to engage in what doctrine would call counterpropaganda activities. Ironically, it was the controversial Peter Arnett, himself distrustful of Pentagon "disinformation," who helped the US military understand the significance of information campaigns. For the first time a reporter powerfully, although unwittingly, demonstrated to the US military what it meant to be on the defensive in an information war.

The consequence of those four insights was that public affairs needed to be integrated into strategic thinking and planning. The actual task, though, took some time. In 1991 there was no information operations doctrine, nor was there a public affairs doctrine in the making. As late as two years after the Gulf War the *Joint Doctrine for Command and Control Warfare* was published. The document – the predecessor of the *Information Operations Doctrine* published only in 1998 – did not address public affairs at all. The US military lacked the conceptual tools to grasp the strategic significance of what it meant to have the media become a permanent feature of the battlefield. If the media were like the weather, like rain, the Marines may have managed to operate "wet" in the Persian Gulf War, but they did so in a rather improvised fashion. Not only would there need to be more public affairs planning if the same war would have been fought in the global information environment a decade later – military thinkers would also have to create some meteorological knowledge and develop an amphibious strategy, to remain in the metaphor. They needed to understand the dynamics involved and develop a public affairs strategy that deserved the name. The last decade of the twentieth century, the decade of experimental public affairs, laid the intellectual foundation and created the experiential and conceptual knowledge required for just that: strategic public affairs.

6 Experimental public affairs
Somalia, the Balkans, and Afghanistan

The information environment of the 1990s was characterized by two simultaneous developments in the global media system. First, rapid technological development in consumer electronics at the dawn of the twenty-first century equipped war correspondents with transmission capabilities that were unimaginable in earlier conflicts. In 1991 satellite phones in the hands of reporters were an exception, in 2003 they were the rule. Second, the global media system was continually diversifying. In 1991, the BBC and CNN had a virtual monopoly on the distribution of global video imagery. Ten years later this was not the case any more. Competition, a result of diversification, made it almost impossible for media organizations to resist the temptation to break a story. Not only had al-Jazeera and later al-Arabiya entered the scene in the Arab-speaking world, consumers in any given country could now receive satellite channels with affordable satellite dishes. Most significantly, however, the internet transformed the business of war reporting as it was both a source of global news for the consumer and a source of global information that could be recycled by news organizations. Consequently, the Pentagon launched its website, *defenselink.mil*, in October 1994. Ten years later bloggers, one-person online media publishers, began to populate the internet, and the publicly available information supply broadened and accelerated. Both trends, technological progress and diversification, were speeding up war coverage: "Fed by the internet, fed by television, anything that is published or put on the air has the capability of going around the world instantly," military leaders had recognized.[1]

In the wars throughout the 1990s, the US military slowly came to grips with this new information environment, conceptually as well as practically. On the practical side, several smaller operations offered a source of valuable experience and a test bed for what it meant to engage in military operations in the information age. Somalia demonstrated the media's power, the wars in the Balkans showed the enemy's sophistication to use this power, and Afghanistan helped to find a way out of the dilemma. Throughout those smaller wars in the era of experimental public affairs, but particularly in Afghanistan, the idea to embed reporters with military units was reluctantly but successfully tested. On the conceptual side, the Joint Chiefs of Staff as well as the services started to adapt their doctrinal publications to the new information environment. Information operations evolved as a discipline out of more technical Command and Control Warfare and, at first, was envisaged without taking its public dimension into account. At the same time, but somewhat disconnected, public affairs doctrine was improved and adapted to the new environment. At the dawn of the twenty-first century these two schools of thought, information operations thinking on the one hand and public affairs thinking on the other hand, still coexisted without synergy.

Somalia

During the preparations for Operation Desert Storm, on 1 January 1991, Central Command conducted a non-combatant evacuation order in a small war torn country at the horn of Africa. Civil war and chaos had gripped Somalia. Operation Eastern Exit evacuated 281 people from the US embassy in Mogadishu, the country's capital, after Mohamed Siad Barre's dictatorship and the government of Somalia had dissolved. By early 1992 the country had fragmented, all government authority had collapsed, and several warlords competed for power. Two of them, General Mohamed Farah Aideed and Ali Mahdi Mohamed, sought to control Mogadishu. Continued conflict between clans led to growing chaos, a drought caused mass starvation. The world witnessed the plight of the civilian population on television. To stop widespread famine and civil war the UN Security Council adopted Resolution 751 in April 1992, and a variety of different humanitarian aid organizations entered the country to help its people. Operation UNOSOM I was launched to monitor the ceasefire between Aideed and Mohamed, and later to protect the distribution of humanitarian aid. But the situation in Somalia deteriorated further. General Aideed threatened the UN peace-keeping force and eventually, in November, attacked and killed several Pakistani troops at the airport. The UN force, it became clear, was unable to provide security for humanitarian activities. On 3 December, the Security Council authorized the US-led Unified Task Force, UNITAF, with the objective to create a secure environment for humanitarian aid. Operation Restore Hope was more complex than a regular joint or combined operation. Not only did all four US military services participate, action had to be coordinated with the State Department and USAID, 20 coalition countries and 49 different humanitarian agencies which complicated the coordination and cooperation efforts. Finally, the UN was a major player as it would later take over the entire operation under UNOSOM II. Adding to the complexity of foreign actors involved, the security environment in Somalia was extremely dangerous. The public affairs operation in Somalia had a bumpy start and a devastating end.

The beach

On 9 December 1992, an amphibious landing of US troops marked the launch of operation Restore Hope. The world public and, more importantly, the American media were already on alert that UN and American troops would soon arrive in

Africa. Five days before the operation's scheduled launch, Secretary of Defense Cheney and Chairman Powell had given a rather detailed operational briefing in the Pentagon where they announced self-confidently the deployment of a formidable force. When the Navy Seals and the Marines, the spearhead of a total of 25,400 troops, went ashore on hostile territory at night, close to Somalia's capital, they engaged a small force surprisingly well equipped. Seventy-five international reporters occupied the beach, in full gear, armed with floodlights and cameras mounted, determined to broadcast live from the battlefield.

The task force already had about 20 journalists on their ships, assuming that this pool would provide coverage of their arrival. They were not informed that more media representatives would be waiting at the beach. When the soldiers came ashore, the beach resembled a movie set rather than a real strip of African coast, with cameras, bright television lights, and journalists trying to put the clandestine landing right into the focus of world attention.[2] As the soldiers went into this hostile environment they expected, if anything, to meet enemy resistance. Poised for combat and adrenalin pumping, the Marines were somewhat confused to find the international press at the beach – and they were not prepared to react appropriately. Donatella Lorch, a young but experienced war correspondent, recalls a persuasive encounter with one of the soldiers at the beach, her face in the dirt and a gun at her head in split seconds: "Get the fuck down, you wanna fuck me to blow your fucking head off?" the serviceman recommended.[3] In retrospect Lorch defended the soldiers, saying that it was not the Marines' fault but that "a bit of a lapse in communication" was the problem that caused the infamous beach incident. At the nightly beach in Somalia the military's and the media's culture clashed in a most dramatic way.

While the landing forces were not warned by their uniformed superiors, the news media were. The coverage was a deliberate part of military planning, albeit ill advised. The morning before the incident, Robert Oakley, the US ambassador with an important role in the entire UN operation, had briefed a group of reporters at the US military base in Somalia announcing that an amphibious landing was scheduled for about midnight. If the reporters would like to be present and cover the event, they should cross the security gates without their Somali translators, he advised.[4] The intent of this public affairs experiment, according to a textbox in a doctrinal publication of the Marine Corps, was to "send a message" to the Somali warlords.[5] It remains unclear what exactly that message was supposed to convey, or how Somali commanders had interpreted it. It is crystal-clear, however, how US commanders received the message. "The December 9 1992 beach scene in Somalia represented the essence of every commander's fears over the violation of operations security," Charles Ricks, a former instructor at the Defense Information School, pointed out in a study for the Army War College.[6] The camera-wielding reporters not only broadcast a nightly landing, they also illuminated the landing spot as a target area for a potential enemy ambush. The event was a veritable public affairs disaster.

But the beach scene illustrated a general trend. The information environment of military operations was in the midst of change. Commercial media were becoming a permanent feature of the battlefield, with independent technology capable of broadcasting in near real-time. Particularly in low-intensity conflicts it would be nearly impossible to control the media's access to operations in the same fashion as in Grenada, Panama, or the Persian Gulf War. The second incident that contributed to Somalia's legacy would make this clear in a rather painful way.

A dead Ranger

On the 3 October 1993, in the afternoon, a force of 160 troops, 19 aircraft and 12 vehicles set out from their base close to Mogadishu airport to "snatch and grab" leading figures of Mohamed Aideed's Habr Gidr clan and possibly the strongman himself. Their target was the Olympic Hotel in downtown Mogadishu. When the Americans had stormed the hotel and captured several enemy fighters, the situation quickly got out of hand. The task force encountered small arms fire, and two Black Hawk helicopters were downed. The operation escalated into a pitched battle in a typical developing world urban environment: narrow streets, civilians intermingling with enemy combatants armed with AK47 and RPGs. Delta Force, Air Force combat search and rescue assets, Navy Seals, and Army Rangers experienced more than 50 percent casualties in 18 hours fighting against Somali paramilitaries without formal training. When the battle was over, 18 American soldiers were killed, 84 wounded and one, Chief Warrant Officer Michael Durant, the pilot of one of the downed Black Hawk helicopters, was captured. Aideed's troops celebrated their victory by desecrating the naked body of a dead US Ranger and dragging it through the dirty streets of Mogadishu. Initial hearsay reports had it that an angry mob was showing body parts as "trophies," but these were dismissed by the Pentagon. After images of the events in Mogadishu's narrow streets emerged in the news, the story spun equally out of control in Washington's Pennsylvania Avenue.

Paul Watson, a print reporter from the *Toronto Star*, photographed the Ranger's abuse as he happened to be on the scene with his 35mm pocket camera. The reporter later won a Pulitzer Prize for his picture. While the still photos of the battle were taken by an independent western journalist, the moving images shown on CNN came from a questionable source. The Somali driver and stringer Mohamoud Hassan – allegedly associated with Aideed and a former freelancer for Reuters[7] – recorded the video of the soldier's corpse being dragged and kicked through the dirt as well as the footage of Durant's interrogation. Hassan had recorded the video early on 4 October and transmitted the Hi-8 cartridge through Nairobi to London from where CNN relayed the footage electronically to Atlanta.[8] Soon the grisly pictures of the dead Ranger's humiliation and the frightened face of the interrogated Durant were broadcast across the United States and the rest of the world. Given that Hassan was able to obtain the video of Durant's interrogation, where presumably no independent local journalist was present, the assumption seems valid that the warlord had an interest in getting the images out. It is thus a plausible and probable assumption that

Aideed and his colonels had an information operations calculus in mind: they intended to penetrate their adversary's decision loop and break America's will. If the images had this intention, they were highly successful.

Major David B. Stockwell, chief UNOSOM II military spokesman from March 1993 to March 1994, argues that it was a legacy of the last war that played out in Somalia. During the Persian Gulf War the public affairs apparatus "created too much of a notion that war was bloodless and had evolved to such a high state of technology that combat was like playing a Nintendo game."[9] The facsimiles of mutilated and interrogated American soldiers contrasted sharply with the expectation to see a surgical and bloodless war. Images of the naked corpse of a US soldier and the battered face and frightened voice of another captured soldier sent shockwaves through the American body politic: "The people who are dragging American bodies don't look very hungry to the people of Texas," commented Republican senator Phil Gramm, reacting to thousands of telephone calls to Capitol Hill demanding the withdrawal of US forces.[10] John McCain, an Arizona Republican on the Armed Services Committee, demanded that "Clinton's got to bring them home."[11] Not only did Congress put pressure on the President to consider a pullout from Somalia; the images had their own direct effect in the White House. National Security Advisor Anthony Lake commented later on the TV footage of the Battle of Mogadishu. The "pictures helped make us recognize that the military situation in Mogadishu had deteriorated in a way that we had not frankly recognized," the President's advisor confessed.[12] Bill Clinton eventually decided to withdraw.[13] The media, it became forcefully clear to the military, were not just becoming a permanent tactical condition of the battlefield, as the beach incident already illustrated; they had become a strategic factor in the *political* environment in Washington, and that factor could determine the outcome of an entire military operation. What is more, the incident undermined the credibility of American military might in the eyes of its opponents for the years to come: if confronted with casualties, they concluded, the Americans would cut and run "with their tail between their legs."[14]

Lessons learned

Two lessons were inspired by the public affairs mistakes and by the coverage of Somalia: the first lesson was that the media had become a permanent feature of the battlefield: "There is no longer a question of whether the news media will cover military operations," an officer graduating from the Army War College argued in his thesis. "As in Somalia, journalists will likely precede the force into the area of operation; and they will transmit images of events as they happen, perhaps from both sides of any conflict." Attempts to leash the media would not be feasible any more, "efforts at control are meaningless."[15] Significant numbers of journalists will already be in theater before operations begin, he argued, as had been shown in Panama or Somalia. General Anthony Zinni, commander of the United Shield rescue operation in Somalia, later drew conclusions regarding the handling of the press under the new circumstances: "On today's battlefield, effective media relations have become an essential ingredient to military success." His advice to commanders is to "never attempt to manipulate the media." The reasoning behind this advice is that the media are going to be there and that they will find out anyway: "If there is bad news, it is best to deliver it immediately rather than be accused later of a cover up."[16] The same line of argument later entered doctrinal documents, with direct reference to the Mogadishu beach incident: "The new reality is that the news media will be with Marines on deployments," a Marine public affairs manual says. And it quotes the incident as an illustration of the battlefield's new information environment: "The word will get out immediately because live coverage is now the norm. As we learned in Somalia in 1993, reporters and news crews will sometimes be on the scene even before the Marines land."[17] The *Doctrine for Public Affairs in Joint Operations* equally refers to the amphibious landing and its "live television and radio coverage" to illustrate that the "environment of the modern battlefield has changed drastically and so has the ability of the news media to transmit instantaneous and often live reports."[18]

Somalia's second lesson was that the "strategic corporal" was recognized. The term was coined by General Charles C. Krulak, former commander of the Marine Corps and Victor Krulak's son: "The inescapable lesson of Somalia and other recent operations, whether humanitarian assistance, peace-keeping, or traditional warfighting, is that their outcome may hinge on decisions made by small unit leaders, and by actions taken at the *lowest* level."[19] This argument has an almost revolutionary potential as it cuts across the traditional three levels of war: the strategic, the operational, and the tactical. Immediately after Somalia, a widely read and extraordinarily influential article appeared in *Parameters*. In *Winning CNN Wars*, Colonel Frank Stech made a similar argument as he reviewed the events that ended the US engagement in Somalia: "The outcome of the Rangers' fight was militarily insignificant," he argues, but "the TV images and lack of a media plan to explain administration policies made the losses politically overwhelming."[20] Major Stockwell, after returning from his job at the Horn of Africa to the US, reflected on his experience in a thesis written at the Strategic Studies Institute in Carlisle: "Somalia reinforced that public opinion is a military operation's center of gravity and that media access to the battlefield is a military operation's critical vulnerability."[21] The argument of the strategic corporal, which was outlined in military journals and masters theses only at the end of the 1990s, had become conventional wisdom several years later as it penetrated doctrinal publications. The theorem is best summed up in the Marine Corps's public affairs manual. After quoting the Somalia amphibious landing incident, the document concludes: "Because of the forward presence of the news media, what used to be tactical- or operational-level situations can now quickly escalate and affect decisions at the strategic or national level."[22]

The significance of the strategic corporal cannot be overestimated. It was the missing link in military thinking. After Panama and Grenada, and indeed still in the Persian Gulf War's aftermath, military analysts, public affairs officers, and even the JCS chairman had argued that operational success was linked to successful public affairs. But they were unable to grasp and show exactly how that link worked. Somalia offered the necessary experience to close that conceptual gap: tactical blunders of little military significance could be magnified through the prism of the global media, thereby elevated to a strategic level, where they could then unfold a political momentum on their own. The picture of a single killed US Ranger dragged naked through a dusty side road in Mogadishu resulted in a presidential decision to pull out US troops. This was the perfect illustration of the strategic corporal. Colonel Rick Thomas, who played an important role in the embedded media program's design and implementation in the 2003 Iraq War, went back to Mogadishu to illustrate the tactic–strategy link: "Somalia may be the better example where a tactical event on the ground had strategic implications in that it changed our policy completely."[23]

The consequences were clear: if you do not want to be controlled by the information environment, control the information environment. The difference between the two is analogous to a reactive and a proactive public affairs policy – which, in turn, had conceptual and practical consequences for the relationship between public affairs and information operations. Somalia marked the starting point of an intellectual movement in the US armed forces that sought to integrate public affairs into the broader and more aggressive concept of information operations. Military culture, however, was not yet ready to make that next step. But another, unanticipated problem added to the pressure. It turned out in the following wars, that not only some progressive US commanders grasped the theorem of the strategic corporal and its wider consequences, but that future adversaries did so as well. And they would try to exploit this distinct vulnerability of the alliance of western democracies they confronted. During the Nato-led Kosovo intervention in 1999 this point was hammered home as the Milosevic regime virtually owned the information initiative.

The Balkans

The wars in the Balkans are complex in their causes as well as in their military history. Two public affairs lessons stand out. At first, in Bosnia, the US Army had troops on the ground and embedded reporters for the first time, but those units and their embedded press did not see combat. Later, in Kosovo, American soldiers saw combat, albeit without embedded reporters. Nato launched a so-called humanitarian intervention to stop "ethnic cleansing" in Kosovo, but the operation was conducted solely airborne which made embedding impossible.

The first time

In the early 1990s the former Yugoslavia saw a fierce ethnic civil war. While the war with its attacks on Sarajevo's civilian population was highly visible and publicized, the US troop deployment that followed is not remembered for any high-profile coverage of combat scenes. The peacekeeping operation in Bosnia, however, was the first time the US Army used an open access press policy and called it "embedding." Sean Naylor is a pioneer of embedding on the journalists' side – he writes for *Army Times*, a publication of the Garnett Foundation, which also owns *USA Today*: "The first one that was done that was actually called embedding that I am aware of was Bosnia," Naylor said.[24] He was one of about two dozen reporters who went into Bosnia accompanying the 1st Armored Division. The reporters were assigned to the Germany-based unit for approximately a week in advance. In the actual deployment in Bosnia, which would last at least two weeks, the reporters gathered experience from inside the operation: they were sleeping on cots in floorless and unheated tents, ate field rations, and shared the deprivations of army life with ordinary soldiers. The division leadership hoped that the arrangement would produce positive stories and boost morale both for the soldiers in Bosnia and for Americans back home. On both accounts the opposite threatened to happen.

One of the most prominent journalists embedded with the Army in Bosnia was Thomas Ricks of the *Wall Street Journal*. The reporter, who traveled with the division's 1st Brigade, had free access to the troops as there was no censorship program or explicit ground rules on how to interview soldiers and how to treat their statements. The unit's commander, Colonel Greg Fontenot, even offered Ricks admission to the brigade's daily staff meetings and intelligence cells. Fontenot had asked the journalist not to report classified information. In late December 1995, around Christmas, the colonel invited the journalist to join him and a small group of soldiers on a reconnaissance patrol across the Sava River into Bosnia. In the pre-mission briefing Fontenot said to two black soldiers that "it'll be interesting to hear what you two see, because the Croatians are racist. . ." In another statement Fontenot said that the US will have a military presence on the Balkans "for a long, long time." Upon return, Ricks finished his story, including Fontenot's statements, and filed it to his editor from the hotel command post in Croatia.[25]

The story was published on 27 December 1995 in the *Wall Street Journal* and was immediately picked up by the *New York Times*. Both the racism quote, but even more so the statement about the duration of the mission, did not play well in Washington. A colonel appeared to question the president's stated policy to limit the mission to one year. Army leaders responded with outrage and pressured to investigate the case. Despite the matter soon being put to rest, Fontenot, who was seen as a rising star and one of the best colonels in the army, was never promoted to general rank. Richard Newman, a fellow journalist also embedded with the unit, wrote a study on the impact of the Fontenot incident, "Burned by the Press: One Commander's Perspective." He reports that "within the Army, Fontenot's story became a kind of word-of-mouth parable on how press attention can be harmful to an officer's unit and particularly to his career."[26] In the military, opposition against embedding was building up. This was registered with concern in the Pentagon. Kenneth Bacon, the department's spokesman, was facing "some resistance to embedding reporters in units,"[27] as he said, and swiftly reacted with a new ground rule: all conversations with troops were to be considered off the record, unless otherwise stated. In practice the rule meant that journalists could not quote somebody by name unless that person knew that he was being quoted. Naylor, a fellow journalist of Ricks in Bosnia, said that the military tried to avoid situations where "you stand in a dining facility and some guy says something and you look at his name tag and it appears in the *Washington Post*." The so-called Ricks-Rule was henceforth standard text in public affairs guidance: "All interviews with service members will be on the record."[28]

Despite the row about the Fontenot affair, embedding was regarded as successful by the commander of the 1st Armored Division, Major General William Nash. Some reporters, the general wrote after his tour, had "developed a high level of expertise" and had a "great potential to wield influence" which he wanted to tap by giving them "true access to the soldiers."[29] Nash's assessment was echoed by other army officers looking back to the Balkan experience before the Iraq War: "In Bosnia we did it, and it worked," Shields had argued.[30] Despite this positive assessment, embedding would not be the policy in the next operation.

Magnified blunders

The conflict environment, not officers' skeptical attitudes reinvigorated after the Fontenot case, made embedding in Kosovo impossible: "The war was fought mostly from Aviano Air Base," DeFrank pointed out later. The operation's exclusively airborne nature created an unprecedented public affairs challenge. Since there were no troops on the ground, there were not any troops with which to embed reporters: "You can't embed somebody in an F-16 fighter jet, there is only space for one person," he added.[31] Because there were no journalists telling Nato's story on the ground, the "humanitarian intervention" in Kosovo, which claimed the moral high ground by definition, elevated public affairs to unexpected military significance. The war was almost as much about public opinion as it was about the destruction of targets in Serbia, in the words of the Supreme Allied Commander Europe (Saceur), General Wesley Clark.[32] The Milosevic regime in Belgrade was committing crimes against humanity by killing and expelling the Albanian civilian population from the province of Kosovo, yet is was the Atlantic Alliance that was publicly accused in western news outlets of inflicting harm and hardships to the civilian population by destroying the wrong targets, as many senior Nato leaders, civilian as well as military, saw it.[33] This was the effect of the strategic corporal. Relatively isolated tactical blunders – less than 1 percent of all ordnance erred – were magnified by their coverage in the international news media and elevated to strategic importance.[34] Two events stand out.

On 14 April 1999, the twenty-second day of the airstrikes, US Air Force F16s mistakenly attacked a civilian tractor convoy near the village Djakovica in Kosovo. At least 20 refugees were killed by Nato bombs.[35] After the misguided bombing of the refugees the regime in Belgrade tried to exploit the occasion for information operations purposes. Journalists in Belgrade were offered free transportation to the site by the Serb government in order to get them to report on the alliance killing civilians.[36] CNN's Alessio Vinci, escorted to the scene by Serb officials, filed his descriptions of mangled tractors and minibuses. Graphic images of burned and bloodied corpses, and limbs scattered among destroyed vehicles, were on the front pages and in TV reports for several days. A blood-stained baby doll made a powerful symbolic motive for the Nato-caused pain of the ordinary population. CNN quoted a Serbian official calling the attack a "humanitarian catastrophe." The event drew an intense reaction in the media. CNN alone broadcast 60 reports on Djakovica.[37] "Civilians Are Slain in Military Attack on Kosovo Road," ran a front page headline of the *New York Times* on 15 April. Also on its front page, the *Los Angeles Times* concluded that the "Convoy Deaths May Undermine [Nato's] Moral Authority." Nato officials were ill-equipped to deal with a PR disaster of such magnitude. Initially Clark had blamed the attack on the Serbs, and Kenneth Bacon, the Pentagon spokesman, asserted that "we only hit military vehicles." Eventually, after five days, Nato responded in an official briefing to the Djakovica convoy attack, and the com-manding Air Force General of the 31st Expeditionary Wing conceded after an inquiry that civilian refugees were bombed by the F16 pilots by mistake. By waiting too long to respond as well as by contradicting itself on the facts, the alliance created the impression that it had something to hide.

The Djakovica incident had a profound impact on Nato's public affairs opera-tion. The heads of state of the United Kingdom and the United States, Tony Blair and Bill Clinton, had invested considerable political capital in the conflict and saw a "serious problem" in the dismal coverage and the eroding popular support. When they discussed Djakovica on the telephone shortly after the acci-dent, the two leaders decided to act. Alistair Campbell, a talented and experi-enced communications specialist who had excelled as manager of Blair's election campaign, was sent to Brussels to "assess the weaknesses" of Nato and streamline its communications effort. P.J. Crowley, deputy spokesman of the NSC, and a competent team of experts from the State Department, the Pentagon, and the White House reinforced the public affairs team in Brussels, increasing it to a staff of 60. Nato's communication bureau in Brussels had initially started with three people. Jamie Shea, the charismatic spokesman with the distinctive East-London accent, first thought was that he would be fired, as Javier Solana, then Nato's Secretary General, was in no position to reject the "offer."[38]

A second memorable event occurred three weeks later. On 7 May, at 2350, several allied missiles hit the Chinese embassy in Belgrade. In the attack that seriously damaged the embassy complex and the neighboring buildings, three Chinese citizens were killed and approximately 15 injured. Flawed intelligence provided by the CIA had identified the Chinese embassy as the Yugoslav Federal Directorate for Supply and Procurement.[39] The US government later apologized to the Chinese government and agreed to pay compensation. Quanti-tatively, the incident was the most publicized single event of the entire war. CNN carried 212 reports, and – as in the Djakovica case – rumors spread that the target was hit deliberately. Although the coordination of the official reaction within Nato had been largely improved, it took the alliance three days to respond to the accidental bombing of the Chinese embassy.

Both incidents illustrate the increased significance of the "information battle-space."[40] Although the Serbs did not control the element of surprise – which was actually created by allied bombs going astray – the government in Belgrade was able to exploit occasions and to "gain and maintain the information initiative," as the US Air Force would call it several years later.[41] The adversary was in control of the pictures and the details. Though in terms of military capability the Serbs were far inferior to Nato, on the information battlefield they almost succeeded to break the coalition's back. Both tactical incidents, through their coverage, had a strategic effect: "After the tractor convoy incident, we stopped daytime sorties; after the Chinese Embassy, we stopped attacks on Belgrade," the alliance's spokesman said.[42] General Wesley Clark puts it even more drastically: "The weight of public opinion was doing to us what the Serb air defense system had failed to do: limit our strikes."[43] The line between military action and the coverage of military action was increasingly blurred, not only on the defense but also on the offense.

On 23 April 1999, at 0220, allied aircraft attacked the central studio of the state owned RTS broadcasting corporation in the center of Belgrade. Between ten and 17 people were killed in the incident. Other than the civilian convoy or the Chinese embassy, the Serb TV studio was destroyed intentionally: "Radio Television Serbia," Nato spokespersons made clear, "despite the appearance, is an instrument of war."[44] The Supreme Commander also justified the RTS attack: "Serb radio and television is an instrument of propaganda and repression ... It has filled the airways with hate and with lies over the years, and especially now. It is therefore a legitimate target in this campaign."[45] Militarily the attack was intended to downgrade both the regime's internal communications (Command, Control and Communication capabilities, "C3," in military idiom) as well as its external communications, its capability to determine the western news agenda by disseminating "propaganda" in the Serb TV only to be picked up by western news organizations. With the attack, the allied command wanted to take away the "information initiative" from the Milosevic regime.

The saturation strategy

The problem the allies were facing had two components. First there were no troops and no journalists on the ground to quell the press's thirst for detailed information; secondly the Serbs were skilled at setting the news agenda by diluting attention to allied blunders. Nato was unable to counter the gruesome details provided by the Serbs with its own detailed accounts. All Nato had was abstract words and denials. The coalition had to find a way to deal with this problem. Masterminded by British communication experts, the alliance embraced an innovative media strategy. Shea explained that "our credo at Nato was just to be on the air the whole time, crowd out the opposition, give every interview, do every briefing."[46] The saturation strategy, as Shea called the new approach in media management in a speech to the Reform Club in London, comprised several elements: quality, quantity, and timing of the briefings – they needed to be good, plenty, and fast. Nato's motto was to "give them [the journalists] the news before they give you the news."[47]

According to Alistair Campbell, Blair's reinforcement to Brussels, it was competition that "drove the broadcasters to put Milosevic's pictures of 'Nato blunders' at the top of their bulletins, and it was our job to try to provide competing stories, pictures and arguments."[48] Briefings needed to be more "interesting" in the words of then Nato's Secretary General Javier Solana – Nato spokespersons needed to compete against the news-value of sensational images showing corpses and destruction. One way to raise the newsworthiness of the briefings were "presentational innovations," Campbell argued, like gun-camera footage combined with satellite imagery, video link-ups, and a charismatic and eloquent spokesman: "We knew that we had to innovate to keep their [the media's] attention. It was vital to try to hold the public's interest on our terms."[49] But the timing and the quantity of the briefings were just as important. In a candid speech after the war the alliance's chief spokesman explained:

> We had an MoD briefing from London late in the morning, and just as the audience was switching off from that, on came the 3 PM briefing [from Brussels], and as soon as the 3 PM briefing was off the air, up jumped the Pentagon, the State Department and the White House.
>
> (J. Shea, *The Kosovo Crisis and the Media: Reflections of a Nato Spokesman*, at Atlantic Council of the United Kingdom, Reform Club, London, 15 July 1999)

The one thing that Nato did well, according to Shea, was occupying the media space. Briefings tailored to CNN's demands were a cheap way for the networks to fill their airtime: "The best way of filling an hour virtually cost-free is to put Nato's daily briefing in the box," he explained.[50] P.J. Crowley was on Shea's staff in Brussels and assisted the PA effort there: "Between our three daily briefings, we were able to command 18 hours of the 24-hour news day. The media dwelt more on our information than they did on Belgrade's."[51]

Lessons learned

Two fundamental lessons were drawn from Kosovo. First, the enemy became increasingly skilled at orchestrating information operations with the objective to undermine public and allied support. An article in *Military Review* argued that "Milosevic's spokesmen used the press to expose Nato's mistakes and collateral damage, in some cases depicting the Serbs as victims of oppression."[52] Wesley Clark, the US commander of the Allied Force, recalled later that the officials in Belgrade "were excellent in organizing press coverage and directing it toward Nato mistakes." The Serbs would do "everything," he wrote, to portray the allied strikes as targeting civilians rather than police and military forces. Serb information operations put the mighty alliance on the defensive in the public debate: "The result was embarrassing for Nato, they could assure world media coverage faster than we could investigate and explain it." The leadership of the alliance was constrained in its strategic decision making and busy trying to reclaim the moral high ground: "Day after day we found ourselves working to explain and clarify. After the first weeks, we were on the defensive."[53] In an article, Air Force Major Gary Pounder argued along the same line: "Visual images rendered strategic importance to a handful of tactical events and threatened to undermine political and military coalitions in the process."[54] The near-success of the information campaign of Nato's adversaries had worrying implications for the future, as *Jane's Intelligence Review* pointed out: "Serbian information operations carried out during Nato's 'Operation Allied Force' were unprecedented in their quality and sophistication and point to the likelihood of increased asymmetric use of information in future conflicts."[55]

The second lesson from Kosovo was a reaction to the first: the development of information operations doctrine. Western military thinkers realized that if the enemy learned to use information successfully against the alliance, they themselves had better improve their own information operations doctrine. The traditionally clear-cut distinction between command and control warfare on the one hand and public affairs operations on the other hand was called into question, practically on the battlefield, as the attack of RTS illustrates, as well as conceptually in doctrinal debates. The terminology and the concepts to grasp the new insights was largely missing. Notions like "information superiority," "information initiative," or even "saturation strategy" were not used in internal discussions in Brussels during Operation Allied Force; only in subsequent debates and publications were these concepts retrospectively applied.[56] Although some military periodicals, and even some specialized doctrinal publications, explored the intersections between information operations and public affairs, those ideas were far off mainstream military thinking at the time. Only the Kosovo experience with its sobering episodes moved public affairs into the focus of military commanders and illustrated the critical dangers of neglecting the public side of modern warfare. The conceptual connection was best expressed by the alliance's spokesman: "Winning the media campaign is just as important as winning the military campaign – the two are inseparable. You can't win one without the other."[57] That insight was essential for what happened two years later.

Afghanistan

The US war against the Taliban regime in Afghanistan was a direct reaction to the 9/11 terrorist attacks against the twin towers in New York and the Pentagon in Washington. Al-Qaeda had its largest operating bases in the landlocked Central Asian country's rugged mountains and cave labyrinths. Operation Enduring Freedom (OEF) was launched on 7 October 2001 with twin objectives: to destroy al-Qaeda's sanctuary in Afghanistan, and to remove the Taliban regime. The military strategy was equally based on two components: Special Forces clandestinely infiltrating the country and recruiting Afghan support, and the Air Force taking out specific targets from high altitude and with high-tech weaponry. Conventional forces were brought in only after nearly two months.

The media–military relationship went sour in the early phase of the campaign. When OEF was launched 39 journalists were aboard American Naval vessels and even more were dispatched to various Air Force bases. But reporters were denied access to the battlefield during and immediately after the attack against the Taliban. The media representatives on the aircraft carrier USS *Carl Vinson*, for instance, had no permission to broadcast until 20 hours after the initial air strikes. Walter Rodgers from CNN, who would be at the tip of the spear in the next war, was on the ship, unable and desperate to do his job: "The Navy locked us down and we could not file live," he complained in a news report on the next day.[58] The Special Forces units infiltrating the country from the ground and assisting their Afghan allies, the Northern Alliance, did their work clandestinely and far from any journalist's microphone, camera, or pen. Had Operation Enduring Freedom been a short intervention like Grenada or Panama, the media management would not have been much different. Only after experiencing problems and making mistakes, for which it had to apologize later, did the Pentagon decide to change its restrictive PA tactics.

News cycling

In the Pentagon, at first, a new concept was tested: provide media coverage from Arlington. On 19 October 2001, Army Rangers conducted a nightly raid against the residential compound of the Taliban leader Mullar Omar. In a morning briefing after the first major ground operation, on 20 October, more than just the usual slides were used in the Pentagon's briefing room. Victoria Clarke's PA office had worked hard overnight and was able to release video footage captured by Combat Camera units the night before. General Richard Myers, the chairman of the Joint Chiefs of Staff, delivered the narrative to black-and-white images of Army Special Forces troopers diving from their aircraft into the dark as well as grainy green video-feeds offering a ground view of soldiers entering abandoned buildings. This was, after all, new. Clarke, the Assistant Secretary of Defense for Public Affairs, and her staff, were proud of their achievement of providing exceptionally swift and vivid coverage in an official DoD briefing – the footage was newsworthy and must-see TV.

But reporters were skeptical. Jamie McIntyre, of CNN, was present at the briefing and expressed his reservations in a live report that immediately followed the briefing. The news coverage, in the words of his network colleague Bob Franken, was "controlled absolutely by the military and the government," as the reporter confronted Secretary of Defense Donald Rumsfeld in a briefing a few days later.[59] The idea to substitute independent reporters for combat camera units on the ground did not bode well with the networks; and the reporters' ensuing skepticism, criticism, and lack of trust, in turn, could not be tolerated by the Pentagon, as it undermined the department's credibility. Just as in the military, the prevailing attitude in the press toward government-provided information was rooted in recent history, particularly Watergate and Vietnam. Lies were commonplace, and trust eroded. A remark by Sarah Chayes, a reporter for *National Public Radio*, illustrates the erosion of government credibility: "When the Pentagon said something and the Taliban said the contrary, the Taliban were usually correct."[60] Others echoed the skepticism. Ulrich Deppendorf, Berlin bureau chief of the largest German TV channel, ARD, expressed his concern regarding the lack of independent sources for the coverage of Afghanistan to the *New York Times*: "We have to rely on what the U.S. government claims, or on what the Taliban via *Al Jazeera* claims, or on information from the Pakistani news agency."[61] An immediate result was that the Taliban had a stage for their own information campaign.

Something had to be done. In mid-November the Pentagon, together with the State Department, launched a proactive media campaign. So-called "Coalition Information Centers," or CICs, were established in Islamabad, London, and Washington. Their objective was to counter Taliban "lies" on civilian casualties and the progress of the war. Kenton Keith, a former American ambassador, was sent to Islamabad with a staff of eight to set up and run a center. In an interview he explained the rationale behind the effort:

> The fact is that Islamabad is 10 hours ahead of Washington and it was discovered that a lot of the accusations and misinformation that were coming from representatives of the Taliban were simply being allowed to circulate and sink in for 10 hours before there was a response. It was decided to try to do something about that and that was the genesis of the coalition center here in Islamabad.
> (Keith, Kenton, quoted in J. Branstein, "Afghanistan: Media Center in Pakistan Hopes to Counter Taliban Propaganda," *RFE/RL*, 26 November 2001)

The idea to set up those centers was masterminded by Clarke and her British counterpart, Alistair Campbell. The CICs had two characteristics. First, they were tailored to the 24-hour news cycle. When a rumor or a false account appeared in the local media 10 time zones away from Washington, European media would likely pick the news up, and eventually the story would leapfrog into major US outlets, whose journalists had to meet their deadline another six hours later and were happy to use the predigested bits of news coming in from Europe. Like in Kosovo, the US could merely react to the enemy setting the news agenda if working under such a system. The information centers were explicitly modeled on techniques successfully used during the Nato campaign in Kosovo to counter the enemy spin on the events. Secondly, they were proactive instead of reactive. The campaigners developed a concerted "message of the day" with the objective to "dominate global media coverage" with positive stories: humanitarian assistance for locals or building a representative Afghan government.

The most successful example of such an infused story was the women-campaign: on 16 November, Vice President Dick Cheney's political adviser

Mary Matalin held a conference call on Afghan women with women Cabinet officials and female members of Congress. Later in the day, Under Secretary of State for Global Affairs Paula Dobriansky met with leaders of NGOs to discuss the situation of women in Afghanistan. First Lady Laura Bush gave a radio address to the nation a day later. In Europe, Cherie Blair, the British prime minister's wife, joined in with a televised address on 19 November; that same day Clarke had a conference call with women business leaders; Karen Hughes, who masterminded the campaign, talked to female editors and publishers on the following day; and National Security Advisor Condoleezza Rice raised the topic in TV talk shows. The women story developed its own dynamic and many details were picked up by media outlets all over the world, often without knowing that it was a government-initiated and concerted public relations campaign.[62] The characteristic photographs of veiled women in Burkas provided the aesthetic backdrop.

The CICs, however, only worked as long as no attention-grabbing "real" news was stealing the limelight from the pre-planned messages-of-the-day. When conventional forces entered the operation in late November, this changed. On 4 December an Air Force bomber mistakenly killed several US Special Forces units as well as several Afghans. The 24 casualties of this friendly fire incident were brought into Camp Rhino, about 80 miles southwest of Kandahar. By coincidence a group of 12 reporters was staying in a large warehouse at the base, waiting for the next pool to arrive in a C130 aircraft, and writing feature stories. The group was already frustrated because they had not witnessed any newsworthy events, and the military had even tried to please the reporters by taking them to promotion ceremonies. With casualties and two plane-loads of journalists coming in, the three public affairs officers on the ground were overwhelmed. Desperate to handle the situation, the officers confined the press to a warehouse. The journalists were not happy with this treatment: "We had greater freedom of coverage of Soviet military operations in Afghanistan then we had at Camp Rhino," Walter Rodgers, one of the confined, later complained in a *Washington Post* interview.[63] The Pentagon officially apologized to the journalists after the event, but it demonstrated that the military–media relationship remained fragile.

Test bed for embeds

While the Coalition Information Centers were producing proactive public affairs on a strategic level, insufficient information was offered on the tactical level and embedding was a way to deal with that problem. In an awkward coalition, the pressure to embed journalists with military units came not only from the Washington news media bureau chiefs; the Marine Corps, although for different reasons, was also pushing for a more open public affairs approach. The military's embedding experience in Afghanistan falls into three phases.

First, the Marines took the initiative. With a large conventional offensive coming up, Davis wanted his service to get good press. And he knew that putting the reporters into units would have that effect. He "worked the hallways" in the Pentagon trying to persuade Clarke's office to allow embedding instead of the unsatisfactory pool deployment.[64] Because of security concerns about Army Special Forces units operating already in Afghanistan the office was reluctant. DeFrank explained why they were hesitant to allow access:

> The reason was, the operation didn't support it, it was mostly Special Forces, often operating with tribal or warlord type organizations, some of them wanted media, some of them didn't. And in some cases, they just couldn't do it because it would give away their TTPs [tactics, techniques, and procedures] and if it was ever covered then they wouldn't be able to use it again. So as long as it was mostly small scale and Special Forces operating with irregulars, media embedding didn't lend itself to that conflict.
>
> (DeFrank, James, interview by author, Pentagon, 27 February 2004)

Against significant reluctance in the Pentagon, the Marines succeeded in having a small number of journalists on their ships to be embedded during the assault. Central Command's chief public affairs officer, Rear Admiral Craig Quigley, finally cleared the 16 journalists.[65] Shortly before operation Swift Freedom was about to be launched, on the night of 25 November, Brigadier General James Mattis invited five reporters to join him in a classified briefing on the USS *Peleliu*. The journalists were about to be embedded in one of the longest amphibious assaults in military history.[66] Some research into media reports of the operation later showed that the coverage "skyrocketed" with more than 350 individual news stories in two months featuring the Marines in Afghanistan.[67] The Marines took the journalists with them without Clarke's explicit consent – a few days later the Washington bureau chiefs heavily criticized Clarke for not activating the DoD National Media Pool and questioned the benefit of the coalition press office in Pakistan.[68]

A second embed arrangement was organized a few weeks later by the Army. In December 2001 *Newsweek*'s Donatella Lorch received a telephone call from the Pentagon. As a senior war correspondent she had experience with tough situations. Lorch had reported from Mogadishu in Somalia, one of the world's most dangerous places for journalists, and had covered almost every major war of the 1990s. And she had excellent personal contacts to the Pentagon's public affairs staff. Her contact asked her to be secretive: "It was very hush hush, we had to keep it quiet, only a few slots. I was amazed that they were doing it."[69] After weeks of pressure from bureau chiefs the decision in the Pentagon was taken to embed a select small group of reporters, among them Lorch. By late December, when they embedded, most of the fighting had ceased, and the journalists were merely reporting the daily life of a Special Forces A-Team. This, however, was newsworthy in itself:

> It was an amazing, fascinating week for me. To spend and live a week with an A-Team, 11 people, they were all seconded to Afghan commanders, and I was in the A-Team that came into Mazar[-i-Shareef] with Atta

Mohammad. And it would have been a lot nicer if I had been there when the A-Team was doing some fighting, but I got there when they were already in Mazar.

(Lorch, Donatella, interview by author, ICFG, Washington, DC, 25 February 2004)

Lorch wrote a positive piece on the Green Berets after her trip for *Newsweek*: "On the ground with the 5th Special Forces who turned the tide – and just lost one of their own," the article was titled. Sean Naylor, long standing *Army Times* reporter who was himself embedded later in Operation Anaconda in Afghanistan, thinks that the Army deliberately chose units that were not going to be engaged in combat for that first embedding arrangement, because "not much happened on those missions." Naylor thinks that the units were "carefully chosen for that reason."[70]

Several weeks later US forces tried a third and more daring embedding experiment. The major offensive of the war was being prepared. Operation Anaconda had the mission, as its name implied, to encircle and squeeze the estimated 2,000 remaining from the well armed and motivated al-Qaeda and Taliban forces hiding in the inaccessible and heavily fortified Shah-i-kot Valley, a terrain similar to the battlefields on which the Soviet's 40th Army had suffered horrendous casualties against the Mujahedeen two decades earlier. After the good experiences with both the Marines' initial embed during the amphibious assault and the 5th Special Forces Group's embeds, it was decided to allow a few journalists to take part in Anaconda. During a fierce two week battle more than 2,000 coalition soldiers were engaged, eight were dead, and more than 80 wounded, and scores of enemy fighters were killed. Half a dozen reporters were embedded with the 101st Airborne Division's 3rd Brigade in Kandahar to cover the operation, with CNN's Martin Savidge and Sean Naylor among them. Naylor embedded from January 2002 until May 2002, most of the time with the famous Rakkasans, as the 3rd Brigade is nicknamed.[71] Just like Lorch, the few reporters were hand-picked by the Pentagon. A couple of days before Anaconda started, Naylor and his photographer were pulled aside by an officer on the military base camp in Kandahar. The officer would not tell the reporters what was coming up, but quietly said: "Just be prepared to leave at an hour's notice some time in the next few days, don't tell anybody else."[72] The 101st took the reporters up to Bagram, and then from there into battle: "I think Anaconda is the first time that they knew there was going to be combat and embedded in the modern era," Naylor said later.[73] Embedding in Afghanistan had a very different character than the embedding in Iraq. Only a small group of journalists was embedded, the responsible officers were still in a reluctant and insecure experimentation mode, and live reporting, because of operational security concerns, was not permitted.

Lessons learned

The military's experience with embedding in Afghanistan, in sum, was good. The command brief of the 10th Mountain Division – a wrap-up presentation for internal use – included lessons on embedding the media in Anaconda. The gist of it was that embedding had worked and that it was the way for the future, as the division's commanders saw it.[74] One layer up the chain-of-command, at the Army Component of Central Command, (ARCENT), an After Action Report echoed this positive assessment. Colonel Melanie R. Reeder worked as a public affairs officer in Afghanistan during Operation Enduring Freedom. Later she participated in writing the public affairs chapter of a CALL report which focuses on the Combined Force Land Component Command's performance in Afghanistan, as ARCENT is called when at war. In an interview she said that "when journalists were provided access, the accurate story was told. When they were not provided with information, the result was speculation, misinformation, and inaccuracy."[75] The Army Component's chief public affairs officer, Colonel Rick Thomas, agrees: "When the marines landed and went into Kandahar, they had around twenty journalists with them ... it was mutually beneficial."[76]

The military benefited from the open access policy because the journalists helped them – wittingly or unwittingly – to counter rumors and the Taliban's version of the story. Air Force Lieutenant Colonel Larry Cox provides some insight to the US military's learning experience during Afghanistan. He served as chief of the press desk in Kuwait City during the Iraq War, and was a public affairs operations officer for the chairman of the Joint Chiefs of Staff. In an interview with the *Columbia Journalism Review*, he pointed out that "many of the things, including the embeds and other aspects that we're seeing today, evolved from lessons learned, revelations, experiences out of the Afghanistan period." Other senior officials in the Pentagon agree: "Afghanistan was the watershed event," Captain Terry McCreary said, the JCS chairman's special assistant for public affairs, who would later initiate the Iraq War's embedding program. In an interview he described his frustration with the dynamics in Afghanistan's information battlespace:

> You raid a camp, there wouldn't be any press with you, you do an operation, you leave, the enemy comes back, the press come in, and everybody tells them you murdered innocent people, you slaughtered them, and that becomes a story for the next 48 hours until you can fix it.
>
> (McCreary, Terry, interview by author, by telephone, 12 May 2006)

The enemy, the planners were certain, exploited the US military's slow internal communication channels and cumbersome official reporting chain: "Reacting from Washington to the enemy in theater is painful," McCreary said.[77] Operation Enduring Freedom's main lesson was, consequently, that embedding could be used as an instrument to counter the enemy's information.

The Taliban were able to invent civilian casualties, misreport the progress of the war, spread rumors in the Arab and European media, and thus set the news agenda in the US. The idea to have independent journalists operating on the battlefield was not born out of democratic idealism for transparence or checks of the armed forces by the free press. Rather, credible news stories from the battlefield were expected to balance the enemy's information more effectively. From the military's point of view, the ingredients of a dangerous mixture were an IO-savvy adversary, global media organizations working in real-time, a 10-hour time difference, and a lack of credibility of military spokespersons if contradicted by a journalist. The remedy was embedding. In McCreary's words:

> The only way you can counter deception was to have the truth told first. The only way to do that is have an independent truth-teller tell it first. The only way to have an independent teller tell it first, is to have them with us. And the only way to have them with us was to embed.
>
> (McCreary, Terry, interview by author, by telephone, 12 May 2006)

This three step argument was not new, but, in the words of Larry Cox, one of McCreary's aides, it "became crystallized in the months after the start of the war in Afghanistan."[78] This new rationale paved the way for a truly strategic public affairs operation in the next war.

Part III
A case study of strategic innovation

Truth can be propaganda
(Mike Birmingham, public affairs officer, 3rd Infantry Division, US Army, 2004)

7   Retrieving past experiences?

The first part of this book introduced a model of organizational learning as a conceptual lens to view the US military's growing sophistication in media operations. The second part demonstrated, through that lens, that many influential thinkers in the US military stopped to regard journalists' access to the battlefield as a vulnerability. The lesson of Vietnam – keep the press out – proved counterproductive in subsequent operations. Very slowly a change in attitude toward the media gained ground in military academies and headquarters. The military's unlearning of the legacy of Vietnam was a necessary precondition to innovate and use the mass-media coverage as a force multiplier in Iraq.

From an organizational learning perspective, this latter argument falls into two components: retrieval and implementation. In order to qualify as a strategic innovation, experiences need not only be cached in the institutional memory and reorient old lessons. Two additional steps were necessary to perform a veritable organizational learning process. First, the recorded individual and organizational experiences in military public affairs needed to be retrieved from the organization's stored body of knowledge during the planning process that predated the operation. Second, the retrieved lessons needed to be brought to bear on current decisions: the plan had to be implemented.

In retrospect, the US military's public affairs policy in the first phase of the Iraq War with the embedded media as its centerpiece was very successful. The military, the media, and the American public mostly agree on this positive assessment. Mark Mazzetti, who covered the war for *US News and World Report*, was embedded with the Marines. He thinks fondly of the military's handling of the press: "They gave us a perspective of the war we never would have had otherwise. I would take in that exchange again for a minute. It was great."[1] When Katherine Skiba from the *Milwaukee Journal Sentinel*, one of 67 female embeds, returned home from Iraq, more than 150 emails were waiting for her. Readers and members of military families from all over the country were thanking her for her coverage of the 101st Airborne Division – an experienced shared by many of her colleagues. One journalist even found 1,200 emails upon return.[2] One of the program's chief organizers who made Mazzetti's and Skiba's experience possible, Bryan Whitman, the Pentagon's deputy spokesperson, agrees strongly: "I think that the journalists did a phenomenal job in covering the conflict from their very unique perspective."[3] Such unanimity in praise of media–military relations is unprecedented in recent American history.

This assessment raises two questions: did the media coverage of the invasion of Iraq go according to plan? And was that plan – with the embedded media program at its center – developed by drawing lessons from mistakes and successes of earlier military operations? This chapter will proceed in two steps. First, it will look at the lessons as contained in systemic knowledge assets. DoD's approach to media management on the battlefield was – in theory – determined by the joint and service doctrines on information operations and public affairs, as well as the guidelines and directives issued by the Secretary of Defense and his staff. Accordingly the official and authorized approach to public affairs as prescribed in the 2003 versions of related doctrinal publications will be outlined. Doctrinal publications contain a contradiction between two lines of argument: information operations doctrine is incompatible with public affairs doctrine. The IO-mindset and the PA-mindset are two competing theories-of-actions, or mental maps, prevalent in the department's communication branches. Second, it will look at the planning phase. How rigidly did military planners adhere to the officially sanctioned doctrine and directives when they turned embedding from an idea into a thorough program with its own staff, its resources, guidelines, and logistics to accommodate an initially requested 917 reporters?

Explicit knowledge: doctrine and the information campaign

In order to appreciate and understand the conceptual revolution in military thinking on public affairs, some background in the theory of war is necessary. A look at the relevant doctrines, directives, and debates in military journals offers a snapshot of the role that the media occupied in strategic thinking before the launch of the Iraq campaign. "War," Carl von Clausewitz wrote around 1830, "is an act of force to compel the enemy to do our will."[4] Arguably this is the most comprehensive and the most widespread definition of war that has ever been spelled out. The Prussian general-turned-philosopher can be regarded as the intellectual godfather of strategic thinking and education of the US armed forces, and of many other militaries as well. Clausewitz was a career officer in the Prussian army at the turn of the seventeenth to the eighteenth century. His main and – according to his own assessment – unfinished book *On War*, particularly in its 1970 translation by Peter Paret and Michael Howard, is the main source of inspiration for the post-Vietnam intellectual elite of the US armed forces. After the lost war in Southeast Asia a whole generation of officers was thirsty for conceptual redefinition, and Clausewitz met the demand.[5] One of the central themes in his philosophy of war is the significance of "moral factors" as opposed to the merely physical forces used to wage war. He views violence instrumentally, as a means to an end. His extensively quoted definition views war as an act of force to *compel* the adversary to do something he would otherwise not have done, not necessarily to destroy his forces or his cities' infrastructure. Together with Clausewitz, the ancient Chinese writer Sun Tzu is the second outstanding strategic thinker on top of the reading lists of strategy courses in US military academies. Despite its more than biblical age, Sun Tzu's *The Art of War*, written in approximately 500 BC, is an eminently important strategic essay extensively quoted in US doctrinal publications. His main line of thought is centered on the psychological dimension of war as well; hence the focus on deception and winning without fighting: "For to win one hundred victories in one hundred battles is not the acme of skill. To subdue the enemy without fighting is the acme of skill," is one of Sun Tzu's most popular aphorisms.[6] The ancient Chinese strategist advises to attack the plans and the strategy of the adversary, not his army. Clausewitz's and Sun Tzu's philosophies of war are an important part of the modern commander's conceptual equipment. General Tommy Franks, the commander of Central Command in the wars in Afghanistan and Iraq, recounts in his memoirs how the "accumulated wisdoms of Clausewitz and Sun Tzu" prepared him for his task.[7] And their lines of thought are continued and refined in contemporary US doctrinal writings.

The Marine Corps' capstone manual, *Warfighting*, is widely regarded as the most sophisticated doctrinal document of any of the US military services. It has a markedly Clausewitzian character: "The object in war is to impose our will on our enemy," the manual says. "It is through the use of violence, or the credible threat of violence, that we compel our enemy to do our will."[8] The document explicitly widens Clausewitz's definition of war to include not only the actual use of force but also the *credible threat* of violence by military force.[9] As a result, the display of force becomes part of war itself, even if ultimately no shots are fired and no bombs are dropped. From recognizing the strategic role of credible threats it is only a small step to see how the media blend in as an instrument and a means to achieve a given strategic end, albeit a step the Marines have only reluctantly taken. A second idea which can be found in Clausewitz's conceptual toolkit, however, proves even more useful to understand the military significance of news coverage.

The center of gravity

One of the most important concepts Clausewitz helped introduce to American military discourse is the so-called *Schwerpunkt*, translated as "center of gravity." Clausewitz viewed war as a "duel on a larger scale" and asks his reader, for "reasons of simplification," to imagine a "pair of wrestlers," where the immediate aim of each of the two is to "throw" his opponent in order to make him incapable of further resistance. After using the wrestler analogy, Clausewitz introduces his definition of war: war is thus an act of force to compel our enemy to do our will. The idea of the center of gravity has to be understood against this background. In German, the word *Schwerpunkt* not only means the center of gravity of a physical object; the same term refers to the balance-point of a human body, be it a dancer, an acrobat, or a wrestler. Its application to matters of war was – originally at least – clearly metaphoric. Clausewitz understood the center of gravity as "the hub of all power and movement, on which everything depends . . . the point at which all our energies should be directed."[10] The official *DoD Dictionary of Military and Associated Terms* defines a center of gravity, similar to Clausewitz's original grasp, as "those characteristics, capabilities, or sources of power from which a military force derives its freedom of action, physical strength, or will to fight."[11] US military thinkers and planners apply the term center of gravity rather liberally and productively to entirely new situations the Prussian general could never have imagined, such as aerial warfare, naval operations, or information and computer warfare.

Add to the center of gravity the distinction between offense and defense. Not only the adversary possesses centers of gravity which can be attacked to take away his freedom of action or to undermine his physical strength or will to fight. One's own strength and will, consequently, rest on friendly COGs (the US military abbreviation for centers of gravity). Friendly vulnerabilities need to be protected and defended against an adversary's attempts to target them. This has two immediate implications. On the one hand, detailed knowledge and understanding of how opponents organize and make decisions is required to identify adversary centers of gravity. To recognize tactical centers of gravity, for instance the location of an artillery battery, reconnaissance and target information is needed. The same, of course, applies to strategic centers of gravity. The so-called "decapitation strike" that marked the beginning of the Iraq War was an attempt to kill Saddam Hussein as the Iraqi regime's most important center of gravity. On the other hand, one's own weaknesses have to be acknowledged appropriately. In the Persian Gulf War, for instance, Iraq, itself under attack by the American-led coalition, fired Scud Missiles on Israeli cities. For the American leadership it was clear that a military response by the Israel Defense Force against Iraqi targets and Israel's de facto participation in the war would disintegrate the coalition which included several Arab states. Accordingly, the US worked hard to defend the coherence of the coalition as a critical center of gravity by keeping Israel out of the war. It is against this background that one of Sun Tzu's aphorisms is quoted so often in strategic publications: "Know the enemy and know yourself."[12] Know the strengths and weaknesses of your enemy, avoid and exploit them; know your own centers of gravity, and protect them.

The media and COGs

A free and open press is an essential institution in every democratic society. TV watchers, radio listeners, newspaper readers, and users of electronic outlets not only inform themselves through the media; editorial pages and news broadcasts are also platforms where opinions are formed and political attitudes are shaped – the opinions of the average consumer as well as the opinions of political decision makers. Congress and the civilian political leadership in Washington are using the media as an important source of their information and as a thermometer to measure the public's mood. The political attitudes of policy makers themselves are heavily influenced by a handful of media outlets like the *New York Times*, the *Washington Post*, Jim Lehrer's *News Hour*, *60 Minutes*, or *Meet the Press*. The media, in a nutshell, forms part of Washington's decision-making process. If the nation's leaders decide to engage in military conflict, they need to have the public's support and they need to maintain the public's support. Evidently, then, national support of the administration's security policy has an impact on strategic decision making.

Doctrine recognizes the importance of public opinion: "American public support is critical to the success of all joint operations," says the first draft version of the new joint information operations doctrine.[13] Because support is so critical, it is a strategic center of gravity: "It is important to identify friendly COGs so they can be protected," one of the most important joint doctrines, *Operations*, explains: "National will also can be a COG, as it was for the United States during the Vietnam and Persian Gulf Wars."[14] And the need to actively defend public support against enemy attacks has clearly been recognized in doctrine. Reviewing the air war against Serbia in 1999, Air Force Major Gary Pounder commented on the vulnerabilities of the 19-country Nato coalition: "In an era of relentless, real-time coverage, the media has an indelible impact on public opinion, long identified as a critical center of gravity for any US military campaign." He concludes that "a more direct, aggressive, and systematic approach in public information might have bolstered public support for the air campaign and eased any lingering doubts."[15] Strategic thinkers underscore the primacy of moral factors, and regard those as centers of gravity: "If they are friendly centers of gravity, we want to protect them, and if they are enemy centers of gravity, we want to take them away," a Marine manual says.[16] The media coverage of war, accordingly, can serve two separate military functions. One the one hand, with respect to the necessary public approval of armed intervention, the media coverage can be defensively used as an instrument of "counter-information," shielding the public against "enemy propaganda"; on the other hand, it can be offensively used as an instrument of "perception management" and psychological warfare against the enemy.

The target audience is the distinguishing element. The intended recipients of counter-information are the American and allied publics; the target audiences of perception management are adversarial. In military terminology as well as organization, the target audience splits the role of public information in warfare into two entirely separate realms, public affairs and information operations. The first is talking to the American people, the latter targets adversarial decision makers. Not only with respect to the most important target audience "PA" and "IO" are distinct, a detailed institutional division of labor has evolved: PA officers and IO officers receive separate educations and training, they follow diverging career paths, they work for specialized sub-organizations, they think in contrasting mindsets and philosophies of war, and they do not read the same publications and doctrines. Both approaches to information in warfare are explicitly discussed and developed in joint and service doctrine. Mainly three types of doctrinal publications are relevant for news media coverage of a military operation: most evidently manuals on public affairs; psychological operations doctrine (PSYOP); as well as guidelines on information operations. With regard to their attitude to public information, US military officers fall into two schools of thought (those schools of thought are not coextensive with the groups of PA officers on the one hand and IO or PSYOP officers on the other hand.) One school, called the PA community for reasons of simplification, primarily has the American domestic public in mind and its right to truthful information. They tend to be proud and idealistic patriots who would like the greatness, the merits, and the dedication of their service's troops to be reported in the national media. The other school, the IO warriors, has primarily the adversary in mind. These officers mostly think pragmatically in a warrior's mindset, willing to use the media as a means to put psychological pressure on the adversary or to deceive him. At times the two philosophies contradict and IO warriors and the PA community wage their own little war. The conflict and indeed a contradiction between those two schools of thought is mirrored in doctrinal publications. Accordingly there is a dissonance between doctrinal publications on information operations and psychological operations on the one hand, and public affairs doctrine on the other hand.

Public affairs doctrine

Any military use of the media as an instrument undermines its credibility. We cannot treat the American people as a target group just like the adversary leadership or population. We should never again lie to the American people. Those are some of the arguments that are put forward by the "PA community" within the Department of Defense. If public affairs is ever subsumed conceptually, institutionally, or practically under the umbrella of information operations – which targets foreign and adversary audiences – it would lose its foremost asset: credibility. This line of reasoning not only plays a role in military journals and debates, it permeates official military doctrine and its legal foundations.

Public affairs doctrine regards the news media as the principal means of communicating information about matters martial to the general public. Military correspondents are appreciated as "the principal source of communication with military personnel, civilian employees, and family members [of DoD employees]," the *Joint Doctrine on Public Affairs* explains.[17] A common distinction is the one between so-called internal audiences and the general public. Internal audiences are DoD-related groups, such as family members, retired personnel, reservists, civilian employees, the civilian leadership, and soldiers and commanders in the area of operations itself. Given the global information environment and the rapid spread of high-technology consumer electronics, US soldiers (and their families) increasingly consume news media coverage of ongoing operations even while in theater, or soldiers in theatre communicate via cellphone with friends and families who report to them what they saw on TV or read in the paper. Americans who have no personal ties to those internal audiences are referred to as the external public. Both internal and external publics are subsets of the American electorate, the most important recipient audience of military public affairs.

Public affairs doctrine identifies several instruments to facilitate the communication to internal and external domestic audiences. A media pool is one such instrument. Characteristic of a media pool is the selection of a group of reporters. As a result, a pool arrangement makes it more difficult for journalists and their editors to claim ownership of a story. This is one reason why those arrangements are unpopular with the media, as the pool's distribution logic runs counter to the journalists' competitive drive for the scoop. Doctrine holds commanders responsible for providing communication facilities to pool members to file their products, for physical transport of the pool, as well as for medical treatment. This gives the military a high level of control over where the pool goes and what reporters can see, another reason for it being disliked by journalists. Contrary to the experience of the 1980s and 1990s, the 1997 PA doctrine demands that pools are not to be used as a standard means of covering US military operations. Sometimes, though, a pool might be the only feasible way to provide news coverage at all, particularly during events "at extremely remote locations or where space is limited."[18]

A second public affairs instrument are so-called Joint Information Bureaus (JIBs).[19] Such facilities are established in theater in an ad-hoc fashion and serve as the main interface between the military and news media representatives. Their main function is to "ensure a continuous flow of timely information"[20] via the media to the domestic and international public. According to doctrine, a JIB answers media requests, arranges interviews with commanders, issues news releases, and conducts briefings, often using combat camera material. Information bureaus in theater also register news media and give credentials, provide communication facilities, arrange logistics, monitor the media coverage, and occasionally give ad-hoc media training to commanders. Depending on the nature of the operation, a JIB is staffed by members of all services, and in the case of allied operations doctrine recommends to include coalition PA personnel to represent their nation's interests.

A third instrument is the public affairs guidance (PAG). The public affairs guidance is first and foremost a tool to communicate public affairs policy to the vast web of defense agencies and military commands. The public affairs guidance "is a primary tool that guides commanders and PA leaders in the application of doctrine and policy during operations. PAG provides the PA force at all echelons standard operating procedures."[21] The guidance is a "source document" for military personnel in situations where they have to reply to requests put forward by media representatives or the general public.[22] In theory and according to doctrine, the guidance is developed and proposed by the operational commander's PA staff upon receipt of a so-called "warning order" from higher headquarters. Once the guidance is developed, it is forwarded through public affairs channels to the Pentagon's spokesperson, the ASD/PA. There, the proposed public affairs guidance (PPAG) is approved, staffed and sent to all relevant DoD components (prior to the Iraq War, the final PPAG was coordinated on 15 January 2003 with the State Department).[23] The document usually contains the ground rules accredited journalists must adhere to. Those rules, doctrine demands, should "conform to operations security and the privacy requirements of the members of the force."[24] Journalists in a combat zone are required to abide by a set of security-related ground rules intended to protect the security of the military operation and the lives of servicemen and women.

Commentary and guidelines on embedding are spread thin in doctrine. At the onset of the Iraq War, the joint PA doctrine's then-1997 version as well as the superseding document's 2002 draft version entirely fail to mention embedding as an instrument to manage news coverage. Joint doctrine did not use the term a single time. Neither did the Army's field manuals specify embedding in detail. The land force's 1997 public affairs manual is merely noting, without going into any detail, that embedding can be one of several possible ways of "media facilitation." The document defines embedding as:

> the act of assigning a reporter to a unit as a member of the unit. The reporter eats, sleeps, and moves with the unit. The reporter is authorized open access to all sections of the unit and is not escorted by public affairs personnel.[25]

Traditionally, the Marine Corps is more adept in promoting its image than any other service branch of the US military: "We think the best way to get the story out is to have embedded reporters with Marine units," explained Davis, acting director of Marine public affairs during the wars in Afghanistan and Iraq. "The best spokesperson for the Marine Corps is the 22 year old corporal, he's the most honest. They don't need coaching."[26] Historically, the service's public affairs manual points out, the Marines have benefited from embedding news media into the force. By "adopting reporters as honorary members of a particular unit," the document says, embedding "fosters mutual trust and understanding." Because the reporters themselves are in harm's way, along with the unit to which they are assigned, they have a "vested interest in complying with security concerns,"[27] and will not disclose sensitive information that might be of use to the enemy. The historic example the manual quotes as a success story is the 1st Marine Expeditionary Force's experimental embedding in the Persian Gulf War in 1991.

But despite the overall sophistication of the Marines' understanding of public affairs, they remain strongly in a pure PA tradition which focuses exclusively on the US public. The document repeatedly states that "public affairs is the discipline of communication that informs and educates. It is *not* designed to influence."[28] The Marines' PR specialists clearly and explicitly refuse to see their plea for embedding as an integrated element of an overall information operations approach that targets the mind of the adversary: "Any influence certain information may have in the minds of our adversaries or anyone else is merely a secondary result of our consistently providing timely, unclassified information. It is *not a design or intent of our public affairs program*."[29]

All this shows that military pubic affairs specialists have a rather sophisticated understanding of the target audiences they are talking to. Those include not only "the public," but particularly their own political leadership and indeed the troops themselves. Soldiers and their families at home in the US, and increasingly service personnel in the theater of war, are using state-of-the-art consumer electronics to follow the events they are shaping via the media. For military personnel, watching the media is like looking into a collective mirror, albeit with significant distortions and blind spots at times. The first joint doctrine on public affairs has recognized this introspective effect of public affairs already in 1997. It emphasizes the tantamount role of credibility with various audiences: "Accuracy and timeliness of the information made available to the public are essential in establishing and maintaining credibility with the news media, the Congress, the general public, our allies, and the operating forces," the document says.[30] In the same spirit, the DoD principles of information emphasize the timely and accurate flow of information to the public, particularly the internal public: "A free flow of general and military information will be made available, without censorship or propaganda, to the men and women of the Armed Forces and their dependents," DoD directive 5122.5 states.[31] But before the war the level of strategic sophistication in the discipline of public affairs was very limited. Officers plainly refused to accept public information as a vehicle to reach out to the enemy. Public affairs doctrine regards the media as apart from the battlefield, not as a part of it.

The strategic rationale behind information operations – and psychological operations as a subset of IO – stands in stark contrast to public affairs. And it is strategically much more sophisticated. Information operations explicitly target adversary and foreign audiences, not the American public. Doctrine draws two sharp lines both of which have legal implications: between domestic audiences and foreign audiences; and between the methods that are used to address or target these audiences: "PSYOP use specific techniques to influence favorable behavior or beliefs of non-US audiences," explains the joint doctrine on psychological operations.[32] The intent to *influence* behavior and to *manipulate* the thinking of a target audience is a thought abhorrent to a public affairs officer. It is spelled out more clearly in PSYOP doctrine: "Psychological operations are planned operations to convey selected information and indicators to foreign audiences to influence the emotions, motives, objective reasoning, and ultimately the behavior of foreign governments, organizations, groups, and individuals."[33] This stands in stark opposition to the traditional PA mission. The entire 61-page joint doctrine on joint public affairs in its 1997 version does not even use the phrase "information operations" once, and it only briefly refers to PSYOPs in order to distance itself from the practice in clear and unambiguous language: "*Joint PA operations should not focus on directing or manipulating public actions or opinion*," it says in emphasized print. "While they reinforce each other and involve close cooperation and coordination, *by law PA and PSYOP must be separate and distinct*."[34] The law the doctrine is referring to is the Smith-Mundt Act of 1948.[35] "Under no circumstances will public affairs personnel working in PA functions or activities engage in PSYOP activities," it continues.[36] Public affairs, the manuals leave no room for doubt, is distinct from information warfare. Information warriors, however, clearly view this differently. Public affairs, they argue, is a subset of information operations and, consequently, a weapon of war. The philosophies of public affairs on the one hand and information operations on the other hand seem mutually exclusive and even contradictory. Doctrine leaves the reader puzzled on which view to take. Both perspectives make sense. With the possibility of war in Iraq becoming ever more probable during 2002, the key question regarding the public affairs strategy is as obvious as it is intriguing: which argument prevailed during the PA planning before the Iraq War?

Information operations doctrine

To understand how information is used as a weapon, it is worthwhile to look at IO-thinking in some more detail. On 9 October 1998, less than six months before operation Allied Force in Kosovo, the US military published its first *Joint Doctrine on Information Operations.* Two months earlier, in August that year, the Air Force had developed and published its own IO doctrine, *Air Force Doctrine Document 2–5.* General Ronald R. Fogleman, Air Force chief-of-staff in the mid-1990s, underscored his service's commitment to information warfare in a speech to the Armed Forces Communications-Electronics Association in April 1995. Fogleman described information operations as the "fifth dimension of warfare" and argued the new discipline would be critical to success in the future. In the terminology of the US military, a "dimension" refers to a separate environment in which human activity takes place. Joint doctrine uses the term to distinguish four such dimensions: land, sea, air, and space. The "information dimension" has been introduced as a fifth dimension. The 1997 version of the *Air Force Basic Doctrine,* its capstone doctrine, acknowledges already that "information superiority" is as "critical to conflict now as controlling air and space, or occupying land was in the past."[37] But in those early days of information warfare in the mid-1990s, with its focus on electronic warfare and command, control, and computers, nobody gave much thought to public affairs operations as a cornerstone of the information campaign. This has changed.

Information operations doctrine has adapted the almost philosophical language to grasp the dynamics of information warfare. According to the authorized joint definition, information operations are "actions taken to affect adversary information and information systems while defending one's own information and information systems."[38] The definition is deliberately abstract. From the overall context of the discussion it becomes clear that the term "information system" includes human as well as mechanical "systems." Information operations doctrine spells this out more clearly. The objective of IO, according to a revised definition, is to "influence, disrupt, corrupt or usurp adversarial human and automated decision making while protecting our own."[39] The document goes a step further and discusses the fifth dimension of war, the information dimension. Information resides either in the mind, the physical world, or in the electromagnetic spectrum. It has human properties as well as physical and electronic properties. During a military operation, public affairs, in this view, is to be located on the informational dimension.

The 2003 revised version of the Air Force Basic Doctrine spells this out most comprehensively. It subsumes all "non-kinetic actions" under the umbrella of information operations and acknowledges that such operations must be integrated into warfare "in the same manner as traditional air and space capabilities."[40] The document distinguishes IO's three main categories: first, electronic warfare operations try to control the *"electromagnetic battlespace,"* or electromagnetic spectrum, including radio frequencies, as well as optical and infrared regions. Second, network warfare operations are used to dominate the *"digital battlespace"* and any collection of systems transmitting information, such as radio nets, satellite links, computer networks, telecommunications, and wireless communications systems. Finally, influence operations are the third category of IO, and their aim is to "achieve desired effects across the *cognitive battlespace.*" The goal of those operations is to change the adversary's decision process: "The elements of influence operations," according to the US Air Force's Basic Doctrine, "are counterpropaganda operations, psychological operations, military deception, operations security, counterintelligence operations, and public affairs operations."[41] The news media, consequently, assume a strategic function as a channel to influence enemy decision making and behavior. From the view of information operations doctrine, public affairs is merely a subset of information warfare. Public affairs, then, can be used defensively or offensively.

Defensive media operations

Defense is a reaction to offense. A defensive public affairs strategy is a reaction to an offensive enemy attack (real or imagined) which uses the news media as a platform. The need to defend the "cognitive battlespace" in the mass media would arise if the adversary is trying to use IO against the US or the coalition. Indeed, it is argued in the DoD that adversaries are getting better at using "disinformation" and "propaganda" against the United States. External commentators, journalists, or television watchers who are not trained to think in strategic terms, tend to dismiss this argument. The US government, in this view, just wants to wage its own "propaganda war" in the mass media. But there are compelling reasons to believe that the adversaries the US is facing are getting ever more sophisticated in using the media for their own military objectives. Even as far back as in Vietnam, this calculus might have played a role. Bui Tin, a former colonel who served on the North Vietnamese Army's general staff, discussed the strategic rationale of the Tet offensive in a *Wall Street Journal* interview: "Tet was designed to influence American public opinion," the paper quoted him in 1995.[42] The North Vietnamese Army employed a guerrilla strategy of hit-and-run raids in all major cities of South Vietnam, including an attack of a small team on the US embassy in Saigon. The Tet-offensive was a staggering military defeat for the North Vietnamese on an operational and tactical level. But strategically – from the perspective of the VC – it was a success; Johnson decided to start peace negotiations in Paris and did not run for re-election. Referring to the American anti-war movement, Tin argued that:

> those people represented the conscience of America. The conscience of America was part of its war making capability, and we were turning that power in our favor. America lost because of its democracy; through dissent and protest it lost the ability to mobilize a will to win.

Historians may question whether Colonel Tin's analysis is correct, and strategists may question whether the North Vietnam military leadership indeed planned and executed the Tet offensive with such a sophisticated strategic calculus in mind. But from a strictly analytical point of view, both questions are of secondary importance. It is evident that the relevant decision makers in the US military *believe* that adversaries are getting ever more sophisticated in using the media against American interests. IO doctrine spells this out very accurately: "The US can fully expect an adversary to use the media to their own advantage by spreading disinformation and propaganda in an attempt to undermine the US position and objectives."[43]

How did the DoD react to the prospect of confronting an adversary with a high level of media sophistication able to attack "the national will" – as the US Joint Chiefs of Staff and the North Vietnamese general staff reasoned? The answer is to engage in counter-information or, as some DoD documents prefer, "counter-propaganda" activities: "Public affairs is the first line of defense against adversary propaganda and disinformation," explains a 2004 joint guidance on information operations.[44] It then underscores the defensive role of public affairs against the adversary's information campaign: "This capability allows PA to help defeat adversary efforts to diminish national will, degrade morale, and turn world opinion against friendly operations." The instruments to use public affairs as a first line of defense fall into three categories.

First, credibility is tantamount. If military spokespersons are not considered credible sources by the media or the general public, their statements will have little effect – even if the officials adhere to the facts in the accounts of events they give during press briefings. The truthfulness of a statement may be determined by *what* it actually says, but whether the statement is credible is often determined by *who* it says. Or, to be more precise, the credibility of a message is first and foremost a function of the sender's reputation from a particular recipient's point of view. Doctrine recognizes the significance of credibility and reputation: "The credibility and reputation of the US military organization in international news media is a crucial factor in combating adversary propaganda," the Air Force underscores. "It is absolutely imperative," the text stresses, "that this credibility is maintained; otherwise news media and the public may lose confidence in what our spokespersons say."[45] The reputation for trustworthiness is thus recognized as an operational asset and as a military capability that gives momentum to messages: "US and friendly forces must strive to

become the favored source of information by the international news media –
favored because we provide truthful and credible information quickly."[46] Several
documents are unequivocal on the military uses of the mass media coverage, and
they intend to harness the power of public communication for strategic purposes.
If public information is used as a weapon, credibility is its thrust.

> If credibility is not maintained, our operational ability to use public affairs
> operations for combating adversary propaganda, for providing informational
> flexible deterrent options, virtual force projection, or maintaining national
> will, could be permanently and irreparably damaged. Providing fast, truth-
> ful, credible information to the news media is operationally essential in
> order to maintain this capability.
>
> (US Air Force, *Information Operations*, AFDD 2–5, 1998, p. 27)

Second, speed is key. In mechanized warfare, momentum and speed are essential ingredients of success on the battlefield. During the invasion of Iraq, maneuver speed was one of Central Command's most important assets: "If highballing
armor units could sustain that speed for days and nights on end," Franks
described the plan, "they would own the initiative, and our momentum would
overwhelm Iraq's ability to react – tactically and strategically."[47] The US military applied just the same logic to the information dimension. In public affairs
strategy, credibility guarantees that a message has momentum; but speed is just
as important for words and images as it is for armor and projectiles. Speed represents a mass of its own, and just as in mechanized warfare the goal in media
operations is to "own the initiative." In the language of IO doctrine, speed is
used to gain the *information initiative*, and it is an essential ingredient to success
on the "cognitive battlefield." The 2002 draft for the new joint public affairs
doctrine extends and revises its 1997 predecessor considerably, and assumes the
language first spelled out in the Air Force information operations doctrine:
"Gaining and maintaining the information initiative in a conflict can be a powerful weapon to defeat propaganda," the document argues. And it underscores the
significance of setting the news agenda by providing the first version of a story:
"The first out with information often sets the context and frames the public
debate. It is extremely important to get complete, truthful information out first –
especially information about friendly forces' mistakes and blunders, so that
friendly forces are exposing those errors and putting them into the proper
context."[48] Doctrinal debate in military periodicals, headquarters' hallways, and
academies' classrooms touches on the interplay between public affairs and
information operations. An entire bundle of terms in that debate refers to speed:
information initiative, information superiority, information dominance, framing,
agenda setting, or the arguments in favor of a proactive approach essentially
mean the same – to be faster than the adversary in getting information into the
public domain. As often in war, the goal is to exploit the element of surprise by
putting the adversary into a position where he has to *react*. The essence of surprise, in Clausewitz's words, is to "give the opponent the law of action."[49]

The third element of defensive public affairs is dominance – Jamie Shea coined an alternative name, "saturation strategy," during the Kosovo War. Its idea is closely related to the information initiative and refers to the attempt to maintain it over an extended period of time. Information dominance (the term "saturation strategy" is not used in US doctrine) has two components. On the one hand messages should have a sufficiently high news value. Journalists are trained to recognize the newsworthiness of an image, statement, interview, or report. The news value is determined by the timeliness of a story, the credibility of its sources, the unexpectedness of the reported event, and the quality of the pictures available. The US military tried to cater to that. On the other hand timing is essential. The potential of a good briefing is not exploited if it takes place at the wrong time, either at the wrong time of the day or too late after a particular event has taken place. Both of those insights had been learned the hard way in Kosovo and Afghanistan. Brigadier General Vincent Brooks, the Central Command's spokesperson in Doha during the OIF, called this synchronized time plan of briefings in theater, London, and Washington the "PA Battle Rhythm."

Offensive media operations

Defensive media operations use credibility, initiative, and dominance to shield against the adversary's information war. The offensive use of the media goes a significant step further. Again a look at the theory of war helps our understanding. "The real target in war is the mind of the enemy commander, not the bodies of 17 of his troops," Basil Liddell Hart, a British general and strategist, is quoted in the Air Force's information operations doctrines. Liddell Hart developed the so-called "indirect approach,"[50] essentially continuing the same line of thought that already preoccupied Clausewitz and Sun Tzu: the primacy of moral factors in war. The *Doctrine for Joint Operations*, which stands at the top of the doctrinal hierarchy, recognizes that the "real target" in war is not of physical, but moral nature.

> JFCs [joint forces commanders] will employ an integrated and synchronized combination of operations to expose and attack adversary COGs [centers of gravity] through weak or vulnerable points – seams, flanks, specific forces or military capabilities, rear areas, and even military morale and public opinion and support.
>
> (US Department of Defense, *Doctrine for Joint Operations*, JP 3–0, 2001, p. III-23)

This argument effectively turns the news media into a weapon. It acknowledges that the news coverage can be used deliberately to communicate messages to the enemy; that it can be – in typical doctrinal jargon – part of an integrated and synchronized combination of operations. Information operations doctrine is more concise: "The public media allow a JFC [Joint Force Commander] to inform an adversary or a potential adversary about the friendly force's intent and capability."[51]

The contrast to traditional attitudes of commanders toward the press could not be starker. Operational security concerns always were the first thought that popped into the head of a commander facing the press. No information of value should be given to the enemy, such as details on future operations, effectiveness of enemy assaults, weapons systems, or hints on a unit's location. This old military concern predated Vietnam and reaches back to the first encounters between fighting men and writing men on the battlefield.[52] The US military's increasingly open-minded attitude toward working with the press contradicts military culture and wisdom:

> Conventional wisdom holds that release of information will be detrimental to military operations. However, commanders should consider the possible advantages of releasing certain information to demonstrate US resolve, intent, or reparations. Rather than providing an advantage to an adversary, the carefully coordinated release of operational information in some situations could deter military conflict.
> (US Air Force, *Information Operations*, AFDD 2–5, 1998, p. 16)

Doctrinal documents formulate what could be called a theory of the offensive media operations. This theory falls into two components. First, the concept that the press can be a used as a channel to address the enemy; and second that the messages sent via the public domain can be used as a deterrent against the adversary.

The three main disciplines under the umbrella of information operations – psychological operations, public affairs, and civil affairs – each have different methods and target audiences. But this traditional structure is called into question by changes in the information environment. Not only the authors of IO doctrine, who tend to be more pragmatic and creative, understand this; public affairs documents have begun to acknowledge that it is impossible to channel separate messages to specific target groups via the mass media. The Army's public affairs field manual on tactics, techniques, and procedures puts it well: "Information campaign objectives cannot be neatly divided by discipline, such as PA, CA [civil affairs] and PSYOP. The responsible organization cannot be easily determined solely by looking at the medium, the message or the audience," the manual says. Accordingly, the recipients of integrated information operations are more diverse than previously acknowledged: "The relevant audiences important to the commander are not limited to soldiers and the American public, but are also international as well as local to the operation," the manual continues.[53] The new version of the joint PA doctrine equally departs from the traditional focus on the US domestic public as the most important and the only legitimate target audience of public affairs. For the first time a public affairs manual not only includes passages which acknowledge that the adversary is receiving messages via the media as well, but according to the document public affairs could and should be used offensively. The text contains thoughts very much in line with Sun Tzu's philosophy: it suggests "using public information to attack an adversary's strategy." Such an attack in the media uses the "virtual projection of military force to show domestic, allied, coalition and adversary publics what the commander is actually doing to prepare for conflict."[54] The change in public affairs thinking is significant. Even joint public affairs doctrine recognizes that the boundaries between the disciplines are blurring. The global information revolution with mobile phones and internet access in remote places forced the US military to integrate public affairs into the overall information operations effort: "PA operations are an important element of the commander's overall information operations (IO) effort."[55]

Media coverage, second, can be used as a deterrent. Traditionally information operations doctrine, which focuses solely on using all possible aspects of information in war, has been more explicit on the offensive use of the media than public affairs doctrine. The revised *Joint Doctrine for Information Operations* includes the section "leverage global influence and deterrence." Deterrence is not confined to scenarios of nuclear confrontation during the Cold War, it is a genuine military term used as soon as the use of force, including the *threat* to use force, comes into play. To deter means to dissuade an opponent from action by fear of the consequences: "Deterrence," the DoD defines, "is a state of mind brought about by the existence of a credible threat of unacceptable counter-action."[56] The concept is a brainchild of the strategic thinkers taught at US elite military colleges: Liddell Hart's focus on the "mind" of the commander, Clausewitz's definition of war centered on the "will" of the opponent, or Sun Tzu's philosophy that "the acme of skill" is to win a battle without fighting. Information operations officers attend those schools and they learn to use their craft for the purposes of war. The spectrum of tools is broad, ranging from technical to human: electronic attacks on power grids, communication facilities, or computer networks target primarily hardware; dropping leaflets, sending e-mail messages to selected military officials in Iraq, broadcasting radio shows from EC-130E Commando Solo planes – all are executed for their psychological effect.

The ultimate objective of both lines of attack is the same: "Making these audiences aware of United States military capabilities and United States resolve to employ those assets can enhance support from allies and friendly countries and deter potential adversaries."[57] In the 2002 Air Force *Information Operations* doctrine, some particularly eager and acronym-loving officers even wanted to establish an abbreviation for the new weapon at their hands: "One way that public affairs operations can be used in an offensive counter information role is by using a virtual force projection IFDO." The contraction IFDO stands for "Informational Flexible Deterrent Options." The more recent and more authoritative *Joint Doctrine for Public Affairs* adopts this idea's essence, although it manages to resist the acronym's lure. In its most condensed form the new concept can be stated as follows: "*Communicating military capabilities to national and international audiences can be a force multiplier for commanders.*"[58] That phrase has turned into standard doctrinal parlance. The strategic use of public affairs is summed up concisely by the Air Force:

The synergistic effects of integrating PA operations into IO planning significantly enhance a commander's ability to achieve military objectives. ... As weapons in the commander's arsenal of information operations assets, PA operations can be a force multiplier that both assesses and shapes the information environment's effect on military operations.

(US Air Force, *Information Operations*, AFDD 2–5, 2002, p. 29)

The US military, it is fair to say, *learned* that mass-media coverage can be a defensive as well as an offensive force multiplier. In sum, the use of public affairs as an instrument of war became an integral part of doctrinal thinking prior to the Iraq War. It was absorbed into the organization's explicit knowledge. But whether the second dimension of the initial thesis holds true is still unanswered. Was this knowledge actually *used* in the PA planning and execution before and during the war in Iraq, when officers had little time to read doctrinal prose? The next section will examine if and how this lesson was retrieved from the institutional memory during the planning process of the Iraq War's information campaign.

Retrieval: designing the information campaign

The idea to embed the media did not originate in doctrine or media guidelines. Those are only a reservoir of ideas that have been articulated elsewhere. The space where ideas originate can be a meeting, a brainstorming session, a coffee break, or hands-on encounters with practical problems – in a foxhole or the interior of a tank. Even for insiders, it is hard to say where the idea to do embedding first materialized. DeFrank, who was the Pentagon's director for press operations during the war in Afghanistan, tried to remember where and when he had first encountered the concept: "I have to say," he explained in his spacious office, "I've been a public affairs officer for 25 years, this is something we've always talked about and wanted to do."[59] His statement is representative for most public affairs officers. This indicates that the idea did not originate at the top of the civilian or military hierarchy just before the Iraq War, but that it "was around" already for a considerable period of time.

A war against Saddam's Iraq became a probable scenario in early 2002. Upon Rumsfeld's request, Central Command began to draw up plans for a possible operation. While the actual war plan was designed in Tampa, Florida, the public affairs aspect of the operation was taken care of in the Pentagon. But Chairman Myers's special assistant for public affairs did not think that the media planning was going well. McCreary had the impression that the preparations were not done in "a thorough manner," and that media planning and operational planning were conducted in a disconnected fashion, which would become a problem in a modern maneuver war. By repairing this old, potentially damaging problem, the JCS leadership in turn wanted to create another new and hopefully beneficial disconnect.

General Myers was a veteran of the Vietnam War. He remembered coming home from a tour in Vietnam and being told at his Air Force base upon arrival: "Don't travel home with your uniform, you'll have things thrown at you or people will spit on you," as recounted by his assistant. During Vietnam the military had become a symbol for a misguided policy, and the anti-war movement's anger and the public's frustrations were unloaded upon the returning officers, creating a crisis in morals for the post-Vietnam army, and resulting in that "generation of embittered officers." In a war against Iraq, Myers and his staff wanted to avoid such a scenario: "We knew," McCreary said, "that there were probably as many people who disagreed with the policy of going to war as agreed." So the challenge for America's highest ranking soldier was to stress a crucial distinction, the separation of policy from the support of the men and women in uniform. The embedded media program was seen as the vehicle to educate the public, to "make the consumer of news a much more intelligent consumer," the officers reasoned. With remarkable sophistication and foresight, the Pentagon's planners wanted to enable TV watchers and newspaper readers to understand this difference. The consumer should be able to say, in McCreary's words: "OK, I like this war, I hate this war, I take the choice – but I really feel that these troops are doing a damn fine job because they're doing what they country asks them." This particular argument in favor of embedding, maybe because of its pessimistic implicit assumption, was never discussed with the Secretary of Defense, who was aggressively pushing the idea to go to war: "I don't remember that it was ever discussed with the secretary," said Clarke, who interacted with Rumsfeld on all press-related issues.[60] Neither was it discussed with Franks, or formally communicated down the chain-of-command. No official document or presentation used in the subsequent internal planning process makes this rationale explicit. But this logic was probably intuitively understood by many, and it was only one selling point among others.

The argument that sold the policy internally to the commanders, who would then have to carry it out, was less political but more operational. Media operations, as public affairs is internally referred to in the Pentagon, consists of three major directorates: the press office in the Pentagon; the media support branch, which arranges interviews and travel photographs for the Secretary; and the Defense Visual Information Directorate, responsible for imagery and Combat Camera throughout the services. The director of press operations, DeFrank, explained: "This was born out of our concern that the Iraqis were masters of propaganda and disinformation." The argument iteratively developed in many meetings and conversations in the ASD/PA's office went as follows:

> We knew from our previous experiences in dealing with them [the Iraqis] that they lied, that they staged events, that they distorted the truth. We all believed that the truth was our friend; the truth was on our side. There was nothing that we could do that would be as bad as what they were trying and say we did. Skeptics around the world, but particularly in the Arab world, would be predisposed to believe the Iraqi side rather than us. What we needed were credible, third party observers present with us, and so we started talking about including media.
>
> (DeFrank, James, interview by author, Pentagon, 27 February 2004)

Whitman, Clarke's deputy, echoes this view: "We knew that information warfare would be very much a part of any sort of conflict."[61] The experience of the 1991 Gulf War, with CNN's Peter Arnett reporting the civilian casualties his Iraqi minders were presenting to the excited journalist and his crew, were seen in the Pentagon as a reminder of the propaganda skills Saddam's regime had developed: "We knew that Saddam Hussein was a practiced liar, who used denial and deception to deceive the international community," Whitman said. Iraq's anticipated attempts to shape the international and domestic perception of the war were seen as a vital feature of the invasion's political context. The Pentagon's media operators were eager to find tools to deal with that problem: "one of the things that came to mind was exactly what the reporters, editors, and bureau chiefs were asking for, and that was to put independent objective observers throughout the battlefield."[62] It was primarily this counter-propaganda rationale, not Myers's calculus of militarily managed political education, that sold the program within the DoD.

The process to get the program running involved three steps. First, the idea had to be pushed upward, in order to get it authorized by the Secretary of Defense. Second, the concept to do embedding needed to be operationalized, turned into a plan, and moved down the chain-of-command to get support of the operators. Third, embedding builds upon a close mutual relationship of trust between military commanders, soldiers, and reporters. Such a network of personal relationships could not be ordered from the top-down; it needed to be created horizontally. The program would not have been possible with middle-managers fostering a deep-rooted post-Vietnam hostility towards journalists: the division, brigade, regiment, and battalion commanders were crucial. The following paragraphs will trace this up-down-horizontal process that made embedding possible.[63]

Up

In the summer of 2002, McCreary went to Myers, expressed his concerns regarding the public affairs planning for the looming war in Iraq, and outlined his suggestions. "Well," the chairman in the end said, "fix it." His aide took this as a license to go ahead, informed Clarke's office, and established the "Iraq PA Planning Cell." The innovative and risky public affairs strategy needed leadership support if it ever was to become reality. The most important military leader who needed to approve the assignment of journalists directly to military units was Franks; the highest ranking civilian leader required to give the program a go was the Secretary of Defense.[64] Both were already acquainted with the idea to do embedding from Operation Enduring Freedom, but needed to be persuaded by Clarke and her staff that embedding could be done on a much larger scale in Iraq. But before she could go to her boss, the Pentagon spokeswoman needed something sufficiently solid and thought through to present to Rumsfeld and Franks. She needed a tangible concept, and preferably some data. Rumsfeld held a PhD in mathematics, and he still liked numbers.

The planning cell would provide them. A small group of specialists labored for one week, from 2 to 7 October 2002. Nine participants from all four branches of the military as well as from joint commands looked at the possibility of embedding in detail. How many reporters could each division take in? What would be the major troubles and obstacles? The group's objective was to come up with some recommendations that could be turned into a plan. The JCS planning cell was headed by Captain Brian Cullin. The Navy public affairs officer was assigned by McCreary to lead the task force because he had extensive experience in public affairs during military operations. He had served in Somalia, the Balkans, and as Director of Public Affairs at the US European Command during Operation Enduring Freedom (OEF). The cell called colleagues all over the country, talked to Central Command and various division headquarters, and pulled together information from a variety of sources, both publicly available information as well as internal military documents. The planners studied the Sidle Report and some of the lessons learned from the Persian Gulf and the Balkans. But one event was particularly important to enable the group to successfully develop a set of recommendations for the next steps, more important in fact than any of the knowledge assets they had studied: a look at the war plan. Through the JCS chairman and McCreary's assistance, the planning cell was able to look at an early version of the war plan as it stood in October 2002. Cullin recounts that this early insight into the operational plan was essential for the group's work.[65] The cell initially estimated a number of 240 embedded journalists in total.

At Central Command, at that point in time, few officers gave much thought to public affairs and the press – a topic that traditionally ranges on the lower end of a commander's priority list, if it appears at all: "You gotta remember," the 3rd Infantry Division's chief public affairs officer, Mike Birmingham, explained, "at the point in time when I was making planning assumptions in the summer of 2002 media wasn't on the mind of the brigade commanders. What's on their mind is: they're warfighting. That's why they hire public affairs officers."[66] Franks's staff was under immense pressure to plan one of the largest invasions since the Second World War. Unlike in the Persian Gulf War in 1991, it was not mass and the number of troops on the ground that was considered a decisive factor, but rather the unprecedented speed of the units' movements and the equally unprecedented momentum of their joint precision firepower. "We would not apply overwhelming force," Franks said, referring to the so-called Powell doctrine of overwhelming force.[67] "Rather, we would apply the overwhelming 'mass of effect' of a smaller force." From an operational point of view, "speed and momentum" were paramount in this war, as Franks, who called himself a "speed freak", often emphasized.[68] Rapid, decisive movements of ground units were built into the war plan from the earliest stages.

From time to time, drafts of the operational war plan would, through the Joint Chiefs of Staff, be passed from Tampa to the Pentagon. McCreary knew that the war's maneuver scheme would create the working environment for the public affairs, and considered it essential to read the cell's planners into a draft of the war plan, which was "very very narrowly held," he recalls. The synchronization of the media plan with the war plan influenced the resulting public affairs strategy by far more than the content of some doctrinal document: "So if we're going to have press operating relatively effectively on the ground they need to be embedded with the units and not just stroll in while this is a very rapid movement," Cullin explained. The way maneuver warfare was planned in turn limited the options of PA planners. The insight that embedding was basically the only feasible option given the new rapid maneuver dynamics on the battlefield was only possible because PA planners were read into the war plan at an earlier stage than in any other war in US history.

When asked about the often presumed intentional co-option of journalists, which could have been another strategic calculus in favor of embedding,[69] Cullin placated: "I knew that that would come out of it, the whole Stockholm-syndrome type of thing."[70] But this line of thinking – many who were involved in the planning of the embedded media program credibly emphasized – did not figure prominently in the planning process: that prediction was rather speculative, soft, and insufficiently reliable for an organization that favors unambiguous chains-of-command and hard control.

Eventually the JCS planning cell concluded that media embeds would be "necessary and desired" in all components: ground, air, and sea. It recommended to "train and equip" the journalists adequately, and to develop some logistical help for the media products' transmission in order to avoid time-consuming blunders that had plagued the coverage of the Gulf War 12 years earlier. The task force also advised the Pentagon and Central Command to develop a "selection authority," and to come up with more concrete numbers on how many journalists could be embedded within units. Cullin's group suggested an initial 400 embeds. "But this is something that's going to need to be worked," Cullin remarked to Clarke when he presented the findings and recommendations to her.[71] The group delivered the draft of a public affairs guidance (PAG) and the recommendation to send out a so-called P4 message to all operational commanders in order to make clear to them that their support would be essential for the public affairs plan and that it would be in their own operational interest to follow it. Five arguments were recommended for the P4 message from the Secretary and the chairman to the combatant commanders: that operational success is linked to the PA mission; that the operational support for PA is key to victory; that it is the commander's responsibility to participate; that the media are an "integral part of the battlespace"; and finally that the tactical play is where public affairs is at risk. Ultimate responsibility lay with the commanders on the ground; their support was essential.

The next step up the chain-of-command was to secure leadership support. Clarke and her staff supported the idea to do embedding. Now Clarke needed to persuade the two relevant leaders to support the new policy: Tommy Franks and Donald Rumsfeld. While the initial idea to put the journalists close to the troops was not new, the way it was communicated internally was unprecedented. Colonel DeFrank, a public affairs officer by training, provides some insight into this internal persuasion of the relevant leaders:

What we did was we tied our communications objective to operational objectives, working on the Sun Tzu concept that the acme of skill is to win the battle without fighting it. So you could encourage them [the Iraqis] to defect to surrender before we came; it was better for us and we didn't have to kill as many of them. Because the object of war, of course, is not to kill people and destroy things, the object of conflict is to get in the decision-makers head and persuade them to do what you want them to do. What we did is we applied military objectives to our communications objectives. We made them the same. This is how we presented it.

(DeFrank, James, interview by author, Pentagon, 27 February 2004)

The pragmatic and target-oriented argument secured the support of the top military and civilian leadership: "We presented our communications objectives in operational terms and showed very clearly how we intended to use communication to help accomplish operational objectives," DeFrank said.[72] The language the public affairs staff in the Pentagon used to promote the idea to embed reporters with military units was plugged into the operational logic of winning the war, and fully integrated into the war plan. And Rumsfeld supported a "robust and engaged" communication strategy.[73]

Donald Rumsfeld, several of his staff emphasized in interviews, always wants to know your assumptions before you brief him. Accordingly, Clarke had to lay out her assumptions before she was briefing the Secretary on the planned public affairs operation, carefully decorating her argument with some math and numbers: "Given 24/7/365 instantaneous news," he was told in the briefing, "information flow plays a major role. There will be a cascading effect of bad information – replicates to nth degree." Clarke did an excellent job in presenting the public affairs strategy as a cost-benefit analysis. The potential costs and risks, on the one hand, were considerable. She laid out a list of things that could go wrong:

> Journalists in Baghdad killed or captured; WMD on US forces and journalists – high casualty rate; OPSEC violation by a journalist that comprises an operation or a unit; Host country does not allow journalists; Embedded journalists pulled out by commander based on unforeseen circumstances/miss the action; Unilateral/independent journalists cause problems; Access denied in error; Terrorist posing as a journalist gets access and hurts or kills coalition member; Attack on family members as a result of media coverage; Transmission of media products delayed.
>
> (V. Clarke, *Communication Strategy in the Global War on Terror/Iraq*, Unpublished Presentation: Department of Defense, 2002)

But the benefit side, on the other hand, apparently outweighed the potential costs. In her presentation of the "general objectives and tactics" of the information campaign to Rumsfeld, Clarke, who saw the media operation as "an integral part of the war plan,"[74] used the same five phase scheme Central Command was using: pre-phase I, preparation; phase I, pre-hostilities; phase II, commencement of hostilities; phase III, engagement; and phase IV, post hostilities. The presentation contained several objectives, some of which were limited to single phases of the war. The first objective, constant in all phases of the entire operation, was to "preempt disinformation" by the Iraqi regime. "Denial and deception" briefings, early public reminders of risks such as environmental terror, or frequent interviews with military analysts, were thought to have a counterpropaganda effect. This was the defensive dimension of the PA strategy, what doctrine calls "counterpropaganda." A second objective was to "encourage dissent and defection" amongst the Iraqi civilians and soldiers. The demonstration of US military capabilities as well as the promise of the inevitable regime change in Iraq combined with a message of "care for the Iraqi people," communicated via the Arab media, should dissuade the country's population from opposing the US operation. A third objective was to "demonstrate success." As soon as hostilities began, the public affairs planners in the Pentagon relied on two major channels to demonstrate the successes of US operations, "embeds reporting" and "briefings." Other objectives presented to Rumsfeld were to manage expectations, and to achieve and maintain "information dominance" through strategic Pentagon briefings, operational theater briefings, and embeds reporting from a tactical perspective, already internally referred to as the "soda-straw" view. The PA planning cell's recommendations and Clarke's presentation stressed that public affairs was not just considered a feedback loop from the battlefield to the TV-watching American people; embedding had an integrated strategic function in the overall war plan. After the Secretary was briefed and read the draft of a message outlining the program to all combatant commands written by McCreary, he signed it almost without any changes. Rumsfeld looked at the so-called Personal For message briefed to him by Clarke, he looked up, and said: "Well, it's a big gamble, but it's probably one worth taking."[75]

Now the still skeptical combatant commander needed to back the program. While the public affairs staff in the Pentagon were discussing the pros and cons of the embedded media program, Franks and his staff at Central Command's headquarters in Tampa were busy trying to meet their deadlines for the war plan. The CINC, the commander-in-chief, was not only busy, he did not like the press to begin with. At one point, Franks asked Rumsfeld to send him an appropriate director of "strategic communications" because he tried to avoid media encounters. Franks thought of himself as being less press savvy than his predecessors. General Norman Schwarzkopf had proved to be an excellent and eloquent briefer during the Persian Gulf War, an inept description for Franks: "I don't give a rat's ass what you do with 'em," he would later say to his media director referring to the many reporters who wanted to cover the war from the ground, "just keep them out of my hair."[76] James R. Wilkinson was 32 when he was borrowed from the White House and named spokesperson of Central Command on 13 November 2002. The Texan was a protégé of Karen Hughes, a close public relations advisor to President Bush, and was a lieutenant in the Navy reserve for five years. During the Afghanistan War he had managed a so-called Coalition

Information Center for the White House: "We've learned that you either start the news wave or you're swamped by it," he had commented on his experience in Afghanistan.[77] And for a public affairs handler he was remarkably IO-savvy: "The goal of information warfare is to win without ever firing a shot," he had said in an interview on psychological warfare, somewhat reminiscent of Sun Tzu.[78] Before Wilkinson went to his new assignment he was briefed by Clarke and her staff on the embedded media program. The concept fitted his progressive public affairs thinking. Wilkinson arrived in Tampa with a "brilliant" and "innovative plan for print and electronic media coverage of the operation, should we go to war," recounts General Franks.[79]

At first, however, the CINC was skeptical: "When I heard the term 'embedded media,' it sounded dangerous." Franks was troubled by two issues – logistics and security: "Assigning newspaper and magazine writers and broadcast correspondents to combat units could present problems: transportation, support, and liability. And there were concerns about operational security, in this age of satellite phones and Internet video cameras." The commander was one of the few remaining Vietnam veterans in leading military positions, and his anti-press reflexes might well be a leftover of the molding experience in South East Asia. The former artillery soldier at the head of Central Command, however, was willing to think twice: "When Victoria [Clarke] and Jim [Wilkinson] briefed me on the details of the program, I saw it as a winner." The argument that finally persuaded him was the media's access to the troops and the reporting from the soldier's perspective that was expected to come from the embeds, based on the lesson from earlier wars: "One of the reasons the press coverage in Afghanistan had been so error-ridden and mediocre – and often anti-military in its bias – was that the journalists had been kept away from combat operations," the general reasoned. This was just about to change. "If the media were actually living and marching with the troops ... they would experience war from the perspective of the soldier or marine." The resulting intimacy, it was clear for the designers of the embedded media program, would result in a more knowledgeable and detailed coverage of the operation. The military has long been unnerved by the obvious lack of expertise on the side of the war correspondents they had to deal with. The press people, soldiers would often complain, were so badly informed that they confused an F16 with an M16.[80] "At least they'll get their facts straight," the general said. "Besides, the American people deserve to see the professionalism of their sons and daughters in uniform," he reasoned.[81]

This last patriotic argument was echoed by many higher ranking officers involved in the planning process. Soldiers who have been successful in their career tend to be proud of their service. Colonel Thomas explains: "We have an obligation especially to Americans to let them know what we are demanding of their sons and daughters." The ground soldiers were held in high esteem by their superiors. Thomas sees the embedded media coverage as a win-win situation, as a two way street. On the one hand, "there was never any doubt that we would defeat them [the Iraqis]. Just show how good those soldiers were." The US military is the best trained, best equipped, and most highly motivated troops, it was argued. On the other hand, he saw the press coverage as an incentive for the soldiers, as a way to "reward soldiers by putting them in the media."[82] Consequently, for the first time official policy was changed. Journalists were allowed to "name names," that is to include rank, first name, last name, and the soldier's home town in their story – provided that the soldier at hand concurred. Colonels (captains in the Navy), generals, and admirals were ordered to identify themselves. By late November in 2002 Clarke advised Franks that there could be as many as 600 embeds accredited to his command: "If we conduct this operation, General," she said, "it will be the best covered war in history."[83] The general agreed.

Down

Once the plan to embed the media had leadership support, it had to be communicated down the chain-of-command. When Air Force officer DeFrank later gave a presentation to an audience of his service about the public affairs performance during the invasion of Iraq, he stressed the "critical importance of strong support and direction from top leadership" that was necessary to get the program running.[84] To add leverage to that support, McCreary and Cullin had advised Clarke in their briefing in early October to disseminate the Personal For message to all combatant commands. During the long pre-invasion phase a P4 was issued two times by the Secretary of Defense and the JCS chairman. The message, headed "Command Support of Public Affairs Activities in Potential Future Military Operations," was sent out to all commands on 14 November 2005, and retransmitted on 21 February 2006. It bore Rumsfeld's signature and was distributed by McCreary even before the political decision to go to war against Iraq was officially made. The message, aimed at the operators, attempted to link the media operation to their success on the battlefield:

> Media coverage of potential future military operations will, to a large extent, shape public perception of the national security environment now and in the years ahead. This holds true for the US public; the public in allied countries, whose opinion can affect the durability of our coalition; and publics in countries where we conduct operations, whose perceptions of us can affect the cost and duration of our involvement.
> (T. McCreary, "Command Support of Public Affairs Activities in Potential Future Military Operations," *SECDEF-CJCS P4 Message* 2003)

The P4 demands to organize and facilitate access of national and international media to US forces, explicitly to those units engaged in ground operations. The motivation for this openness was "to get it right from the start, not days or weeks into an operation." Speed was essential, the "information initiative" in doctrinal terms or, as in the briefing to Rumsfeld, "information superiority." The rationale was denying the adversary to spin the media, and preventing rumors. The commanders' main motivation to take the operational security risk that inevitably came with embedding was to use PA as a counterpropaganda tool, and this was mirrored in the P4: "Let's tell the factual story – good or bad – before others seed the media with disinformation and distortions as they most certainly will continue to do."[85] To guarantee a quick reaction to events, the leadership delegated the authority for declassification and release of media products to the lowest possible level. This was a lesson from Afghanistan, where time zones got in the way of a quick authorization of news releases. At the time when those authorizations were required, the relevant decision makers in the Pentagon were often asleep because it was in the middle of the night at the East Coast. To avoid an overly restrictive and cautious handling of the press by the newly empowered commanders, the P4 advises them to "approach these decisions with 'why not' rather than 'why?'" The authors of the message tried to shift the burden of proof in favor of the open media policy:

> Operational planning should incorporate and support these efforts and include a push/pull mechanism to make the products readily available to a wider DoD audience for eventual use in a variety of public communication activities. These plans should also support the expeditious movement of media products that tell our story – both good news and bad – from the front lines. The goal for moving both media products and images should be minutes or hours not days.
>
> (T. McCreary, "Command Support of Public Affairs Activities in Potential Future Military Operations," *SECDEF-CJCS P4 Message* 2003)

In order to guarantee the accelerated transport not only of the media's reporting, which would be done by the technologically well equipped journalists themselves, but also of the military's own imagery, the message suggested they "put in place mechanisms and processes for the rapid dissemination of weapons systems video, ISR [intelligence, surveillance, and reconnaissance] footage, and operational combat camera footage before coalition forces move."[86] Even if the public affairs effort is not explicitly spelled out in a task list, the message demands, it is to be regarded as an implied task for "almost" all missions. The two messages were a major attempt to change default routines and standard operating procedures.

On 10 February 2003, the "Public Affairs Guidance (PAG) on Embedding Media during possible future military operations" was sent from Clarke's office in the Pentagon to the public affairs offices of all authorities related to national defense, the White House, the Secretary of State, the National Security Council, and several military commands. That guidance was only one of several PAGs distributed throughout the build up to war, but it was the most authoritative and comprehensive one. Just as doctrine demanded, the information's credibility and timeliness were important themes. The guidance explicitly states that no single reporters will be offered embed opportunities, but that the news organizations would determine which individuals they would send: "Embed opportunities will be assigned to media organizations, not to individual reporters," a measure designed to deflect criticism of hand-picking reporters.[87]

The media guidance was designed to make sure that journalists traveling with the units would be able to report and react to events in a speedy manner, largely echoing the P4. It was tantamount – in doctrinal language – to gain and maintain the information initiative: "The standard for release of information should be to ask 'why not release' vice 'why release.' Decisions should be made ASAP [as soon as possible], preferably in minutes, not hours." But the requirement to process public information fast included not only its approval but also the transmission of media products. Though modern communications technology would preclude many of the difficulties the military and the media had encountered in the Persian Gulf War, the guidance still called for adequate preparation in case of unexpected transmission problems: "Units should plan lift and logistical support to assist in moving media products to and from the battlefield so as to tell our story in a timely manner," the guidance demanded. So important was a speedy information transmission by the media, that the directive even prepared for calamities: "In the event of commercial communications difficulties, media are authorized to file stories via expeditious military signal communications capabilities."[88]

This acceleration raises the question of security risks, and their control: "Media products will not be subject to security review or censorship," the document's authors wrote. But the guidance also acknowledges that the "nature of the embedding process" may involve that reporters get access to sensitive information which could, by combination with other available information, disclose classified information. Examples of such sensitive information are future and actual troop movements, friendly capabilities or vulnerabilities, or the effectiveness of enemy tactics, such as electronic attack. The guidance calls for "prudent precautions" to be taken by commanders to protect such information. One such precaution, called for in the public affairs guidance, could still be a security review, if a mission's coverage is of particular significance:

> In instances where a unit commander or the designated representative determines that coverage of a story will involve exposure to sensitive information beyond the scope of what may be protected by prebriefing or debriefing, but coverage of which is in the best interests of the DOD, the commander may offer access if the reporter agrees to a security review of their coverage.
>
> (US Department of Defense, *Public Affairs Guidance on Embedding Media During Possible Future Operations/Deployments in the US Central Command's Area of Responsibility*, PAG1, 2003)

The guidance explicitly states that such a security review would not involve any editorial changes. Rather it was intended to protect classified information and operational security. In the war, such security reviews proved to be the exception rather than the rule,[89] although the Secretary of Defense explicitly prohibited commanders to disclose classified information to media representatives: the guidance "does not authorize commanders to allow media access to classified information."[90] During the operation this rule would later be bent and outright ignored, and several reporters would even be invited to participate in classified meetings. The "prudent precautions" the guidance was calling for turned out to be mutual trust rather than security reviews. In practice, an important element of that mutual trust was that the reporter, as a potential leak of sensitive information, was traveling with a particular unit. Disclosing sensitive information to the enemy would not only endanger the unit, but also its embedded reporters. Most reporters understood that risk. And most commanders understood that most reporters understood.

From the perspective of many commanders, the plan to do embedding was not a new idea. The P4 message fell on fertile ground since many units and commands had already begun to think along similar lines long before Captain Cullin's planning cell in the Pentagon was brainstorming about a new approach to media management on the battlefield. Before the public affairs planning in the Pentagon took shape, some commands had independently begun to develop their own plans: "Regardless of what DoD policy was gonna be," Birmingham recalls of the 3rd ID's planning, "we had already made plans, starting that summer, to embed some media with us."[91] Others even give earlier dates. The plan to embed the media had already been under way since March 2002, according to Thomas, Director for Public Affairs for the Combined Force Land Component Command (CFLCC, pronounced sea-flick). The services, like the Marines or the Air Force, are not the only autonomous organizations; joint commands like CFLCC or even a single unit, like the Army's 3rd Infantry Division or the 1st Marine Expeditionary Force, act in their own interest and have their own lessons-learned mechanisms. And those sub-organizations sometimes ignored or acted against explicit guidance from the Pentagon.

The 3rd Infantry Division is a particularly interesting case because the formation would have a decisive role in the invasion of Iraq under Major General Buford Blount's command. In the summer of 2002 Birmingham invited Sean Naylor, a journalist for the *Army Times* and a frequent contributor to *USA Today*, to come down to Fort Stewart, in Georgia, the home of the Marne Division, to speak about embedded media in Afghanistan. Naylor is an experienced war correspondent with an impressive network of personal contacts within the US Army. The young journalist with the distinct English accent had been embedded with US forces in Afghanistan, where he was one of the very few reporters who covered Operation Anaconda. He had also covered Somalia, Haiti, Bosnia, Albania, Kosovo, and would later embed in Iraq. Naylor was one of the first embedded reporters in Bosnia. At that summer day in Fort Stewart, his audience was the 3rd ID's leadership, battalion level and up. Commanders like David Perkins or Terry Ferrell, who would later be at the forefront of the Iraq invasion and skillfully worked with the media, were listening to the reporter's presentation.

Birmingham explained: "I brought him down there to give a presentation to battalion and brigade commanders, and primary staff, and the command group on embedded press operation – as well as other press operations – during OEF."[92] Birmingham wanted to educate the commanders about the benefits of having an embedded reporter with them, and the *Army Times* reporter had a deep understanding of matters martial. In retrospect Birmingham doubts that the commanders were really getting the gist of where his PA plan was going that day. Just as the strategists in Central Command, they were focusing on the operational war plan, and not on the media who would report on their work. But their PAO realized that the media had become "just a condition of the battlefield," as Lieutenant General William S. Wallace would put it later,[93] the commander of the Army's V Corps which included the 3rd ID. And Afghanistan had shown the best way to deal with that condition of the battlefield: "I thought embedded media was the best case scenario because there is gonna be media on the battlefield anyway. So why not?" Birmingham said.[94] Like his colleagues in the Pentagon, he was rather cautious in the early phases with respect to the numbers of embeds he could take in: "I settled in between 20 and 30 for the entire division. That was a planning assumption based on the fact that we would thumbly embed no less than what they were embedding in Anaconda."[95]

An entire community of likeminded public affairs officers was promoting the idea to embed the media. Colonel Guy Shields, the Kuwait press center's director, said: "I think you can talk to any military PAO, we've been saying this is the way to go for a long time."[96] That explains why seemingly disconnected organizational units were coming up with similar contingency plans. The organizational culture was receptive to the innovation, which had been discussed in communities-of-practice among public affairs officers in the past. This emerging common sense made it easier for the leadership to persuade operational commanders some levels further down the hierarchy, a point stressed by the 3rd ID's public affairs handler:

> Junior commanders during the Gulf War who basically have learned to live with media since that time and have basically looked back and said we wasted one hell of an opportunity during the Gulf War. They were company commanders back then, now they're LTC [Lieutenant Colonels] and battalion and brigade commanders, so they were more willing to embrace the media and bring'em in to cover.
>
> (Birmingham, Mike, interview by author, Pentagon, 6 April 2004)

Central Command in Tampa, Florida, already began to develop plans for large-scale embedding in Iraq in early 2002, during the Afghanistan operation, concurrent with planning in the Pentagon. In June the command's leadership was briefed on embedding. From 9 to 11 October 2002, just after Cullin's planning cell had delivered its recommendations, officers from various components and the Pentagon discussed the embedding issue, and other aspects of the Iraq War's strategic communication, in a planning conference in Tampa. Each component – air, naval, and land – briefed its public affairs plan. It became clear that there would be three levels of war coverage, and the estimate of how many journalists could be accommodated was adjusted to 400.[97] Shortly after the meeting CFLCC began to move its headquarters to Kuwait.

Horizontal

Even after the embedded media policy was communicated down to a receptive working level, it needed rehearsals and trainings to establish the new routine. Many observers and even scholars of military innovation seem to assume that a military organization's chain-of-command functions as reliably as an electronic circuit. This is hardly the case, and even less so in the realm of public affairs. The ASD/PA is outside the chain-of-command, and the Goldwater-Nichols Act of 1986 even clarified that the chairman of the Joint Chiefs of Staff is not part of the formal chain-of-command during military operations. The chairman's influence depends strongly on the personal relationship between him and an operation's commander-in-chief, as well as on the personality of the Secretary of Defense. The line of authority directly runs from the Secretary to the combatant commander. The Pentagon's civilian spokesperson has no formal authority over the postures of combatant commanders. And even if their formal superiors, the Secretary of Defense or Central Command's CINC, support a particular policy toward media access, the leadership's support would not necessarily result in that policy's smooth implementation by the operational and tactical commanders. In an actual military contingency, where the fog of war blurs the overview, there are significant grey areas in which lower-level commanders can use their power without explicitly disobeying orders. One example was the Marines' initiative to embed reporters in Afghanistan; another example is the 3rd Infantry Division's initiative to equip their embedded reporters with their own vehicles.

While the US military prepared for the media onslaught with presentations, contingency plans, task forces, and P4 messages behind closed doors, journalists and bureau chiefs began to speculate and to prepare for the invasion as well. In October 2002 significant numbers of journalists started to travel to Kuwait. In November the number had swollen to about 300 journalists. Thomas acted as the chief spokesperson Combined Force Land Component Command, the joint command overseeing all US ground forces in the entire area of responsibility of Central Command, mainly the Middle East. The colonel and his staff initiated two things: first, they started a weekly briefing that the spokesman was giving in a suite in the Kuwait City Hilton Hotel, initially with a small number of journalists. By February, more than a month before the start of the war, up to 700 reporters were attending military briefings in Kuwait. A second initiative was more vital. Birmingham recommended that the division's 2nd Brigade Combat Team train with journalists before the war started. From late 2002 until the start of the actual operation in March, large numbers of American troops were arriving in Kuwait and Qatar. Beginning in early November, exercises and simulations were conducted in the desert terrain of the neighboring coalition countries, and from December to January more than 85 press representatives trained with the troops for three to five days, including the coverage of the rehearsals. Both writers and warfighters benefited from this early experiment in Kuwait's deserts.

The training did two things. First, as Thomas explained, "it acclimated the soldiers in the units to having journalist with them all the time."[98] During the last large-scale military operation in the Persian Gulf War, reporters only had contact with military minders, the PAOs, not with ordinary corporals and sergeants. The troops usually did not encounter journalists while they did their regular work. They had to learn how to deal with the reporters and build confidence and trust. But the experience was a two way street: "The second piece of that learning curve was for the reporters," Thomas said. "They learned what it took to operate in a desert environment and to be dependent on the military unit they were embedded with."[99] Some sensitive pieces of the new high-tech equipment the journalists were carrying did not hold up well in the dust and sand and heat of the Kuwaiti desert. The press learned various tactics to get a better vantage point, or how they could use a Humvee battery to run their plastic-covered laptop computer. The rehearsal-embeds reported from the training, which in turn reassured commanders: "Commanders around the military saw the mutual benefits of having journalists," said Colonel David Perkins, commander of the 2nd Brigade Combat Team, who took part in the pre-war training and served as a positive example for his fellow commanders by demonstrating that embedding could work: "By God, if Dave Perkins can do that, I can do it better," as Thomas sums up their reaction.[100] While the troops under CFLCC's aegis were training in the desert during the build-up phase, their numbers continually grew. As a result, the estimate of embeds the land components could take in was continuously reassessed based on the most recent training experience. The training, Thomas remembers, "tremendously increased the number of embeds."[101] Birmingham's initial estimate for the 3rd ID, the single formation with the largest number of reporters, grew from 25 to 85; the total number rose from 240 to 671.[102] Finally the training helped to overcome some logistical problems that could have thwarted the entire embed operation. As the estimated number of possible journalists was growing, the problem of equipping those journalists with protective masks and suits against chemical and biological weapons grew as well: "Had the war kicked off three weeks earlier," Thomas insisted, "we would not have embedded reporters."[103] The positive assessment of the preparation phase is echoed by the media: "The U.S. Army was nothing short of brilliant in terms of the way they prepared us for it," said CNN's Walter Rodgers, who embedded with the 3rd ID's 7th Cavalry squadron:

> [They] let us go out a week in advance, get to know the troops, build trust. It's just like any reporter in any situation. You get to know the people you're covering. You talk to them. They know you. You know them and you build rapport. And that rapport stands you through the whole time very well.
> (Rodgers, Walter, quoted in A.C. Shepard, *Narrowing the Gap: Military, Media and the Iraq War*, Cantigny Conference Series, Chicago: McCormick Tribune Foundation, 2004, p. 30)

According to Thomas, this common learning experience in the deserts of Kuwait had a greater impact on the embedded media program than the boot camps, several week-long training camps organized for reporters in the continental United States before the war. And some of the experiences in Kuwait's deserts, several weeks before the invasion of Iraq was launched, seemed to contradict Pentagon guidance which was issued earlier. Brian Cullin and his task force had pre-drafted the public affairs guidance in October. When the text was finalized, its authors could not have anticipated how well embedding would be received when it was tested prior to the war. Thus, the PAG explicitly prohibits to equip the media with their own vehicles: Paragraph 2C1 makes clear that "embedded media are not authorized use of their own vehicles while traveling in an embedded status."[104] The leadership of the US Army's 3rd Infantry Division decided to ignore that rule. The division's chief public affairs officer reasoned that his unit would get a better media coverage if they provided Humvees to their fellow journalists: "Better picture, better sound," Mike Birmingham quipped, when asked for the rationale behind the decision to provide 12 vehicles to the division's reporters. CNN or Fox News were among them. The large TV networks in particular had a lot of technical equipment that would not fit easily into the already overcrowded military vehicles. The Pentagon had security concerns, but Birmingham's unit decided to be less cautious: "We didn't think that they would be wandering off, frankly," he said. After all, the media were in hostile territory, in the middle of a vast desert, with an enemy who might not be willing to make subtle distinctions before shooting, distinctions between a journalist and a soldier climbing out of identical US military vehicles: "We just felt that we had worked with this concept during training in December and January, December especially, that we thought that we had a good working relationship," the PAO said. And as predicted, the 3rd ID would get a rather satisfactory coverage: "What did you get?" Birmingham asked rhetorically, sitting in a cafeteria in the Pentagon a year after the invasion, "you got great pictures, tight shots, panoramic shots." Just as some of the doctrinal documents were arguing, the 3rd ID's intention behind this open access policy was to use the images of superior US military forces as a deterrent: "Again, the hope was, if the images were being displayed worldwide and somebody was seeing these images, maybe, just maybe, if it saves a few lives because people stayed home, people stayed indoors, soldiers went home, the [Iraqi] air force didn't fly."[105]

Some of the arguments used to justify embedding internally were already articulated in doctrinal publications. The significance of doctrine, however, should not be overestimated. Doctrinal writings, particularly when published by the "wrong" service, were simply ignored or even unknown to the people they were produced for. And for a joint planning effort, like the embedded media program, doctrinal manuals are particularly problematic. Joint doctrine tends to be a compromise between the different services' approaches. As a result, the *Joint Doctrine for Public Affairs* is too abstract and too slow to adapt to changes in the information environment. Doctrine, contrary to its intention, is a description of past practices more than a prescription of best practices. Cullin, the PA planning cell's head, thinks that doctrine often "is just something to take a departure from." The group did not use any doctrinal writings as background reading or as sources of their research: "I was typically Navy and did not use any doctrine," recalls Cullin. Asked what role doctrine played in the embedded media process, Colonel Thomas was unambiguous in his answer: "There does not exist any solid doctrine on what we did in Iraq." Several officers who were involved in the planning and execution of the embedded media program simply raised an eyebrow or smiled at the evidently naïve and academic question about whether they used doctrinal writings to prepare their work.

The view that the final idea was invented and moved up and down the chain-of-command is too simple. This technical and narrow view does not bear witness to the evolution and the change of the plan during its actual implementation. The final concept evolved during the process itself. The program's initiators embraced it because they hoped to avoid a rerun of the military's post-Vietnam experience; the PA-community embraced it because the program improved media–military relations and created mutual understanding; the IO-warriors embraced it because the program effectively used the media as a defensive counter-propaganda tool and as a means to demonstrate US capabilities to the foe they were facing; the commanders embraced it because the rationale of embedding was explained to them in the language they could understand; and leadership embraced it because so many good reasons led them to believe that the potential benefit was worth taking the risk.

8 Strategic public affairs
Iraq

Organizations in turbulent environments face much more data than they sensibly can process. Perception filters and attention directing mechanisms are needed to deal with over-complexity. Experienced decision makers are equipped with mental models and tacit framesets that enable them to act swiftly in the face of complex situations. If the idea sits on our nose like a pair of glasses, the concept of the center of gravity serves as spectacles through which commanders view the strategic environment. It directs their attention, reduces complexity, and ultimately guides action.

The center of gravity is a simple but crucial conceptual tool for modern strategic and operational planners. In his memoirs, Franks goes into some detail explaining the way the concept was used when he and his staff were planning the invasion: "CentCom would apply the necessary lines of operation to attack or influence what Clausewitz had described more than one hundred years before as the enemy's 'centers of gravity'."[1] Already in December 2001 Central Command's planning cells were working on a contingency war plan for the invasion of Iraq. The general and his staff drew a working matrix, combining the most important targets, the centers of gravity, and the means to attack those targets, the lines of operation, in a cross-table. They identified nine columns or "slices," as the planners preferred to call centers of gravity, which kept Saddam in power: the most important ones were the regime leadership with the dictator himself; internal security; the Republican Guard and its special forces; the regular Iraqi army; the country's infrastructure; and the civilian population. Accordingly, suitable lines of attack were included in the working matrix: operational fires; Special Forces Operations; maneuver warfare; information operations; the support of opposition groups; but also civil–military operations to deal with the civilian population during the attack and particularly after hostilities had ceased. The prime objective that guided the planning was to topple Saddam's regime. Franks did not see it as part of his responsibility to question his civilian superiors and their preeminant concern with regime change, nor did he consider the strategic consequences of this narrow focus. The commander of all US forces in the Middle East did not divert any of Central Command's planning resources to the much more challenging task of stabilizing Iraq once its authoritarian government would be gone. Instead, he zeroed in on bringing down the regime. With Saddam's fall, the war would somehow end, it was assumed. Accordingly, the most important center of gravity was the dictator himself. He was the target with the "highest value," and killing Saddam at the top of the enemy regime's organizational pyramid was internally referred to as "regime decapitation."[2]

Operation Iraqi Freedom

On Tuesday, 18 March 2003, the CIA disclosed to Central Command that it had an intelligence report by reliable sources on a possible meeting of Saddam Hussein and his sons over the next day. For a brief period the US military leadership, with the help of the clandestine service's assets, thought it would be able to determine the dictator's location. An occasion to strike this high-value target was emerging. Immediately the information on the whereabouts of the dictator was checked as thoroughly as possible. Michael "Buzz" Moseley, the air commander, told his staff that the CIA was 99.9 percent sure (the information later turned out to be wrong).[3] Should the United States attempt to kill the dictator? President Bush was in charge of a decision with such historic proportions. The US president and his advisors were busy contemplating the attack in Washington while the Air Force prepared two stealth F-117 Nighthawks, equipped with bunker busting bombs, and the Navy programmed a synchronized strike with 45 unmanned Tomahawk cruise missiles, each carrying a 1,000 pound warhead, to hit an additional list of targets in downtown Baghdad. The two bombers, codenamed Ram 1 and Ram 2, would be able to fly in, drop their explosive freight, and return before daybreak, the commanders hoped. At 0312 hours, Qatar time, Central Command was informed about the direct presidential decision ordering to execute the decapitation strike. Twenty-five minutes later, the planes departed from Al Udeid Air Force Base, racing against dawn toward the site coded Dora Farms where Saddam was suspected to meet his sons, still waiting for their final target coordinates to be transmitted in flight.

The sun was almost above the horizon when the two planes approached their target. A blanket of clouds made ground observation nearly impossible for the pilots, and only in the last moment they were able to find a whole in the clouds and pierce through to identify their targets visually. Each F-117 dropped two bombs at once, leaving the GPS-guided weapons falling to hit their aiming points. Not knowing whether their mission was accomplished successfully the pilots returned to Saudi Arabia. Journalists from the Palestine Hotel's rooftop filmed the dark skies filled with the Iraqi Air Defense's red tracers and illuminated by the blazing blasts of the Tomahawks hitting their targets in the city. At 0541 hours on 19 March 2003, Franks sat in front of a television screen and flipped through several satellite channels. He saw a reporter on a balcony of the Palestine Hotel reporting "heavy explosions" south of the city and in the western suburbs. While the general was watching this on TV, Central Command had no information about the stealth bombers' attack yet, for security reasons, all communications with the planes were cut during the mission. It was 2141 hours in

Washington and Americans bore witness in real-time to the initial strikes of a new Iraq War.

While the stealth bombers were still on the way to their target, the President's staff was already considering giving the first press conference to announce the beginning of the war. Because this first day of the war was a strategically significant moment, Donald Rumsfeld needed to clear the presidential statements to the press with his commander-in-chief of Central Command. The information Bush would release in his remarks in front of US cameras and the eyes of the world could potentially harm the security of the operation, or convey a wrong impression to the wrong audience. It was critical. Rumsfeld called the combatant commander in Qatar to clarify the details. Even before the Tomahawks or the F-117s had reached their targets at Dora Farms, Franks pointed out to his civilian boss that "Baghdad is full of foreign reporters" who would report the attack instantly. The physical impacts of the missiles and the bombs would be visible to the world via the international press assembled in the Palestine Hotel enjoying a good view over the city from the tall building, and this would have a psychological impact on the adversary as well. "We're looking at a real CNN moment," he said. Franks knew that the Iraqis would not need CNN to tell them that "kinetics" – contemporary military speak for fighting – had begun. The commander argued that he did not want the President to speak in a way that sounded good to the domestic US audience but would compromise the plan. Franks also did not want to leave the enemy too confident after a relatively brief attack by playing down the magnitude of the assault or what was to come: "We don't want to let the enemy think this is another pinprick TLAM strike that got lucky," the general said to Rumsfeld, using jargon for Tomahawk Land Attack Missile. He tried to avoid giving the Iraqis the impression that the US was just sending in those weapons from a safe distance, like it had been doing before.[4] But the commander also did not want to give away the element of surprise by disclosing too much information about what was to come and when: "But we also don't want the Iraqis to start gearing up for G-Day right this minute," he said to the Secretary.[5] The "G" in G-Day stands for "ground operations" and refers to the day when the ground war is scheduled to start. The statement for the President's speech that the two men would agree on to reconcile those contradictory strategic concerns was: "These are in the opening stages of what will be a broad and concerted campaign."[6]

The scene makes clear how important the media have become in war. Senior military and civilian leaders had a clear understanding of the multiple audiences they were talking to, and they acted accordingly. The same applies to the middle-managers of the war. The responsible division, brigade, and battalion commanders knew as well that talking to the media meant talking to the enemy in Baghdad, talking to their families at home, talking to their uniformed comrades in Saudi Arabia, Kuwait, Qatar, and Afghanistan, talking to their civilian superiors in Washington, and talking to Congress at the same time. In doctrine as well as in the planning process, the international mass-media coverage was viewed as a dimension of the "cognitive battlefield."

During Desert Storm the US-led coalition had deployed 560,000 troops in 14 divisions. Warfare used to be linear: "There's a line, with an offense, a defense, they huddle, they clash, the line moves," as Davis, who took part in the 1991 Gulf War, put it.[7] In the high-tech environment of the 2003 Iraq War, the situation on the battlefield would be different. The operation was non-linear. Operation Iraqi Freedom was staffed with fewer than half the number of troops, organized in five divisions. The total number of ground troops was about 175,000, and many of them were not in a position to fight when the war started. The size of the attack force was considered less important than the tempo and the flexibility of its maneuver. Instead of conventionally and slowly advancing broad front-lines, the commanders planned to apply fast, rapid, and decisive maneuvers simultaneously at key points, throwing the enemy off balance. The Iraqis would not be able to react to the US Army's fast maneuver speed. An almost obsessive belief in the overwhelming effect of speed and momentum was guiding the planners: "Just as in physics, the effects of mass increased with velocity", Franks thought, as did some military historians.[8] "As with the French in 1940, every decision of the Iraqi high command would already have been overtaken by events when made."[9] That modern "blitzkrieg"[10] had profound consequences on how the war could be reported.

The information environment

Communication technology had advanced dramatically in the dozen years since the Persian Gulf War and it provided the media with unprecedented broadcasting and recording capabilities. Donatella Lorch has covered about every US military operation since the Persian Gulf War, where she had worked for the *New York Times*. In Saudi Arabia in 1991 she was carrying a typewriter and had no satellite phone: "I had to beg the networks to use their satellite phone to file my stories. I had no means of communication," she remembers.[11] Usually, in those days during the Gulf War, she fully had to rely on the military to file her stories. Lorch and her print colleagues would use a satellite telex for the first time in Mogadishu in 1993. No earlier than two years later, in 1995, she started to work with a satellite phone, with the size and weight of a suitcase. In 2003, by contrast, portable satellite phones were standard equipment for print and radio journalists, and even TV crews had the ability to broadcast digitally with video-phones, eliminating all logistical obstacles of the past. This radical change in the media environment has well been recognized in the Pentagon. As Whitman said:

> In 1991, reporters didn't have the type of technology and capabilities that exist today. They did not have the ability to file from the field like they can today. There was not the option of sending images and video lugging along tremendous amounts of equipment.[12]

Thanks to this technological development, reporters had unprecedented capabilities to file their stories, fast and almost without the military's logistical support. This was very clear to public affairs handlers in the Pentagon: "Reporters, for the first time, have the ability to get their stories back real time without relying on the military," Davis acknowledged.[13]

The repercussions of this revolution in reporting affairs for the military were almost contradictory: "Technology was an enabler and at the same time it was one of our greatest concerns," Thomas said after the war.[14] The new technology and the sheer speed of global information flows were a problem for the military: "The speed that these reports made it for often outpaced the military's communication channels," an Army War College report said.[15] Journalists tend to find favor in this development. Nik Gowing, BBC World's chief presenter, labeled the acceleration of news reporting "real-time tyranny of the present" in a lecture he gave in 2000 at the King's College Liddell Hart Center for Military Archives in London. Gowing believes that the shortened "time-line" plays to the media's advantage and to the military's disadvantage. Official spokespersons would be forced to react to journalists' questions at press briefings in Brussels or Washington without knowing what had happened only a couple of minutes ago in a war on the other side of the world. This, he argued, would empower reporters and would allow them to outpace and outwit the military which lost "the control of the information edge."[16]

This view, however, entirely ignores the benefits for the military. The new media technology helped the military to deal with the new blitzkrieg's maneuver speed. The journalists who are able to file from the field without using and occupying military equipment create three benefits for the military. First, the military saves badly needed logistical assets because media products do not have to be moved via military communication channels or airplanes any more. Second, the armed forces save time by outsourcing the reporting to professionals, as passing tactical details up the military's hierarchical reporting chain takes many hours. Third, and most importantly, the new technological equipment of the media provided the military with a new weapon in the information war. Depending on whether one views the media as a channel or a target group, the embeds were providing the information initiative to the US forces or they were taking it away. The BBC's Nik Gowing is taking the latter view; Terry Ferrell, commander of the 3rd ID's 7th Cavalry, a squadron designed for fast-paced armored thrusts, equipped with M1 tanks, Bradleys, 155 mm artillery, and Kiowa helicopters, was taking the first: "CNN," he would say after the war, "became a part of the organization from the aspect that I did not have to put any additional focus on moving them, securing them, or ensuring that they were prepared to do as we were doing along the way."[17] The media became – at least temporarily – part of the mission by serving its communications objectives. Clarke was even worried about the media's equipment: "One concern was technology would fail us, but it didn't," she said.[18] Embedding, in this sense, ceased to be a metaphor.

The commander's objective

The commander's objective is to win the war. The information revolution had not only transformed the way a war would be reported; even more so it had transformed the way military conflicts are fought and won. To understand how radically different the view of the embedded journalists was in comparison to the view from military headquarters, it is helpful to have a look at the CINC's command center. Network Centric Warfare was the concept that had occupied the US forces for the decade prior to the Iraq War. The term emanated in the computer industry in the early 1990s. Applied to military operations, the idea was to transform the military into a gigantic armed computer network, transgressing unit and service boundaries. Jointly the military was more effective and more lethal.

Network-centric operations relied on the Global Positioning System, GPS. In 2003 almost every vehicle and every aircraft of the US forces carried a GPS transponder that constantly transmitted encrypted data via satellite to headquarters. The received data contained information on coordinates, direction, and speed of all friendly vehicles (it was those data that the F-117s en route to the decapitation strike of the first day did not transmit to avoid being detected, and to preserve the element of surprise). Once these data are combined, computers can assemble the big picture. During the invasion, large plasma screens in the Pentagon, at Central Command in Tampa, and in the coalition headquarters in Qatar showed the friendly force formations in clusters of small, bright blue boxes. Due to the color of the friendly forces the system is called "Blue Force Tracker." By clicking on the data boxes on the screen, the commanders in headquarters could zoom in on smaller and smaller units, from corps, to division, to brigade, to regiment, to battalion, to company, "down to a single Armored Cavalry scout troop in Bradleys," as Franks described the system with awe.[19] On a second plasma screen the commanders at the Qatar headquarters could see "Red Force Tracker," representing the positions of enemy formations. Iraqi tanks and missiles, of course, were not transmitting their positions via GPS satellites to the US military. But the coalition was gathering and analyzing data from a whole range of sources and loading them into the "enemy database": Unmanned Aerial Vehicles (UAVs) roaming the skies over Iraq provided live-video feeds and high-resolution imagery, medium and high-altitude reconnaissance aircraft delivered still photos and were even able to pierce through sandstorms with their infrared equipment, and satellites and a growing net of spies in the country were sending in data to complete the picture. Technically it would have been easy to put the positions of the adversarial red force and those of the friendly blue forces on the same screen. But this would have provided a distorted view. The intelligence on enemy formations was incomplete, delayed, and often faulty, so the red force icons on the screen in effect showed an image that was inadequate and unreliable. The blue force screen, by contrast, represented near real-time and comprehensive movements.

Building 217 in the huge command complex in Doha, Qatar, housed the operation's technical nerve center. Its encrypted satellite voice and data links, video conference facilities, and internet and media capabilities used bandwidth equivalent to that of a large US city. The air-conditioned command warehouse with the blue and red force tracking system was the modern field marshal's hill, giving him a truly strategic view of an immensely complex war. Blue Force Tracker is indeed a very controversial tool among experts because it creates an incentive for strategic commanders to micromanage and meddle in tactical engagements. But it is essential to get an appreciation of the commander's perspective in order to understand what the embedded journalists did not see. In the early days of war reporting it was possible for correspondents to get the overview of a battlefield just by overlooking the moving troop formations from an elevated vantage point, and to get an overview at least approximating that of a general. In 2003 this had changed. Most reporters only had the very limited view from a unit's perspective, the soda-straw view, rich in human and tactical detail but poor in abstract and strategic oversight. And the embedded journalists often lacked the military knowledge to put their eye-witness accounts into perspective: only 19 percent had served in the military.

The reporter's objective

The reporter's objective is to produce a rewarding story. That reward oscillates on a spectrum with sensationalism on the one end and investigative journalism on the other end. Those more on the sensationalist side favor fame, money, or a prestigious prize, and see their reports' truthfulness or objectivity as secondary. Those on the investigative side care more about the quality of their product and want to get as close to the facts and their sources as possible, and view fame and prestige as secondary. Journalists like Geraldo Rivera or Peter Arnett probably are rather on sensationalism's side, reporters like Anne Garrels or Sean Naylor tend toward the investigative end. Both types of reporters nevertheless had strong incentives to embed with the military. The first incentive was to come closer to the sources. Networks and news-editors were keen on embedding and interested precisely in the type of coverage that would come out if it: live close-ups from the front, possibly combat scenes and soldiers in action. This was particularly evident in the early phases of the operation. As the war started, the live pictures of the advancing troops had the highest news value, even if they were just showing plains of sand and occasionally a military vehicle in an unsatisfactory resolution and quality. But the images were broadcast live from a moving frontline on a battlefield for the first time in history. The reporters' second incentive to embed was to come closer to their career objective. Many journalists sensed the chance to turn themselves into celebrities: "Essentially," as the *Washington Post* quotes an anonymous network news producer who spent months in Kuwait observing the competition among his correspondents, "every correspondent sees this as their way of becoming a household name."[20] Competition for the best "slots" between networks, and even more so within the media organizations themselves, was fierce.

General Dwight D. Eisenhower, later to become president, concisely described the conflict of interests between the media and the military in an often quoted aphorism:

> The first essential in military operations is that no information of value shall be given to the enemy. The first essential in newspaper work and broadcasting is wide-open publicity. It is your job and mine to try to reconcile those sometimes diverse considerations.[21]

Prior to the invasion of Iraq, these considerations ceased to be diverse. The new information environment and the embedded media program created conditions in which the commander's objective and the reporter's objective largely converged. The traditional zero-sum thinking of opposed interests and structural conflict between the two institutions gave way to a positive-sum logic.

New routines: implementing the information campaign

Operation Iraqi Freedom's information campaign was largely designed in the Pentagon. The five-cornered structure is said to be the largest office building on Earth, and the US Department of Defense is the world's largest employer. In its introductory presentation, "DoD 101," the department compares itself to America's biggest companies. With more than two million employees working all over the globe, it ranks itself first followed by the private sector giant Wal Mart with approximately 1.3 million employees. Mirroring those dimensions, the campaign in Iraq involved almost 200,000 soldiers, sailors, airmen, and support staff working around the clock and the globe. The operation was a gigantesque logistical and financial undertaking which triggered an immense media interest, second only to the terrorist attacks against the World Trade Center and the Pentagon on 11 September 2001. But in contrast to the spontaneous and ad-hoc media coverage of the 9/11-strikes, the Iraq War's information campaign was designed, planned, and executed by military men and women as well as by civilian administrators in the Department of Defense. An entire army of 2,500 journalists and their staff traveling to Iraq and the neighboring countries were registered by the American military, and around 775 reporters were embedded with coalition troops when the line of departure from Kuwait into Iraq was eventually crossed. Public affairs officers, information officers, former civilian journalists, and PR specialists with a private sector background were there to help. As the previous chapter has shown, the public affairs planning for Operation Iraqi Freedom absorbed significant resources: intellectual, administrative, financial and, most importantly, time.

Information to the public was principally provided through three channels: a strategic, an operational, and a tactical channel. The strategic picture of the war was presented to the international press corps in briefings in Washington, mostly in the Pentagon's press room and sometimes in the White House; the operational briefings were held at Central Command's headquarters in Doha, Qatar; and the tactical view from the ground was provided by reporters embedded with troops. On all three levels communication and the media were – just as planned – deliberately used as a channel to address an entire bundle of audiences at the same time: the US public, the enemy leadership, the Iraqi population, the coalition troops, allied publics, and potential future adversaries. On each level, the media cooperation was motivated by specific operational intentions. The communication strategy, in short, was tied to the war strategy.

News from Washington

The embedded media as well as the news editors did not have access to battlefield intelligence. The embeds only had an outlook from the ground and lacked the bird's-eye view. To officers, this imbalance in perspective had been obvious before the war started: "The reporters filing their stories from the maneuver units would not have access to the Blue Force Tracker. For many, their perspective would be limited to a single company or battalion's Area of Operations," Franks had noted.[22] His vantage point, by contrast, offered the most complete picture of the battlespace. It would be informed by his subordinate commanders, video-feeds from reconnaissance UAVs, satellite imagery, human intelligence sources, and the reports broadcast by the embedded journalists. The CINC had, in military jargon, the maximal available situational awareness – which still was incomplete – while the journalists, by contrast, were represented by just one little blue dot on a large plasma screen. Commanders understood the importance of battlefield intelligence and situational awareness, and anticipated that the embedded media's limited overview would not be without effect. It was crystal clear to experienced officers that the view from the ground would result in both too many detailed impressions and too little contextual information:

> We knew from the start that each journalist would get what we called a soda-straw-view of the world, through that very narrow perspective. Of course, it had to be that way, they were embedded with units; they would get a very narrow view, but rich and deep.
> (DeFrank, James, interview by author, Pentagon, 27 February 2004)

The "soda straw" was only one of several metaphors that were invented during the discussions in the Pentagon and Central Command to describe the lack of overview, which would not only affect the reporters themselves, but also their readers and watchers. DeFrank preferred the metaphor of a "dragonfly's view" of the world. Like in a compound eye, in his thinking, each single soda straw provided one pixel, the sum of which would provide an "overall view of the environment, but each one was individual and discrete." Others, like Brooks, Davis, or Robert Gaylord, US Army director of public affairs, used the image of a "mosaic chip" to refer to the same problem. Usually the allegory of "700 mosaic chips of the battle" was used in the military to argue that there was nobody systematically putting the entire mosaic together in order to show the entire image, that there was a danger the public could get a distorted vision of the war.[23] The soda straw, however, would become the most popular metaphor, and it was widely adapted by journalists and pundits all over the world. The almost lyrical creativity the Pentagon developed in inventing new metaphors to describe new phenomena illustrates Nonaka's argument that new tacit knowledge is articulated with the help of metaphors and allegories.

Rumsfeld, however, wanted more than just to understand the new dynamic. He felt that he had to call the reporters' attention to the soda-straw problem. In a press briefing on the second day of the war, 21 March 2003, he used yet another metaphor to describe the journalists' narrow view: slices. He not only knew that many of the embedded reporters would probably succumb to the illusion that they had an excellent overview of the war.[24] Their editors and many television watchers, which included congressmen, politicians, and administrators in Washington up to the highest levels of government, would be led to believe that they know what is happening at the frontlines in Iraq. After all they could witness it in real-time and in multiple perspectives. This dynamic was indeed unprecedented. Rumsfeld pointed out that it would be "somewhat historic" to have 24-hours-a-day news coverage of an ongoing operation, accessible all over the world via the internet, with hundreds of representatives of the international free press accompanying the military campaign. He continued his warning: "What we are seeing is not the war in Iraq," apparently irritating some journalists with that statement, judging from their subsequent commentary:[25]

> what we're seeing are slices of the war in Iraq. We're seeing that particularized perspective that that reporter, or that commentator, or that television camera happens to be able to see at that moment. And it is not what's taking place. What you see is taking place, to be sure, but it is one slice.

In other words, the soda-straw effect, or the slices metaphor, implied that important things were happening without journalists documenting the events. The reports coming from the embedded correspondents were not providing an empirical basis solid enough to assess the progress of the entire operation. The coverage lacked context and background.

Here the strategic briefings come in. The news conferences in Washington had the purpose of providing context to the details coming from embedded reporters, and putting the tactical information into strategic and political perspective. The DoD News Briefings were held daily at around 1330, sometimes as late as 1600 EST. The briefers usually performed in couples, a civilian spokesperson in the forefront and a general serving as a military expert in the background. During the first two days of the war, the Secretary of Defense and the chairman of the Joint Chiefs of Staff briefed the press corps in the Pentagon, and then took questions. In the first days of the war the Secretary usually started the briefings by restating the objectives of the entire operation. At the first briefing, only a couple of minutes after the air war had begun, Rumsfeld laid out the objective of Operation Iraqi Freedom: "Our goal is to defend the American

people, and to eliminate Iraq's weapons of mass destruction, and to liberate the
Iraqi people." The Secretary thanked the coalition and the 45 nations that publicly associated themselves with the military effort in Iraq, and continued with
political statements justifying and legitimizing the military action the US had
initiated against Saddam's Iraq: "We did not choose this war. Saddam Hussein
was given a choice by the international community: Give up your weapons of
mass murder, or lose power. He chose unwisely, and now he will lose both."
After those general remarks, Myers gave very broad summaries of what had
happened in Iraq. He described early battlefield preparations, the destruction of
the Iraqi air defense two days earlier, and he informed the journalists about
reconnaissance Special Forces Units which took down visual observation posts
on the southern border of Iraq. He mentioned the leadership target of opportunity, the "decapitation strike," that the Navy Seals had seized two major gas and
oil terminals in the northern Persian Gulf, and that the 1st Marine Expeditionary
Force had "now secured the port city of Umm Qasar and the al-Faw peninsula"
– a detail the Iraqi information minister had denied earlier that morning.

Because the chairman as well as other generals who briefed in Washington
were outside the operation's decision loop they confronted two problems. First,
uniformed spokespersons in Washington were in relatively short supply of operational information, unlike the CINC and his staff in Qatar. As a result they were
often not able to answer the journalists' detailed questions. Just as the BBC's
Nik Gowing had argued, the commercial media indeed outpaced military communications channels. Second, Pentagon spokespersons were constantly pushed
by journalists to enter Franks's turf and make statements on intentions of US
maneuvers, future operations, or other decisions that were made not in Washington but in Doha or, in fact, by a division or brigade commander in the field.

On 22 March, Clarke as well as Major General Stanley McChrystal, the vice
director for operations on the Joint Staff, were the presenters: "The oil fields in
the south are being saved to benefit the Iraqi people. Coalition forces have the
key port of Umm Qasr and are making good progress in Basra," Clarke stressed.
"The Iraqi forces, including some leadership, are surrendering and defecting in
some numbers." She also emphasized that the US would only target military
assets, that the forces would take care to protect civilians, and that the military
would be prepared to distribute humanitarian aid. Later McChrystal would fill in
some data on the operation, for instance that 1,000 sorties were flown against
several hundred targets across Iraq, 400 Tomahawk missiles were launched from
US and British ships, or that the ground components reached more than 150
miles into Iraqi territory and had crossed the Euphrates river. After Clarke's and
McChrystal's remarks they would take the journalists' questions.

Most DoD briefings during the operation followed this pattern. But they
were remarkably different from previous military briefings in one respect.
The Secretary and the Chairman, and their aides, knew that they were simultaneously talking to all major constituencies, including DoD staff, the coalition
troops in the field, the US Congress and public, allied publics, journalists from
Muslim countries, the Iraqi regime, and the public in the target area. Accord-

ingly spokespersons often explicitly identified the audience they were aiming at with a particular statement. On 21 March, Rumsfeld addressed the regime leadership:

> To those in the Iraqi chain-of-command, some words of advice: Do not obey regime orders to use weapons of mass destruction. Do not obey orders to use innocent civilians as human shields. Do not follow orders to destroy any more of Iraq's oil wells or to blow up dams or to flood villages. Those who carry out such orders will be found and will be punished.
>
> (D. Rumsfeld, "News Briefing," Department of Defense, 21 March 2003, 0136 EST)

A day earlier, even before the hostilities had begun, Rumsfeld cautioned against the use of WMD. Subordinates' justification that they were merely following their superiors' orders would not be accepted in trials after the war, he warned. But he also specifically addressed the Iraqi people in that briefing:

> To the Iraqi people, let me say that the day of your liberation will soon be at hand. Coalition forces will take every precaution to protect innocent civilians. Once hostilities begin, stay in your homes and listen to coalition radio stations for instructions on what to do to remain safe and out of the line of fire. Iraqi civilians: Do not go to work. Stay away from military targets and any facilities where Saddam Hussein has moved military assets.
>
> (D. Rumsfeld, "News Briefing," Department of Defense, 20 March 2003)

The US Secretary's words of advice in that briefing were largely identical to the themes featured in Arabic on illustrated leaflets that were dropped over Iraq as part of a broad psychological operations campaign. The rationale was to dissuade and deter adversarial groups, for instance officers within the Iraqi army, from taking up arms against the coalition. The recommendation by threat of punishment not to obey regime orders is an attempt to "get into the decision cycle of the adversary," in the language of information operations doctrine. The briefings are an excellent example of how information operations and public affairs operations became intertwined on a strategic level. Virtually in the next sentence, Rumsfeld addressed his own staff. The intention, of course, was now reversed; he wanted not to discourage the adversary but to encourage the coalition troops:

> To American forces and those of our coalition partners, let me say this. Know that we are proud of you that we stand with you today. We have every confidence in your courage, your tenacity, and your ability to get this job done. All Americans hold you and your families in our thoughts and prayers today.
>
> (D. Rumsfeld, "News Briefing," Department of Defense, 21 March 2003, 0136 EST)

While it was clear to Rumsfeld that he was talking to many recipients at the same time, it was equally clear to him that those recipients would see not only his remarks, but many other news outlets at the same time. Most Americans and the families of his troops would eagerly devour any piece of information on the ongoing military operation in Iraq. They would watch Fox News and CBS, CNN, and even al-Jazeera, they would listen to the BBC and NPR, and read the *New York Times* and *USA Today*, and follow local newspapers with embeds reporting on a particular unit on the internet. In an internet age, the domestic American media and international news organizations were highly connected, using each others' material as well as internet-pages as sources, and in real-time. But both adversaries tried to take advantage of this.

The Iraqi regime's strategic news briefings were held in the Palestine hotel.[26] Representatives of the international press lived in the 18-story tower in downtown Baghdad near al-Firdos square, at the bank of the Tigris. Daily press briefings were given on the second floor, mostly by the Iraqi information minister, Muhammad Said as-Sahaf. In the first official Iraqi statement after the attempted decapitation strike by US stealth bombers, the minister had said that the Iraqi president and his family were attacked in their residence but that they were safe. And he expressed his outrage at the American attack orchestrated from what he saw as a safe distance: "This is a complete disgrace," the minister said, speaking English as well as Arabic in his briefings. "They are a superpower of villains. They are a superpower of Al Capone," as-Sahaf was quoted on CNN the morning after the initial attack. After the attempted killing of the dictator, US marines had crossed the line of departure and taken control of large parts of the Iraqi port of Umm Qasr. The CNN news story the next day quoted the information minister denying that coalition troops took control and insisting the city was "completely in our hands" and that "they failed to capture it."[27] During the Pentagon briefing in Washington a couple of hours later, Rumsfeld contested his Iraqi counterpart's claim:

> The Iraqi information minister declared that the port of Umm Qasr is "completely in our hands," quote/unquote. Quote: "They (the coalition forces) failed to capture it," unquote. In fact, coalition forces did capture it and do control the port of Umm Qasr, and also a growing portion of the country of Iraq.
>
> (D. Rumsfeld, "News Briefing," Department of Defense, 21 March 2003, 0136 EST)

Without the elaborate PA strategy the Pentagon had designed in the months prior, the two statements would have stood against each other, put out by two government officials, and the media consumer would have to judge for himself whom to believe. Americans would probably tend to believe Rumsfeld, many Arabs and skeptics would find his Iraqi counterpart more credible.[28] Several planners in the US military, however, had anticipated that their enemy would be skilled at "disinformation and propaganda," as they called it. After his remarks,

Rumsfeld passed the word on to Myers. The general went on explaining the status of the ground operation under way. He explained:

> Last night, at approximately 10:00 p.m. Eastern Time, the rest of the ground campaign began in earnest when the 3rd Infantry Division rolled into Southern Iraq. There's been a lot of reporting on this, of course, with some of the embedded media. At this hour, our ground forces have pushed close to 100 miles inside Iraq.

Credibility was the thrust and momentum of information operations, and the reporters embedded with coalition troops in Southern Iraq were just providing that thrust to US spokespersons in Washington. And they were providing it in real time. After Myers had mentioned the seizure of Umm Qasr, which was flatly denied by as-Sahaf, he added: "As you've seen from the TV coverage, from embedded media, clearly we're moving towards our objectives."

The DoD news briefings were usually carried live on the major news networks. CNN and others truncated the Q&A parts after the official statements, but media organizations provided an ideal global platform for US spokespersons to communicate to the entire spectrum of target groups they intended to reach. The Secretary and his military and civilian spokespersons were effectively merging information operations, counterpropaganda operations, and public affairs operations in the Pentagon's press room. But several thousand miles and eight time-zones were between the East Coast of the United States and operational headquarters in Doha.

News from Doha

Central Command in Doha gave its first news briefing two days after the war had already begun. On Saturday, 22 March, 0904 EST, Franks and Brooks faced the press for the first time since "kinetics" had begun. Due to operational security reasons, the first briefing had been postponed. The enemy, it was feared, might be able to use the information released at the briefings to his advantage. The physical proximity to one particular target audience, the Iraqi leadership, seemed to have an effect on Central Command's public affairs stance. The enemy was at the forefront of the generals' minds. They assumed that Saddam and the Iraqi leadership were not only watching CNN but also taking for granted what they saw on the American news channel: "Intel had reported that Saddam and his military advisers accepted what they saw on CNN as holy writ, assuming that the cable channel would report all critical developments," the Americans believed.[29] The result of this attitude was that Brooks, the eloquent young general representing the coalition in Doha, conceived of himself not so much as a neutral spokesperson but as an information warrior. Brooks saw himself performing two functions. On the one hand he was doing traditional public affairs, "putting into context what was happening" and giving the "big picture," he said later.[30] Reporters, however, viewed the general's attempts to explain the bigger picture as restrictive handling of information on a multi-million dollar press stage. In one briefing's Q&A session, Tom Feneman from CBS News voiced the growing frustration which was spreading among the press corps in Doha:

> We've been getting terrific snapshots from our embedded correspondents, but we were told we would then get the big picture here from this podium. And instead we have been getting snapshot videos, vague generalities, broader timeline.
>
> (V. Brooks, "News Briefing," *Central Command*, 26 March 2003)

Brooks, however, had a second function of the briefings in mind: the coalition was "engaging in operations in the public domain," as he called it.[31] The general knew that the Iraqi information ministry was observing and responding to Central Command's briefings. This soon became clear to the coalition as the Iraqis were changing the time of their briefings as a reaction to the Doha presentations, and as Brooks observed as-Sahaf was trying to refute US claims in advance, and attempting to "plant his information" on issues and developments that the American briefers would predictably talk about. The Iraqi IO-officers themselves tried to gain the information initiative and to enter the American government's OODA-loop, as Brooks saw it. Central Command's communication staff observed the situation and drew conclusions. As a spokesman observed:

> When I watched that pattern occur, then I knew that I was in fact engaging in information operations, even though the domain was a traditional public affairs domain. But the activity was not a public affairs activity, it was an operational activity.[32]

Two characteristics demonstrate the information operations rationale put into practice in Central Command's press center in Doha. The first was the briefings' standardized timing and content. As of timing, a so-called "public affairs battle rhythm" had been developed. During the wars in Kosovo and Afghanistan, the allied commands had improvised their schedule. In 1999 it was Jamie Shea's ad-hoc "saturation strategy" and in Afghanistan, where the "time-zone disconnect" was even larger, Coalition Information Centers in different time-zones were hastily created to counter the Taliban's propaganda and disinformation efforts on the ground. In Iraq an elaborate public affairs "battle rhythm" – a term normally used to describe the time management of combat – had been designed and planned well in advance. Its intended venues were two televised briefings per day. The Qatar briefing was scheduled for around 1530 Qatar time, and tuned to the morning news at the American East Coast to set the agenda of the daily coverage in the US (the actual briefings usually were done a couple of minutes past five, i.e. nine). Before the briefers in the Pentagon met the press daily at around 1500, they received an update from the commanders at the Gulf via secure video conference (STVC).

The briefings' content was equally standardized. The military spokespersons generally gave a short overview of the current operational situation – which was usually optimistic and therefore not entirely credible in the eyes of many of the journalists in the audience. The media's skepticism, as it turned out later, was justified. The Army's V Corps encountered fierce resistance by highly motivated and well trained paramilitary Fedayeen fighters, who employed sophisticated guerilla and urban warfare tactics. The battles in Nasiriyah, Samawah, Tallil, or Kifl, to name only some of the toughest, were unexpected by the American high command, and temporarily threatened to derail the entire plan. Those harsh realities on the ground were not fully appreciated by Franks, who in the midst of war threatened to relieve the V Corps's commanding general, Wallace, because he publicly voiced the enemy's unexpected strength and the Army's troubles with it. The realities on the ground were even less appreciated in Central Command's press briefings. The briefings' dominant theme was the affirmation of the coalition's precision fire power. This "demonstration of capabilities," as it was called during the planning phase in the Pentagon, was Brooks's task. "Before-and-after images" and gun-camera footage were used to show how effective the coalition's bombardment was. Brooks pounded the assembled journalists with long arrays of pre-arranged videos and split screens, showing the precise and effective destruction of armored personnel carriers in Iraq, artillery equipment, tanks, rocket-launchers, and regime buildings, as well as command and control centers and information facilities. Brooks usually underscored just how well the desired effect was achieved by precisely destroying the targets, even if they were hidden or placed next to a mosque or school, while at the same time the surrounding civilian buildings remained intact. Spokesmen also regularly referred to the leaflets dropped in the PSYOP campaign, and repeated their messages into the cameras of the assembled world press.

The second characteristic feature of the Doha presentations was that the briefers released information selectively according to their strategic value. The embedded media were – in contradiction to what many journalists and TV watchers thought – not adequately witnessing and reporting all key developments of the operation. The sustained attacks by Fedayeen forces on US and British troops while they were heading towards Baghdad from the south of Iraq are an example. The Fedayeen, paramilitary troops loyal to the regime in Baghdad, used pick-up trucks armed with a 12.7 mm machine gun, RPGs, and small arms. These trucks, so-called "technicals," were used to hurt the long and vulnerable supply lines of the advancing US forces on their way to the capital. Although often successful, the attackers suffered high casualties against heavy US armor. The paramilitaries' attacks on the American columns were "one-sided slaughter," at least from Franks's vantage point. But the embedded journalists – inexperienced in combat and unable to put the technicals' assaults into perspective – tended to report the attacks as a serious threat for the advancing US forces. What the journalists did not know was that intelligence gathering drones were able to locate the regional headquarters of the Baath Party and the

Mukhabarat based on the routes of the returning Toyota vehicles. The UAVs then provided target data to the Air Force enabling its pilots to bomb the enemy at headquarters. The US command guarded the new tactics against the Fedayeen, in the CINC's words, "as an operational secret."[33] Brooks and Wilkinson did not brief the press, or rather were not allowed to. "Jeez, General," Jim Wilkinson complained to his commander one day, "the public is going to think we're powerless to counter these Fedayeen attacks. Can't we show them some video of the JDAMs smashing the Baath headquarters in a couple of those towns?" Out of operational reasons Franks refused.

Another example of operational information that was deliberately not released is the sandstorm. The intense storm had a significant effect on the war. On the sixth day a massive cloud of red and brown dust gathered over the Iraq's western desert and with the heavy rain a thick layer of sandy mud descended on 170,000 coalition troops. Visibility and mobility almost went to zero. Helicopters were grounded, drones remained tethered on their launch pads, and finally all movement on the battlefield came to a halt. Several pundits in Washington quickly boasted that the advance was bogged down and started to talk about a quagmire, bringing back unwelcome Vietnam memories. The bad weather, however, equally hampered the Iraqi army and thus presented an opportunity for the technologically far superior attacker: "We can use the sandstorm to destroy the RG formations," suggested Victor Renuart, an Air Force two-star general and Centcom's chief of operations, referring to the Iraqi Republican Guard formations. The US Air Force was able to locate the Iraqis underneath the thick layer of sand through satellite images of Iraqi units taken immediately before the storm and modern reconnaissance technology. By 2000 hours Qatar time on 25 March, only minutes before the afternoon briefing in Washington, an intense bombing campaign was launched. For more than 24 hours B52s, B1s, and an entire range of fighter-bombers jointly delivered precision-guided bombs "through the zero-visibility, zero-ceiling weather," Franks noted later.[34] The commanders in Qatar, somewhat optimistically, were confident that this would be the end of organized resistance. Again the public affairs handlers ran into problems: "I'm taking a beating out there," Wilkinson had complained, pointing toward the Press Center at the far end of Camp As-Sayliyah, where the command room was located. "I've got to tell those reporters something. They're filing stories that we've lost the war." Again Franks's attention was focused less on the US public but on the enemy. "Good," he replied, "we couldn't ask for a better deception."[35]

Franks knew that the media coverage would be sensitive with respect to different audiences. And precisely because the embeds were offering only a limited perspective, it was essential to keep Secretary Rumsfeld, Chairman Myers, and the President fully informed on the events in Iraq: "This would be doubly important because of the media embedded with our forces," the general recounts in his memoirs. "I knew the gang inside the Beltway would be channel surfing from the get-go in this campaign, trying to pierce the fog and friction via Fox and CNN – not to mention Al-Jazeera."[36] Given the detailed and graphic character of the many reports that were coming from the field, the assumption that not only the Iraqi leadership but also many in Washington would accept what they saw on CNN as "holy writ" was very plausible. The embeds' coverage was too graphic and persuasive.

News from the field

Let me give you a picture of how this unit rolls. First come the Kiowa helicopters. Those helicopters are flying quickly. Between 30 and 50 above the ground, 80 to 100 miles per hour. And what they're doing is zone reconnaissance, flying out in front of the tanks and looking for any Iraqi units that may be in the way of the oncoming Bradley Fighting Vehicles and the tanks. One thing very, very interesting, I was riding in one of those tanks and a Bradley. And you cannot believe how cramped the soldiers are in there. Let me give you a visual picture of what it's like to be in a Bradley: The commander of the tank is standing the whole time. They've been choking on dust all the way coming up. Also standing is his loader to his left. The loader is the rear observer and he observes on the left side of the tank. The commander is keeping track of things forward. Down below and forward you have the driver of the tank in a two-thirds reclining position. If these tanks stop for more than five minutes you can bet as exhausted as these tankers are the soldiers and the drivers of the tank will fall asleep. Then there is the gunner, and I sat in the gunner seat on a rolling M1A1 Abrams. It's like riding in the stomach of a dragon. It's growling and screaming all the time. The tank pitches but it actually is very smooth. Tankers call the M1A1 the "Combat Cadillac." Much the same on the Bradley Fighting Vehicle. Very cramped, particularly if you're sitting in the gunner's seat. I was riding with one gunner who was well over 6'5" tall. I believe his name was Walker from Columbus, Georgia and he was 6'5" tall. They called him the "Green Mile." How he ever fitted into that gunner's seat, I'll never know.

(Walter Rodgers, CNN, aired 21 March 2003, 0706 EST)

Walter Rodgers from CNN was embedded with the 3rd Infantry Division's 7th Cavalry, Ferrell's unit. The above excerpt is from a live broadcast from 0706 in the morning of Friday, 21 March 2003, the day after the initial air-strikes on Baghdad. During Operation Desert Storm some 12 years before, CNN as well as its TV watching audience were puzzled and amazed by Peter Arnett's live reports from the al-Rashid Hotel's rooftop in Baghdad, showing the nightly bombardment of the city. The attention-grabbing pictures in the early days of the 2003 Iraq War were also shot from the rooftop of a large hotel in Baghdad, this time the Palestine Hotel near al-Firdos Square. The view provided by the military, in contrast, had changed entirely. In 1991, the sterile and technical images beamed back by little cameras embedded in the warheads of precision guided bombs upon hitting their targets had been the most memorable of the Persian

Gulf War. The cold and technical gun-camera footage was now replaced by the flamboyant and gripping narrative of journalists embedded with military units. This, its tactical facet, was the most innovative feature of the new public affairs strategy the Pentagon had designed.

During the war's first hours and days, the dominating images were vast and empty planes of sand and military vehicles rolling forward in front of a blurry and monotonous desert background. Just as the gun-camera footage 12 years before, the sand footage was provided and broadcast in poor resolution, and did not contain much useful information. But the pictures were "unprecedented" and live. For the first time in military history it was possible for reality-TV conditioned watchers in the US and elsewhere, and for internet users all over the globe, to glance at a real front line, in a real war, with real soldiers, in real time. The mere possibility of real shots fired at an enemy appearing live in the picture was boosting the sand footage's news value. The information strategy, at first, seemed to work, as the coverage from the American perspective had all desired features: it was fast, dominant, and credible. Again the CNN correspondent:

> Bill, imagine for a moment a giant wave of steel sweeping across the southern Iraqi desert and imagine that almost hourly that wave grows in strength and numbers. As we ride through this desert, we can see that the 3rd Infantry Division's heavy mechanized units have moved up. This giant wave of steel that grows every hour is ever pushing northward, ever pushing toward the Iraqi capital. The total goal is obviously to intimidate the Iraqis and pressure them and if that doesn't work then they can smash the Iraqi regime, so powerful is this force which is building out here in the desert. It is bold, it is audacious, it is fast and it is traveling far. The policy of these armored units of the 7th Cavalry, with whom I'm with now, and the 3rd Infantry Division, a heavy mechanized division, is if there is a demonstrably hostile force out there, then the Army is going to kill them. Their goal is to find the enemy, grab him by the nose, they say, and this, according to one senior officer, after grabbing him by the nose, we don't let the Iraqis go anywhere. The 7th Cavalry's mission is to find the Iraqis and to persuade them to give up and if they don't persuade, if the Iraqis don't give up, then they will be pounded, according to the officers we're traveling with.
>
> (Walter Rodgers, CNN, aired 21 March 2003, 0525 EST)

Rodgers and his crew practically lived with their commander through the war. Ferrell appreciated the network's presence and called himself "probably one of the greatest fans of the embedding process." He granted the CNN reporters and his other embeds unrestricted access and briefed them regularly. The boundaries between the media organization and the military organization were indeed blurred in practice. "The military mission," Rodgers said later on CNN, at 0650 on 21 March, is "to force a regime change in Baghdad by intimidation." And the correspondent added that "this kind of military force, the pictures of this military force is one clear pressure." The reporter obviously realized that he and his coverage were in effect used as a force multiplier.

Sean Naylor and his photographer were also embedded with Ferrell. The commander likely had seen the *Army Times* reporter at Fort Steward the summer before, when the division's public affairs officer Mike Birmingham invited Naylor to brief the division leadership on embedding. Now the journalist was on the receiving end as the embeds were read into maps and even classified information on future operations – although they were not allowed to report on these plans, the background information enabled them to put their coverage into context. Lieutenant Colonel Todd Mellman, an officer handling logistics for the 3rd ID, pointed out during a conference in the Army War College that:

> And, yes, they had access pretty much to all the information that we had in the rear of the command post. So they saw what was going on from the tactical side of the house. They also saw what was going on in some of the planning and what our future plans were ... Our embeds were thoroughly briefed on the plan. We had a bond of trust."[37]

Operational security was one of the greatest concerns for the soldiers. The scenario that they wanted to avoid was that Iraqi commanders could use the reports coming from embeds to reconstruct target coordinates and launch an attack. Michael Wilson from the *New York Times* was embedded with Lieutenant Colonel Glenn Starnes, who commanded the 1st Battalion of the 2nd Marine Expeditionary Brigade's 10th Marine Regiment. Sending out an email to the *Times* would trigger incoming scud missiles, they feared. The main reason for the trustful relationship was that the embedded reporters would be harmed by such an attack as well, and hence had a vested interest in not giving away critical information to the enemy: "I never saw one of his stories, never read it beforehand or looked at it. I trusted him," Starnes said about Wilson. "But I trusted him because he was on board with us the entire time."[38]

Providing more information to the journalists in fact increased operational security. Two days before the ground war started the 3rd Infantry Division provided the media a broad overview of the war plan, including rough timelines. The motivation for this openness was "that the media would understand the context of what they were observing and avoid filing stories that would tip intentions to the Iraqis," the division's After Action Report explained. "If media were not provided the context, they could report their observations and unknowingly provide the Iraqis sensitive information."[39] In effect, this was the inversion of the old Vietnam-infused mindset: in earlier days, in Grenada, Panama, and the Persian Gulf War, restriction, control, and denial of access were used somewhat helplessly to guarantee operational security. Now openness and trust were used just for the same purpose. And it worked – even better than many had anticipated.

The result of the almost intimate relationship was a more qualified coverage of the operation, at least from a military perspective: "Embedded media," the report summarized, "had a more realistic understanding and were more optimistic in their accounts than media who were reporting from the Pentagon, from Central Command in Qatar, or from Combined Force Land Component Command in Kuwait."[40] The realistic understanding was a result of the comprehensive background information most of the embedded reporters were provided by their unit's commanders. This was most evident during the extreme sandstorm. Four days after Walter Rodgers's euphoric coverage of the growing and swiftly advancing "wave of steel," the entire US Army came to a halt. Sand, dust, and rain blended into a virtual wave of mud. To journalists in Washington, and even to those in Qatar, it seemed that the situation was out-of-hand. The dominant story line was that the US advance had stopped. Mark Mazzetti was embedded with the 1st Marine Expeditionary Force's mobile command, just as Molly Moore was 12 years earlier. He has a different view: "We noticed during that one week where everyone was saying that the war is going to drag on, it was a quagmire, bogged down and all that." Although the embedded media did not know that the Republican Guard units were being pounded from above the brown clouds, they knew from their commanders that the sandstorm coincided with a pause to rearm, refit, and refuel, and that it would not present any serious problems: "We were watching the reporting coming out of Washington, and we were sort of amazed," Mazzetti said in an interview. The embeds had information on future operations, although they could not report it: "We knew there was a big offensive coming up, we knew that this is far from a quagmire," he added.[41]

But the military–media cooperation exceeded a mutually trustful relationship by far. The army used the media for offensive strategic purposes. On the morning of Friday, 4 April, the 3rd Infantry Division's 3–7 Cavalry Squadron was on its way to take Baghdad International Airport. On the large plasma screens in the commanding headquarters in Qatar, Franks was observing a single icon on the Blue Force Tracker speeding north. He picked up the phone and called David McKiernan, the land component commander, to get an update on this surprisingly fast movement of the Army's tip-of-the spear unit, the 3–7 Cavalry: "Check out Walter Rogers on CNN," Major Chris Goedeke advised Franks in the Command Center while the general was still on the phone. The CNN reporter was broadcasting live with his videophone from a Bradley tank, providing a view through just the right soda straw at the right time.

With the airport in the Iraqi capital's outskirts under US control, the next step was to enter Baghdad. Military planners, and even the President, had been worried about a stiffly defended city – a Fortress Baghdad. Urban warfare in unknown terrain, sluggish progress, bloody ambushes, tough house-to-house and street-to-street fighting was a deeply troubling scenario for the American attackers. The Army's messy battle of Mogadishu in 1993 or the Marine's bloody fight for the Hue during the Tet offensive still lingered large. To avoid such a scenario on a larger scale, the V Corps' planning staff had intensely studied the problem. Wallace's preferred strategy to minimize risk and casualties while maximizing the demoralizing effect on the enemy, was to do repeated audacious raids into the city with heavily armored mechanized infantry units, using the five forward operating bases in the city's outskirts as a staging ground. But while Franks, McKiernan, and Wallace embraced the momentous "thunder runs" as an alternative to avoid getting bogged down in an urban guerilla war, it was less popular with the division and battalion commanders. Blount and Perkins were concerned that the operating bases outside Baghdad would be vulnerable to Iraqi artillery and missiles, that US soldiers would find it demoralizing to give up ground and fight for it again and again, and that the raids would embolden Iraqis to think they would be able to strike the Americans.[42]

The first thunder run, executed by Task Force 1–64 AR, was a charge of a battalion-sized force, 761 soldiers in 29 Abrams tanks, 14 Bradleys and several other vehicles, including M113s. Their mission was to get in and out of the capital, both to test the capabilities of the Iraqi Medina Division and to send a signal to the enemy that the US military was prepared to attack. Lieutenant Colonel Eric Schwartz, who was in charge of the brigade's 1–64 battalion, said that the intention was to "conduct a movement to contact north along Highway 8 to determine the enemy's disposition, strength, and will to fight."[43] The thinking behind this first attack into downtown Baghdad was to create confusion among the Iraqi military inside the city: "It was an attempt to create as much chaos as quickly as I can throughout as wide an area as I can, because our guys are so well trained and disciplined as they can deal with it," explained Perkins, who commanded the task force. The Iraqis, in contrast, would not be able to deal with this "well-planned, synchronized chaos," he reasoned.

At 0630, on Saturday, 5 April, the task force crossed the line of departure. Franks sat together with Renuart and John Abizaid, his deputy, in front of his large Blue Force Tracker screen and watched the little icons starting to move. A Hunter UAV observed the action with its camera from a bird's-eye view and provided a grainy overhead video-feed on a second screen. To complete the picture, an aid was switching channels until he found a jumpy TV broadcast from a reporter who was embedded with the Task Force that was about to raid Baghdad. The commander of the blue icons was Perkins, and behind him in his vehicle Greg Kelly from *Fox News* was broadcasting live. A single armored tank battalion without the usual wheeled supply vehicles – tires and a thin skin were too vulnerable to enemy fire – swept the city. As they entered the urban areas, war had not reached the city yet. Despite the thunderous sounds of guns and columns of black smoke rising to the sky, civilian families were driving in their sedans like it was just another Saturday morning. Many, as it turned out, did not know that the US army was about to enter the city. During the attack it proved impossible to avoid harming civilians, who were using the same highway as the column of American tanks. Opposing paramilitaries and regular Iraqi forces heavily defended against the Americans with small arms, RPG fire, and even air-defense systems installed on the roofs of buildings that fired downward into the streets. The opposing forces were firing from "every niche and cranny," as an official report put it.[44] US troops entered on the strongly defended Highway 8, raided with high speed along a 20 kilometer axis, and quickly left again toward the international airport to meet with the 1st Brigade. During this first thunder run the US Army lost one if its 70 tons A1M1 Abrams tanks, a powerful weapon system with a reputation of near-invincibility.

Back at the airport, two things happened that impressed the American commanders. Despite the fortified streets and the heavy resistance, even those higher up in the Iraqi military chain-of-command seemed to have limited knowledge about the ongoing invasion of their country and the Americans' real strength. By coincidence, the battalion had captured an Iraqi brigadier general during the raid. The general's car almost crashed into an Abrams tank he encountered in the headway traffic as he drove to work. The Americans packed him in one of the maintenance 113s, and took him to the airport for interrogation. The general, who turned out to be the Iraqi Army's principal logistics coordinator, said he was completely caught by surprise and that he thought the Americans were hundreds of miles south of Baghdad, dying by the thousands. "And so at that point," Perkins recounted during a conference at the Army War College in Carlisle after the war, "it became apparent to me that the misinformation that was being put out, was having a strategic effect in that it was falsely emboldening the Iraqis to continue to defend."[45] US military leaders concluded that the propaganda the information minister of the crumbling regime continued to broadcast gave the Iraqis a false sense of security. Even high-ranking members of the Iraqi regime were kept in the dark about the ongoing invasion progress. In interrogations after the war as-Sahaf maintained that he actually had believed what he said, and that his information came from "authentic sources, many authentic sources." Just after the raid had left the city, as-Sahaf brought a group of western reporters to the abandoned and demolished Abrams tank. Using the tank's burned-out casket as a trophy, the information minister cast the thunder run as a defeat for the US Army.

The second of Perkins's insights at the airport was triggered by the BBC's coverage. The British network reported that its correspondents were in Baghdad but that they did not encounter any US tank battalions, concluding that there had been no American presence inside the city, and thereby lending credibility to the Iraqi spokesman who vehemently denied that coalition soldiers would be anywhere near Baghdad and that they were bogged down in the south. Perkins's flippant response to a BBC reporter's question was: "well, I was in Baghdad today and I didn't see the BBC."[46] But in the eyes of the regional, international, and to some degree American public, the BBC clearly had more credibility than an unknown US colonel. The conclusion was clear: the armored tank battalions not only needed to enter the city, they needed to *prove* that they entered the city. And in this game of publicized combat epistemology, the free embedded media would be the ideal instrument to corroborate that the US military was able to enter Baghdad and stay there: "What I really took away from it was maybe there was a psychological benefit to be gained by making sure people knew exactly who was controlling the city, that the war was over," Perkins reasoned.

At the airport several soldiers gave interviews to journalists: "We marched through town and knocked on Saddam's door and said 'We're here, we're taking over'," Captain Jason Conroy, the commander of Charly Company, said to a

Washington Post reporter. His commanding colonel also gave an interview. His face still caked with dust and grime from the action, Perkins chose a more worldly language: "This shows we can go anywhere in the city at a time of our choosing. The world saw today that the American army is, in fact, not bogged down," he was quoted in the *Los Angeles Times*.[47] On the day before the brigade went into Baghdad the second time, Perkins addressed his commanders: "In our mind there's no doubt," the 2nd Brigade Combat Team's commander said, making the point that they had to use the media coverage to demonstrate their capabilities, "but there will be no doubt in anyone else's mind as to who controls Baghdad. That it is the American Army."[48]

The second thunder run was planned for 7 April. Two tank battalions and one infantry battalion were sent into one of the fiercest battles of the war to date. With relatively few troops and a limited objective the thunder run was, at first sight, a tactical engagement with little direct relevance for the fall of Baghdad. But the battlefield, in doctrinal jargon, was extended into a battlespace which included a fifth, cognitive dimension. The raid's world-wide media coverage elevated the attack onto a strategic level. Asked about the intentions of the attack, Perkins replied: "The news media was becoming this battleground for who's in the city, who's in charge."[49] The US military had already taken the airport north of Baghdad, and Iraq's largest city and capital was of critical strategic importance: "It's obvious Baghdad's the center of gravity," Perkins told his soldiers, "and if the city is fallen then all hope is lost." It was necessary to occupy some sights with "symbolic significance," as Perkins reasoned. This was thought of as a way to show to the Iraqis, civilian as well as military, that the US was in charge of the country now: "We had to make sure that in no uncertain terms that people knew the city had fallen and we were in charge of it, because then I think that would end the resistance."[50]

As it turned out, Perkins and his superiors up to the President were fatally wrong with their estimate. But during the ongoing invasion in late March and early April 2003, American political leaders and military commanders were operating under the assumption that the US forces would be greeted and welcomed as liberators. On 7 April the aim was to show that the city was still under the control of the US forces and not, as the Iraqi information minister insisted upon in his press conferences, under the control of Saddam's regime.

Between the V Corps commander, Wallace, the 3rd ID's commander, Blount, and the 2nd Brigade Combat Team commander, Perkins, there was some misunderstanding about the second thunder run's objective. Wallace never ordered an attack into the downtown palace area, let alone to stay there overnight. But as a result of scrambled three layered communications, Perkins had just that in mind. He planned to attack and intrude the center of Baghdad and stay in one of Saddam's palaces at least until the next morning. Several hours before the attack, on the morning of 7 April, the brigade leadership met for a battle briefing. Perkins introduced the meeting and asked the brigade's intelligence officer, Major Charles Watson, to describe the enemy. After estimating the Iraqi's strengths and capabilities, Watson added: "They've done an outstanding job of propaganda." The people, he said, would "actually believe" that the regime is winning against the US military. The brigade leadership knew very well that they would fight under scrutinizing observation by the world's public, including the enemy, and that they carried the burden of proof, competing against the Iraqi information minister. Perkins added: "We have to set the conditions to create the collapse of the Iraqi regime. We're transitioning from a tactical battle to a psychological and informational battle."[51] This view dramatically changed the dynamics on the battlefield, as the pressure to succeed skyrocketed. Loosing a tactical engagement would consequently mean a significant strategic loss; this was the strategic corporal at its best.[52]

When, in the fog of battle, it became clear to the division leadership that Perkins was headed downtown, Bount, his immediate superior, decided to support him. The general ordered the 2–7 Infantry Battalion in and gave his aides the mission to get Ted Koppel, ABC's *Nightline* anchorman, downtown with his camera team, hoping that media reports of occupied palaces would break the Iraqi fighter's will. The media operation had to be abandoned and Koppel did not reach downtown, because enemy resistance was too fierce, and the unit equipped with ABC was needed to defend the supply lines instead. But Perkins had some embedded media with him, *Fox News* and the *Associated Press*, to factually report on his attack into the palace area. The commander knew that it was not enough to set up his command post inside Saddam's palace, he had to prove that his battalion was actually there. Greg Kelly from *Fox News* and his cameraman had accompanied Perkins in the back of the command vehicle. Once the task force had entered and cleared a palace in downtown Baghdad, the embedded journalists set up their camera equipment and prepared for a live interview. The camera was set up with the palace view as a backdrop to the interviewee: "What we have in the city now is an entire armored brigade," the commander said live into the camera. "Right now, we really have control of the center of Baghdad and what is the heart of his [Saddam's] governmental structure." Kelly asked how long the commander planned to stay in the city. "We'll continue to develop the situation," Perkins deferred, after all he did not have orders to permanently occupy the palace or even stay downtown overnight. "We'll see what our tactical requirements are and how they fit into the overall situation. There's a lot of ways we can control this ground, a lot of ways we can control entrance and exit."[53] It was still mid-morning in Iraq and in the middle of the night in the US. The videos and photographs taken in Baghdad would make it into morning news and newspapers in Europe and America. John Moore from AP that day took one of the war's most widely reproduced pictures. It shows US soldiers from the battalion's 7th Infantry Regiment, perched in baroque armchairs in one of Saddam's palaces, rubble in the background, smoking and relaxing on a sunny Baghdad morning.

The example of how the media were used for operational purposes in the thunder runs on Baghdad is spectacular but it is not an exception. The Combined Joint Special Operations Task Force West was a multi-national elite force, stationed in Jordan and made up of the US Army's 5th Special Forces Group, US

Air Force Special Forces, British SAS, and Australian specialists. Its commander was Colonel John F. Mulholland Jr, from the 5th SFG at Fort Campbell, Kentucky. One night in March 2003, a detachment infiltrated behind enemy lines in Iraq's western desert, probably on a covert mission to scout and neutralize Scud batteries that could have threatened Israel. But that was not the mission's only objective. Mulholland's public affairs officer, Lieutenant Colonel Scott Malcom, explained: "One of the initial IO objectives that we had was to demonstrate to the Iraqi regime that we were closer to him than he thought we were. Because we were." The information objective was to put pressure on the adversary, to break his will to fight. On that nightly airborne reconnaissance mission, Mulholland took Lee Cowan of CBS and his camera team with him. CBS filmed Operational Detachment Alpha teams, commonly called the Green Berets, getting off the aircraft and disappearing into the desert. The reporter did not know from his military escort where he had been when he later aired his report: "I told Lee Cowan precious little about the operational details of the mission," Malcom said later. "He didn't even know how far into Iraq we went that night."[54]

CBS aired a report soon after Cowan returned to base: "These are rare pictures of Army Special Forces, operating closer to Baghdad City Center than any other US units," it opined. CBS reported the mission's purpose, specifics of which were also not provided to the journalist: "The swift and precise insertion of special forces ground units – reconnaissance teams – who will disappear into the dark of the desert, well ahead of any invading army behind," the correspondent commented about the green and grainy infrared pictures of aircraft landing, securing an airstrip, and troops swarming out. Cowan, seemingly impressed by the action, ends his commentary by alerting the viewers to a "desert now filled with scores of additional Americans, paving the way for thousands more." And he added that it is risky to get "eyes and ears on the ground this far behind enemy lines."[55] The Task Force's public affairs officer later explained the CBS coverage's operational significance. "This was helpful to us tactically," Malcom said, "because we wanted the enemy watching CBS (and we think they were watching US television) to know that we could move at will anywhere, anytime on the battlefield and that we were watching everything they did."[56] Both cases illustrate how the media inadvertently became an instrument of war by merely reporting the facts.

A note of caution is necessary here. The examples are not to suggest that the media coverage was manipulated, controlled, or masterminded by the US military. Commentators need to mind their verbs. Indeed, the Iraq War has seen both a great deal of improvisation in a military campaign that did not always go according to plan, and a great amount of newscasts critical of the US-led invasion. But the examples epitomize a general problem for journalists. Merely by reporting accurately on military developments, they may produce footage that is of strategic advantage for one party. And in the example described, the odds were in favor of the American attacker: "We realized that the truth is our friend," as Colonel DeFrank had philosophically put it during the planning phase.[57] By having trained, objective observers on the ground, the military and the media were jointly refuting and countering as-Sahaf's and the Iraqi regime's spin.

This raises the question of whether the media were used, or even abused? "If having the media report accurately is using them, then they were used, okay," Perkins acknowledged later.[58] In a discussion about the media coverage of the operation, a colonel of the 3rd Infantry Division who had a prominent CNN embed, candidly discussed how the media was conceptually embedded into the operational planning process: "Did we use IO, and was the media a part of it?" he asked:

> I was at the division level and I was at the planner level. And, yes, we did. We rearranged my division tactical operations by the table where people sat in the latter half of the war to pull together forward our planning staff, the IO officer and our PAO. And, yes, we did.

His remarks also demonstrate the increasingly merged character of information operations and public affairs:

> We are taught in this school here and the other schools that I've been to, is IO, information operations. I had an information operations officer, and I had a PAO [Public Affairs Officer]. And part of our planning process was: how could we maximize the use of that press?[59]

The examples of how the media can be used for military purposes, which the colonel then referred to, are not limited to combat situations, but also include humanitarian assistance and post-conflict reconstruction. In sum, the 3rd Infantry Division, the 5th Special Forces Group, and many in the US Department of Defense used the media as a force multiplier and a platform for information operations on a tactical, operational, and strategic level. This making a weapon of the media, paradoxically, was in the genuine interest of the press. In its After Action Report, the 3rd Infantry Division evaluated the war's invasion phase and includes a section on media and public affairs: "The media we surveyed spoke highly of their experience and stated the embed far exceeded their expectations," the chapter concludes. "Soldiers, media, and the American public were the true beneficiaries."[60]

On 1 May 2003 President George W. Bush landed on the USS *Abraham Lincoln*. The commander-in-chief had himself flown the airplane, touched down on the deck of the aircraft carrier, and famously declared to the American people in a jumpsuit that "major combat operations have ended." The address, with the aircraft carrier as its stage and the jumpsuit as the President's costume, was equally designed to be a veritable public affairs coup. In the administration's screenplay, the so-called reconstruction and post-conflict phase was to follow. For a brief period, it offered real possibilities to demonstrate the military's constructive role in Iraq, and to use the media for that purpose. There were many attempts, some successful, to get positive coverage of the budding electoral process, of infrastructure reconstruction efforts, re-established energy supply, the rebuilding of streets and bridges, of the improving security situation for the Iraqi people, the training of the Iraqi police and military, and of the creation of new governmental institutions and structures. In short, the US government tried to demonstrate the liberation of Iraq. But the Coalition Provisional Authority (CPA) took over, the Iraqi Army was dismantled, thousands of officers where pushed into unemployment and frustration, and local elections were postponed. Those and other mistakes set the course for what was to come, and reality did not follow the administration's script. The war did not end on 1 May 2003, and neither did the embedded media program, although a day after Bush's address the number of embedded journalists had dwindled to 108. Both, however, fundamentally changed their character. The war's nature transformed from a high-speed, high-tech invasion to a stalled asymmetric urban conflict against a diffuse adversary, partly insurgency and partly terrorist network, that employs the full range of guerilla tactics with growing sophistication. The war's coverage transformed as well, as the Department of Defense lost its near-monopoly on the reporting and embedding lost its attraction. Both the administration's misman-agement of Iraq's reconstruction as well as the – in retrospect – shaky reasons to go to war in the first place have undermined the US government's credibility, providing an open flank in the information battlespace. The "truth" ceased to be America's friend.

Part IV

Discussion and outlook

Alone, in your home or with a group of your brothers, you too can begin to execute the training program.

("Mu'askar al-Battar," 1, al-Qaeda online manual published in 2004)

9   The friendly learning loop

This study set out to answer the question why the Pentagon decided to embed reporters in the Iraq War. The question had two dimensions – form and content. The past chapters examined an adaptation *process* in the Department of Defense as well as its *product*: the trajectory of the embedded media program and its rationale. Prior to the invasion of Iraq, decision makers in the Pentagon realized that the media had become a permanent feature of the modern battlefield and that the enemy was ready to use this feature against the United States. Both insights forced military planners to look into new ways of dealing with a new problem. Their favored solution was to have not merely one or a few soda straws on the ground which could be controlled by the adversary, as had been the case with CNN reports of civilian dead in bunkers and milk factories in the first Gulf War, pictures of killed and tortured American soldiers in Somalia, and images of dead refugees and civilian casualties in Kosovo displayed first on Serb television and rebroadcast in the west. The radical changes in communication technology and in the global mass media landscape, it became clear, made it impossible to avoid publicity of war's bloodier side. So it needed to be balanced. The new approach was to have 775 soda straws on the ground, not controlled by the adversary, providing a more complete picture of the war that included its human side: hard-working, well trained, and superbly equipped young American soldiers confronting an evil dictator. Before reporters were embedded physically with units in the battlefield, the media had been embedded conceptually into the war plan.

The military planners' underlying set of assumptions was grounded in strategic theory. Public opinion was recognized as a so-called "center of gravity," a critical point of vulnerability, which, if successfully attacked, could end the war. The media were able to spell defeat. In a modern democracy where the electorate draws its information from a diverse news spectrum, the media are a genuine component of the battlespace. Understanding the dynamics involved was painful but essential for the US Department of Defense, and it allowed its decision makers to act. The embedded media program was a major attempt to control the new risks posed by the novel complex global information environment. It was created with two major strategic purposes. The first strategic objective was defensive, to maintain the political will of Americans to carry out the operation; the second strategic objective was offensive, to break the political will of the adversary by putting psychological pressure on the Iraqi regime and its supporters. Those two military rationales were piggybacked by a third, almost covert political calculus: to shield the military from the anticipated political criticism of the war. So even if the public's support for the political decision to go to war would wane, the good reputation of the hard-working soldiers, airmen and sailors would remain unaffected.

The second dimension of the initial question, whether the innovation was the result of a process of organizational learning, requires a longer answer: organizational learning takes place when knowledge assets, created through practical experience and cached in an organization's memory, are retrieved and used in action. To diagnose whether such a retrieval had happened in the Department of Defense prior to the invasion of Iraq, three steps were necessary: the process of military learning needed to be understood analytically, the learning experience needed to be reviewed historically, and the retrieval and use of the organizational knowledge assets needed to be examined empirically.

The first part of this study fleshed out a model of organizational learning and distinguished four types of knowledge assets: *routine knowledge assets*, manifested in organizational culture, tradition, and standard procedures; *experiential knowledge assets*, in the form of on-the-spot ideas and alternative perspectives drawn from practical experience, as in informal After Action Reviews or conference presentations; *conceptual knowledge assets*, articulated and recorded concepts such as articles in periodicals or lessons-learned reports; and finally *systemic knowledge assets*, officially authorized rules and guidelines, such as doctrine and directives. The model then identified several drivers that facilitate the creation of new organizational knowledge and new performance: change in the external *environment*, the introduction of new *technologies*, the decisions of *leaders* as both blockers or facilitators of learning, the input of motivated teams (*communities-of-practice*), and *organizational culture*. The model assumes a spiral form as the drivers facilitate the creation of new knowledge derived from action, resulting in turn in a change of behavior.

The model sheds new light on developments external to the organization. Both major changes – that the media became a permanent feature of the modern battlefield, and that the enemy engaged and attacked the United States and its allies in the information battlespace – needed not only to take place in the environment. The insights and the knowledge that those changes were taking place, that they were transforming the operational environment, and that this transformation would have wide-ranging consequences for the military, needed to be created within the organization. An appropriate response required an innovative strategy to deal with the new challenges, new solutions had to be found, conceptualized, authorized, and disseminated, as well as trained and implemented as new routines on the battlefield. The spiral model envelops this process and offers three types of organizational learning according to the level of hierarchy involved: *experiential learning* occurs when routines are changed on the spot by lower-level officers on the basis of ad-hoc reflection; *conceptual learning* takes place when new procedures are created by soldiers or teams of soldiers on the middle-management level, and when their suggestions are articulated and disseminated on unofficial platforms; and *systemic learning*, which is the outcome of decisions made by top leaders and communicated down the formal, official chain-of-command.

The second part examined the historical development of the lessons the US military learned from its past military operations. Each time the armed forces went to war they had to deal with the press. In broad brushstrokes, three historic phases of the US military's public affairs were discussed: disastrous public affairs during the Vietnam War led to the lesson that the media lost the war for the military. The nature of the conflict with its inflated *body-counts*, the infamous *five o'clock follies*, and the dramatic reporting of *Tet* resulted in a culturally deep-rooted anti-media bias in the US armed forces. The lesson that the media lost the war for the military corroded into the organization's routine knowledge assets, and impregnated its culture with a persistent anti-media bias. But during the Vietnam War and throughout the 1980s, the US military's public affairs culture and routines were not changed on the basis of systemic knowledge assets, as Nonaka's model would suggest. Not a single official document prescribed hatred of the media. The learning cycle was short-cut on a lower level. Experiential knowledge assets powerfully conveyed and conserved the myth that the media were the stab-in-the-back that precluded victory in Southeast Asia. This myth was stored in the organization's culture and its routines. Although emotionally biased and counter-productive, experiential learning remained dominant.

The phase of restrictive public affairs, a reaction to Vietnam that continued until the mid-1990s, was characterized by tight control and limitation of media access to the battlefield. Operation Urgent Fury in Grenada in 1983 was marked by *improvisation* of the public affairs operation, indicating its low strategic priority at the time, and a strict *denial of access* for reporters on the Caribbean island. Six years later, Operation Just Cause in Panama saw an equally murky management and unnecessary *pool restrictions*. Although *the Marriott incident* demonstrated that independent journalists were increasingly becoming a political force on the battlefield, the two operations, and their similar public affairs handling, demonstrate that the DoD simply lacked the conceptual tools to embed the media into strategic thought and to understand the battlefield as a battlespace. In the model's language, the colonels and generals did not have the appropriate routine knowledge assets to apprehend the emerging new information environment. This lack of understanding is mirrored in a lack of sophisticated arguments in the debate in military journals during the 1980s. None of the refined conclusions and stimulating analyses that appeared in periodicals and doctrinal publications in the mid-1990s can be found a decade earlier. Although conceptual and systemic knowledge assets, such as several thoughtful articles in periodicals, and the final reports of the Sidle and Hoffman panels were created, they had a negligible impact on actual battlefield performance, if any. Conceptual and systemic learning did not take place, and experiential learning only on a minor scale. The period of restrictive public affairs was marked by stasis and the DoD's inability to unlearn the deep-rooted trauma of Vietnam.

A strong distrust of the media and the desire to control the public information flow dominated the Persian Gulf War, with its *briefings* and media *pools in the desert*. A comparison of the *Marine Corps v the Army* showed that particularly the larger land force nurtured the old Vietnam prejudice that the media cannot be trusted. The comparison hints at the strong cultural differences between the two sub-organizations. The Marines, in contrast to the Army, were traditionally keen on getting good press. As a light expeditionary force composed of air, naval, and land components, the Marines were constantly under pressure to legitimize their existence as a separate service; they were culturally "paranoid," in the words of one of their generals, that they might one day be dissolved. As a result, the Marines regarded their excellent reputation with the American people as existential.

Two insights can be gained from Operation Desert Storm and its public affairs. The Marines learned experientially during the operation how to optimize their work with the press. New routines were developed on the spot by culturally open-minded lower-level officers to deal with the new environment, "kind of like the rain. If it rains you operate wet," in the words of Chief Warrant Officer Carlson. Organizational culture thus explains both the Army's restrictive press handling as well as the Marines' more adept media management. Experiential learning was again the dominant mode of innovation, not conceptual or systemic learning. Second, *the Iraqi information campaign* skillfully exploited the presence of international news organizations in Baghdad, illustrating the information environment's new strategic challenges. But like in Grenada and Panama, the dynamics of this new feature of the battlespace were not fully understood by the Department of Defense. Even after the war, the information operations debate in military periodicals neither gained momentum nor produced tangible results. Doctrine had equally little to offer to help understand the increasingly aggressive media environment. In the absence of insightful conceptual knowledge, much less systemic knowledge, necessary routines were also lacking. The Marines' more adept public affairs handling in the Persian Gulf War, on the other hand, was not strategic or target oriented but merely a cultural reflex of a proud and image-conscious organization. A significant change in the organization's environment equally did not translate into a change of its perception filters.

Experimental public affairs policies characterized the operations throughout the 1990s. Militarily a mixed bag, the operations in Somalia (a so-called military operation other than war, MOOTW), in the Balkans (so-called humanitarian interventions), and in Afghanistan (the so-called war against terrorism) were rich in lessons for public affairs officers. The landing at *the beach* in Somalia underscored that the media had irreversibly altered the future battlespace and become a permanent feature of it on a tactical level; the Battle of Mogadishu painfully completed that lesson by showing how a single *dead Ranger* on CNN can have an uncontrollable effect on decision making on a strategic and political level. Slowly the debate in expert circles became more productive and yielded results: the Toffler's book *War and Anti War* went to press in 1993; Colonel Frank Stech's milestone article "Winning CNN Wars" was printed in *Military Review* in 1994; the Joint Chiefs of Staff published *Joint Vision 2010* and soon *Joint Vision 2020*, two much discussed visionary papers about military change in the information age. The information operations debate was in full swing.[1] Although in the mid-1990s joint and service doctrine did not include any of the ideas articulated in that debate with respect to the media's role on the battlefield, public affairs officers started to think and act progressively. Conceptual learning took place as routines were adjusted on the basis of conceptual knowledge assets drawn from the lively debate in the military's intellectual circles. Embedding was tested for the *first time* in Bosnia, albeit in a low-intensity environment without exposure to combat. The experiment helped refine the media ground rules and demonstrated that embedding would be a feasible option to accommodate journalists in future theaters.

During Nato's war against Serbia in 1999, the trend became manifest that the enemy will apply his own IO strategy and deliberately use the media against the coalition to *magnify blunders*. The Atlantic Alliance, in the absence of ground troops, and hence in the absence of embedded journalists who might have offered an alternative view, reacted with a "*saturation strategy*" and attempted to magnify its successes. Its communication experts at headquarters realized the need to cater the information supply to the scheduling demands of a 24-hour news cycle. Initially the public affairs operation at the alliance's headquarters in Brussels was not planned or staffed sufficiently well. During the air campaign a great deal of improvisation and lateral thinking took place; the British PR-expert Alistair Campbell was sent to Brussels to fix the alliance's communications. Again experiential learning was the norm rather than systemic learning. Nato's PR-strategy was more inspired by Campbell's experience in British Prime Minister Tony Blair's recent election campaign than by joint doctrine.[2] Concepts like "centers of gravity," "information initiative," or "information superiority" were hardly used during public affairs planning and execution in 1999: "We were busy doing it, rather than reflecting upon it," as the organization's spokesman put it later.[3] Kosovo marked the arrival of warfare in the information age, and after the operation was reviewed many participants realized that a radical rethinking of public affairs and the media's role in modern war was necessary.[4] Although useful conceptual knowledge assets about the role of the press in war had been created, leaders in the DoD, and even more so at Nato headquarters, were slow to incorporate the new concepts into higher-order systemic knowledge like joint or Nato doctrine.

Only a month after the terrorist attacks on New York and Washington in September 2001, Operation Enduring Freedom was launched against the Taliban regime in Afghanistan. Because the preparations were made under intense time constraints and because the operation was primarily conducted by Special Forces and Air Force bombers, public affairs did not figure prominently in the planning. Time simply was lacking to develop a sophisticated public affairs strategy in sync with the war plan, and the planners' priorities were clearly focused on the operation's logistics.[5] As a result, public affairs improvisation was again the norm in Afghanistan. Coalition Information Centers were hectically set up during the operation, again drawing on the experience of British experts to bridge the large time-zone difference, and to tailor military communication efforts to a global media system which by now had adapted to seamless 24-hour *news cycling*. Later in the operation, Afghanistan offered a *test bed for embeds* in actual combat situations. Again, engaged communities-of-practice within the Marine Corps were driving the innovation by taking the initiative to embed reporters in their amphibious assault in late November 2001. The Marines offered a positive role model for the Army, where many were keen not to repeat the mistakes of the Persian Gulf War which had resulted in bad press or no coverage at all for their service. By now many influential public affairs officers and commanders had understood the battlespace's new dynamics, including its virtual dimension.[6] The extensive information operations debate produced countless articles in military periodicals, graduation theses written at war colleges and academies, conferences, presentations, roundtables, and some doctrinal publications had mainstreamed the view that the media and the twenty-first century's information environment drastically affected warfare itself. Although the media operation in Afghanistan was improvised and makeshift compared to the embedded media program two years later in Iraq, it already assumed a counterpropaganda character, in effect as well as in intention. Although the mode of innovation had risen to the conceptual learning level, systemic learning in public affairs did not occur before the Iraq War.

The empirical third section examined the planning and implementation of the embedded media program in the Iraq War in 2003. To understand whether a retrieval of past experiences had taken place, it was necessary to take stock of the body of explicit systemic knowledge on public affairs, captured in doctrinal publications of the four services as well as in joint doctrine. The US military recognized domestic public support as a critical *center of gravity* and as a decisive vulnerability. This put the *media and GOGs* at the heart of strategic thought. While strategically sophisticated arguments were almost entirely absent from *public affairs doctrine*, this was not the case with another line of military thinking. *Information operations doctrine* discussed the new information environment with strategic sophistication, understanding the news media and the new dynamics journalists created as an element of the battlespace's "fifth-dimension." Some doctrinal documents even distinguished between *defensive media operations* and an *offensive media operations*, with the distinction depending on the target, whether the information in the public domain is directed at the US domestic public or at an adversarial group.

It was then examined whether this rich stock of systemic knowledge assets was consulted during the planning phase and used for the design of the information campaign prior to the war. The department's internal communication process followed the spiral model's middle-up-down pattern, notwithstanding some modification. Explicit conceptual knowledge assets on public affairs management were reassembled (not newly created) by the office of the ASD/PA on a middle-management level. The plan was then communicated *up* to the leadership of the Pentagon and the commander-in-chief of Central Command (PA-Planning-Cell, Clarke's presentation). Leadership authorization was necessary for converting conceptual knowledge assets into systemic knowledge assets. Once embedding had the support of the Secretary of Defense and the combatant commander, middle-managers were able to spread the details of the embedded media policy *down* the hierarchy, using authorized systemic knowledge assets and official channels (Personal For, PAG). The intention of spreading the message was to change routine knowledge assets on the basis of systemic knowledge assets, the hallmark of systemic learning.

However, to effectively change the routines, another step proved to be critical. The build-up phase before the war was extended and prolonged both by the attempt to reach a diplomatic solution in the UN Security Council and, more importantly, by the enormous logistical task of preparing for a major conventional military confrontation on the other side of the globe. In late 2002, and in the first months of 2003, journalists as well as military units had already arrived in Kuwait, waiting for the invasion to start. During those months, trainings and rehearsals in the deserts of Kuwait helped soldiers get accustomed to embedded media in their units and build confidence. It also helped the organizers to get the logistics right and adjust the numbers of embeds they could take in. On the journalists' side, the training facilitated the reporters' adjustment to military life, they learned to understand army jargon and to use their communication equipment in a desert environment. After embedding had been authorized by top-leadership and communicated down the official chain-of-command, the new routine knowledge assets were formed and refined *horizontally*. During the four-month training phase prior to the war, an additional experiential learning loop was inserted before embedding was implemented in the actual invasion.

The Iraq War was fought in a new global *information environment*. A technological revolution that accelerated in the mid-1990s had altered the news business, empowering both the sender – journalists – to instantly communicate from almost everywhere, and the recipients – the news consumers – to choose from an overwhelming variety of new sources and be informed almost anywhere and anytime. Operation Iraqi Freedom was the first major military operation conducted under information conditions dictated by global TV networks, mobile devices, widespread email, online newspapers, and internet blogs. The introduction of the embedded media program seemed to change the incentive system for the military to cooperate with the media, traditionally pitched as adversarial, and turned public affairs into a win–win situation. From the military's perspective, the news media could now be used to get better coverage for one's service at home, potentially shield the soldiers against political criticism, to counter enemy disinformation, and even to put psychological pressure on the adversary. From the media's view, the military had finally allowed front-line access and abolished censorship. *The commander's objective*, winning the war, and *the reporter's objective*, winning the Pulitzer Prize, ceased to be irreconcilable – at least temporarily and on a tactical level.

Not only recipients of the communication effort needed to be separated analytically. Different "channels" were used to reach them. Analogous to the three levels of war – the tactical, the operational, and the strategic – three levels or channels of communication can be distinguished. *News from Washington*, mostly televised briefings by civilian and military spokespersons from the Pentagon's press room, were designed to offer a strategic bird's-eye perspective as well as the political context to the events in Iraq. *News from Doha*, presented to correspondents waiting in Qatar by Central Command's spokespersons, such as Brooks, provided an operational view of troop movements. *News from the field*, the detail-rich tactical ground view of the invasion, was reported primarily by some 775 journalists embedded within US and British military units. As the centerpiece of the DoD's overall communication strategy in the Iraq War, the embedded media program absorbed most of the US military's public affairs thinking, planning, and logistical energy prior to the war, and it produced the most visible news stories of "major combat operations." The examples of the 3rd Infantry Division, the thunder runs into Baghdad, and the division and brigade commanders' sophisticated ad-hoc use of the media, illustrate the significance of the working level's support. The full potential of the embedded media program could only be realized through the inventive and open-minded attitudes of mid-level and lower-level officers.

Discussion

Three different forms of learning have been introduced according to the level of hierarchy that carries an innovation: experiential, conceptual, and systemic learning. The prevalence of experiential and conceptual learning in the history of the US armed forces' public affairs indicates that the spiral theory of knowledge creation needs adjustment. Systemic learning, which mirrors the full knowledge creation cycle suggested by Nonaka, is only the most complete and, at the same time, the most improbable form an innovation may take. The findings of the present study carry this thought even a step further. The historical and empirical revision of the US military's innovation in public affairs indeed suggests that systemic learning is the only way to implement broad reform and mindset change; only by disseminating authorized systemic knowledge through official channels can an organization's lower-management level and the front line employees be instructed in a synchronized, encompassing way. But systemic learning is characterized by an inherent inertia, risk-aversion, and caution. Systemic learning is unlikely to be the motor of truly progressive innovation. A closer look at the determinants of organizational change illustrates this.

Five types of drivers have been discussed: an organization's external environments, technology, leadership, communities-of-practice, and corporate culture. The analysis showed that the external environments of military public affairs – the normative, political, and the conflict environment – all put strong pressure on the organization and limited the number of available options. At the same time, technological change enabled new responses to the challenges of modern warfighting, both through the external information environment as well as through the military's internal "transformation." But it took the US military's public affairs managers two decades, from Grenada to Iraq, to effectively understand and react to the operational environment's two major changes: instant information and IO-savvy adversaries. This indicates that neither the external pressures nor new technologies can qualify as vital drivers of innovation. *New* perception filters, in the form of experiential and conceptual knowledge assets, needed to be created to interpret the altered environment's impact and to understand how to use the new technological possibilities according to the department's operational interests. Conceptually it is therefore more useful to regard the environment as a set of external pressures and technology as an enabler, rather than as separate drivers. Because tacit knowledge and routines reside in humans, actors are bound to drive any innovation process.

Researchers of organizational and military change have traditionally regarded leaders and senior managers as the most important actors in innovation, which equals a focus on systemic learning defined by leadership authorization. The present analysis, however, finds otherwise. Leadership merely had a role as facilitator of reform, neither as initiator nor, in a strict sense, as implementer. Key civilian leaders in the DoD and the White House acted as authorizers and facilitators. Clarke and her staff undoubtedly played an important role when the ASD/PA's office gained Rumsfeld's support which, in turn, helped justify the embedded media program vis-à-vis the commanders. But leaders in the Pentagon, be they political leaders, civilian administrators, or senior military officers, had only some influence on the initial concept's formulation, as well as its implementation on the battlefield. Leadership support was necessary but not sufficient. It merely used knowledge which had already been created *and* tested on the battlefield; it used, that is, the output of previous experiential and conceptual learning processes as an input. This study suggests that systemic learning has a very limited innovative potential.

It is therefore necessary to descend one step further in the hierarchy to find the epicenter of innovation. The initiative and the momentum for the embedded media program came from communities-of-practice, which took different forms. The community of progressive public affairs officers cut across departmental and even service boundaries. Public affairs officers personally meet at the Defense Information School and take part in conferences, or they simply follow discussions in military periodicals or online forums where new ideas are debated. But communities-of-practice did more than just create conceptual knowledge assets; they tested them, too. The Army's 3rd Infantry Division, or the Marine's 1st Expeditionary Force, enjoy a considerable degree of autonomy and independence within the Department of Defense. The examples of the 3rd ID sidetracking Pentagon rules in Operation Iraqi Freedom by providing a dozen Humvees to their embeds; the Marines overriding DoD guidelines and the orders of the commander-in-chief in Operation Desert Storm by inviting journalists to come along in the general's command vehicle; or the initiative of the 1st Expeditionary Force to embed reporters regardless of Pentagon restrictions in their amphibious assault during Operation Enduring Freedom, all illustrate the innovative momentum of communities-of-practice. When large and hierarchical organizations face a swiftly changing operational environment which creates strong pressure to adapt, such agile and initiative-seeking ad-hoc communities on a lower management level can be a powerful enabler and accelerator of innovation.

The role of communities-of-practice is therefore not limited to the creation of conceptual knowledge assets, as Nonaka argued.[7] Communities-of-practice do not just feed knowledge into the spiral and up the hierarchy in order to gain authorization; they actually experiment and test new routines in practice themselves – even in the often exemplary over-hierarchical military organizations. Communities-of-practice change routine knowledge assets on the basis of frame-bending experience or concepts they developed. This deviation from guidelines and formal rules short-cuts systemic learning and speeds up the innovation loop. Conceptual learning, which by definition is fuelled by engaged and self-recruited communities, has the highest innovative potential. Innovative processes accelerated by autonomous internal communities, in turn, create a problem for organizations that do not change their structure accordingly. The speed of experiential learning loops may entirely outpace traditional higher-level evaluation processes, and permanently damage them.

Organizational culture, finally, is generally credited as a powerful determinant of an organization's ability to adapt to change in its environment. It was argued earlier that organizational culture is both an obstacle and an enabler of change. Stable routines, rooted in history and tradition and potentially solidified by competency traps, guarantee operational performance under extreme conditions of stress. But they are also a major impediment to change and make unlearning and reorientation a serious problem. If routines are stable, it is difficult to get rid of them. But by fostering an atmosphere which is conducive to out-of-the-box thinking, playing with new ideas, experimentation, and error-tolerance, culture can equally enable an organization to adapt to its environment. In adaptable organizations, culture should promote both stable routines and stable routine-breaking routines. Thus, organizational culture, translated into the model's jargon, breaks up into two subsets of tacit knowledge: routine knowledge assets, on the one hand, are the locus of procedural conservatism, traditions, stable or highly stress-resistant routines, and competency traps; experiential knowledge assets, on the other hand, provide for routine-breaking routines such as on-the-spot improvisation, informal After Action Reviews, ad-hoc fixes, inventiveness, ingenuity, and a spirit of experimentation and trial and error. If an organization successfully fosters routine-breaking routines, it has institutionalized experiential learning. Culture is a major conditioning factor of experiential learning, but analogously to environmental pressure and new technologies it is a determinant of innovation and does not qualify as an actor. For the success of the embedded media program, it was a necessary condition that the post-Vietnam generation of military leaders had shed their emotional and culturally deep-rooted anti-media bias, exemplified by young officers like David Perkins, Eric Schwartz, or Mike Birmingham.

In sum, it is justified to say that the US Department of Defense stopped perceiving journalists' access to the battlefield as a vulnerability, and learned to use the mass-media coverage as a force multiplier. To regard this as a major achievement, however, means ignoring an essential shortfall. The Department of Defense, in the course of two decades, may have recognized and learned to pay attention to the new dynamics of war in an age of instant information. Countless books have been published, magazine articles written, presentations given, and speeches held, in which the new information environment was the *object* of a collective learning process – but technology was not a *platform* for learning. American soldiers, sailors, and airmen excel at using modern information technology to increase the efficiency and lethality of warfighting, but they are only beginning to understand the potential of modern networked communications technology to create new and faster learning loops. The US armed forces have still not adapted to the new information environment, as accentuated by McCreary in an interview after he was promoted to rear admiral and chief of Navy information: "Some might say it's a giant step," he said about the embedded media program. "I think it's a baby step."[8] America's most important enemy, by contrast, is way ahead. Careful attention should be paid to the way fundamentalist networked organizations adapt. The last chapter provides a glimpse.

10 The adversarial learning loop

The present study examined the trajectory of strategic thinking on public affairs in the US Department of Defense from Vietnam to the Iraq War. Enabled by a new global information environment, both the Pentagon and its adversaries had learned that the media coverage of battle had become part of the battle. This insight forced both to react. While the past chapters focused on the US military's attempt to adapt its public affairs approach to the new environment, this final chapter looks at America's most important adversary in the "war against terrorism."[1] By using the spiral model as a heuristic assistant and applying it to militant Islamic organizations and networks, it becomes apparent that a trend of the past is accelerating: while the US military and its allies are focusing on their own modernization and successfully improving their technical superiority on the battlefield, their adversaries are far more adapt in dealing with the new information environment and exploiting it tactically, operationally, strategically, and most importantly *organizationally* in ways the DoD is not fully equipped to understand and react to.

Before zooming in on the adversarial learning loop, the broader context of the development needs to be taken into consideration. Information is the oxygen that energizes the body politic of twenty-first century knowledge economies. Communication technology, interconnected personal computers, the world wide web, and the mass media are the capillaries providing that oxygen to the circulation system of modern societies, and the internet backbones concentrate the nerve bundles that flex their economic muscle. Information technology has deeply penetrated the fabric of developed societies: politics, diplomacy, public administration, trade, retail, supply chains, finance, agriculture, science, academia, medicine, publishing, schooling and education, pastime interaction, travel, traffic, the visual arts, music, entertainment, sports, and even dating.[2] Warfare, many strategists and experts argued, is in an equally firm grip of the information revolution, to which it has had to adapt and continues to adapt. In the field of the institutional application of violence, the IT revolution thus has produced its own martial offshoot: a new revolution in military affairs, "transformation," as it is called in the defense community.[3]

Transformation is, first and foremost, a process of technological modernization. Military organizations are "functionally specialized in the institutional application of violence."[4] If their operational environment drastically changes – and this change includes the "inevitable public opposition to the indecisiveness of attrition"[5] – armies are forced to functionally adapt their specialization. Military organizations had to reform and transform in order both to reap the benefits, and to minimize the risks of the unforeseen but enormous innovations that were altering their operational and technical environment: "Military transformation," as defined by US defense experts, "is the act of creating and harnessing a revolution in military affairs. It requires developing new technologies, operational concepts, and organizational structures to conduct war in dramatically new ways."[6] Modernization's overall goal is to achieve more speed and momentum with less mass: "Mass would be sacrificed for speed, information and precision killing power," in the words of military historian Williamson Murray.[7] First, speed is increased through an improved ability for rapid deployment, through light rather than heavy vehicles, long-distant airlift capabilities, computer-based logistics, and efficiently managed supply lines, the goal of which is to create a capability for joint expeditionary warfare. Second, joint operations require better information and enhanced battlefield awareness. The creation of a common operational picture at all levels of command is created by digitized communications, various types of drones in the air and under water, space-based reconnaissance and sensors, computer-based command and control systems, such as Blue and Red Force Tracker, but also novel organizational structures to enable the concerted action of previously disconnected units, "interoperability" in the language of transformation. All that, third, enhances the precision, efficiency, and lethality of the joint forces: precision-guided bombs, intelligent munitions, the expanded use of robotics on the battlefield, a sensor-to-shooter time reduction, and improved and real-time targeting information would make "effects-based operations" possible. The most ambitious components of this revolution in military affairs are an airborne laser system, a space-based infrared sensor system, or the use of nanotechnology. Transformation's objective to perform missions more effectively, faster, and with fewer casualties thereby met the demands of a more impatient and casualty-averse electorate. Media operations, in other words, are an integral component of this revolution in military affairs.

Measured against the Pentagon's misconceived and faulty history of public affairs management, the learning curve described in the previous chapters seems to expose a considerable strategic sophistication – it pales, however, when compared to the level of sophistication the adversaries in the "war against terrorism" have developed in using the modern information infrastructure for their own advantages and against their opponents.

Over the past decades, senior US commanders assumed that their adversaries' intelligence officers would watch American television, and theorized somewhat helplessly about the potential psychological impact their communication strategy could have on them: "Maybe, just maybe," the 3rd Infantry Division's Mike Birmingham had hoped, the unit's media coverage would have an effect on the Iraqi army's behavior. From the adversary's point of view, the situation looks very different. The activists, leaders, or supporters of militant Islamic organizations merely have to switch on a TV set or go online, zap to CNN or surf to *nytimes.com*, and they can witness in real-time and first-hand how the leaders of the democracies they have attacked are personally and emotionally affected, struggling to maintain posture as they address their mourning and frightened publics: George W. Bush in the rubble of the World Trade Center, José Maria Aznar losing his grip on power after the Madrid bombings, or Tony Blair immediately returning from a G8 summit to London after the city's subway was struck by multiple suicidal attacks. How, then, have militant groups reacted to the changes in the global information environment, and how do they use it to their own advantages?

Sub-state militant movements have, similar to the US military, undergone a radical process of transformation. Three features of its operational environment have forced particularly militant groups with a relation to Islam "to conduct war in dramatically new ways." First, most of militant Islam's physical sanctuaries under the Taliban regime in Afghanistan have been destroyed in Operation Enduring Freedom, and their globally active American enemy threatens to eliminate new training camps wherever they appear. This forced many of al-Qaeda's leading figures, as well as the organization's fighters, to leave the landlocked country and to disperse to Iraq, Pakistan, Yemen, Indonesia, Russia, the United Kingdom, France, and many other places around the world. The internal communication between the scattered cells and fighters and ideologues, second, has to be conducted under the aggressive surveillance by the world's most sophisticated clandestine services. As a result, organizations like al-Qaeda and its regional branches, Ansar al-Islam, Hezbollah, or start-up insurgent groups in Iraq were forced to decentralize, not only geographically but also organizationally. The threat of western soldiers and spies does not allow clear-cut chains-of-command and channels of communication, which would significantly increase vulnerabilities and create additional risks for networked organizations engaged in terrorist activities. Hierarchically structured and top-down means of control and command had to be abandoned and replaced by decentralized, bottom-up communicational structures.[8] The third environmental feature which had changed drastically, one al-Qaeda shares with the DoD, is the global information environment. Mobile phones, al-Jazeera, and the internet have not only revolutionized conventional warfare, but also irregular guerilla operations. The adaptive strategy of al-Qaeda's transformation, however, is markedly different from the Pentagon's.

Militant activists, for example, use the internet to gather tactical and operational intelligence on their targets, to attract and recruit followers, to raise funds, to reach out to international or neutral observers, to target enemy audiences through psychological warfare, or to plan and coordinate their operations.[9] But modern insurgent organizations do more than just use the information which is readily available in the global information environment; they radically adapted their knowledge creation and learning processes. A first look at innovation in militant Islamic groups illustrates two things: first, the decentralized and highly entrepreneurial structure of networked organizations allows them to run faster learning loops than their hierarchically organized opponents; and second, militant networks run these accelerated learning loops on platforms created and maintained by the very societies they are fighting against.

Routine knowledge assets

Unlike soldiers in hierarchical military organizations, al-Qaeda's activists, its sub-networks, and cells cannot rely on instructions or orders issued by superior layers of the organizational hierarchy. This affects the role of culture and routines in militant Islamic groups. Individuals and their motivation, entrepreneurship, initiative, but also their qualifications and skills gain critical importance. This is where new forms of communication come into play. Tacit components, motivation, and practical skills can increasingly be created and shared via the internet. The activists of terrorism tend to be rather young, well educated, and accustomed to the possibilities of the information age. They are, to borrow a term from the gaming industry, "digital natives" who grew up in the new digital environment and are at ease with new forms of social interaction; "digital immigrants," by contrast, are not.[10] Digital natives have assimilated to a digital culture. It is normal for them to socialize in virtual spaces like social-networking sites, chat-rooms, newsgroups, blogs, virtual message boards, by voice-over-internet protocol, to upload and download personal images, videos, and audio-files. Increased bandwidth and the spread of affordable consumer electronics have turned the internet into an interactive platform for *socialization*, capable of emotionally charged interaction such as creating trust, epitomized by the success of MySpace and Facebook. The internet today is a platform that allows individuals to reinforce and stabilize his or her radical religious views, even while living a seemingly regular life in a secular social environment. For a digitally native Islamic militant, it is no contradiction to live, study, and work in Hamburg, and socialize and exchange knowledge via the internet with like-minded extremists in London, Islamabad, Baghdad, and Groznyy. In his understanding of routine knowledge assets, Nonaka includes passion, motivation, care, and trust. In the case of militant fundamentalists, anger, rage, hatred, and religious zeal have to be added, as they unleash strong inducement and enable organizational members to take drastic action, even to the point of committing suicidal attacks.

"Salaam, right-click this link to download and watch it! A chechen mujaahid slits the throat of a Russian soldier!!!," a participant wrote in the chat room Islamic Awakening in 2004. "It's much better with the volume up!" as Gabriel Weimann quoted a user nicknamed Umm.[11] The graphic display of violence, such as videotaped ambushes on Russian patrols in Chechnya and the soldiers' subsequent torture and killing, are designed for internal as well as external consumption: "The real target audience of violent attacks is . . . not necessarily the victims and their sympathizers, but the perpetrators and their sympathizers," argues Jessica Stern a terrorism expert.[12] Violence can become an instrument to bolster support and recruit followers. High-resolution imagery, videos, and audio-files on extremist websites, however, increase not only the emotional depth of online communication. Many online videos seek to substitute the military training dimension covered in the Afghan camps: "Jihadists have sought to replicate the training, communication, planning and preaching facilities they lost in Afghanistan with countless new locations on the Internet," as the *Washington Post* put it. In 2005 the newspaper obtained an al-Qaeda video library of a series of "high quality training films shot in Afghanistan" that taught how to conduct a roadside assassination, raid a house, shoot a rocket-propelled grenade, blow up a car, attack a village, destroy a bridge, or fire a SA-7 surface-to-air missile.[13] Traditional training camps still play an important role in acquiring battlefield skills, but terrorist organizations use the internet with sophistication both to motivate and to train new members. And those potential recruits do not have to take the risk of traveling to Afghanistan or Yemen or Iraq any more: "Oh Mujahid brother, in order to join the great training camps you don't have to travel to other lands," outlines the inaugural issue of an al-Qaeda training magazine published in early 2004. "Alone, in your home or with a group of your brothers, you too can begin to execute the training program."[14] Today, the internet allows militant groups to adjust and modify the routine knowledge assets of its followers. Consequently, the new information environment becomes a venue and channel for all three forms of organizational learning in decentralized and networked organizations – experiential, conceptual, and systemic learning.

Experiential learning

Personal interaction and immediate face-to-face reflection of actions and routines is very difficult for an organization which takes the form of a global network that operates under the permanent surveillance by the world's best intelligence organizations. Moreover, reflecting and reviewing action is particularly difficult in case of operations which involve the intentional destruction of the unit performing the action, as in a suicidal attack, or a very high casualty ratio against a militarily far superior force. Feedback loops are interrupted. A suicide-bomber is the odd analogue to the Air Force's "smart bomb": as soon as the projectile detonates, alternative sources of information have to be used to assess the damage it created and whether the intended objectives of the attack were achieved. The US Air Force uses gun-camera footage, which is broadcast back to the attacking airplane before the shell detonates, as well as independent reconnaissance imagery from satellites or drones to assess a bomb's damage; terrorist networks, in the absence of alternative sources, use media reports to run feedback loops and to assess the damage efficacy of their techniques. The media provide intelligence to militant groups on all three levels of war: whether the intended object was destroyed and the attack *tactically* worked according to plan, whether it had the intended *operational* impact on the target group's psyche, and whether a *strategic* goal has been achieved by influencing a political decision. The mass media, in the model's logic, are helping violent networks to produce experiential and conceptual knowledge assets. Terrorist organizations highjack western infrastructure to create After Action Reviews and to run parts of their immediate experiential learning loops.

Conceptual learning

Just like the US military, militant networked organizations publish an affluent body of conceptual knowledge assets: websites, chat-histories, maps, photographs, instructions, newsletters, ebooks, magazines, and manuals. *The Mujahadeen Poisons Handbook*, for instance, written by Abdel-Aziz in 1996, was published on the official Hamas website and outlined in 23 pages how to prepare poisons, home-made nerve gas, and other weapons material.[15] Other manuals, usually available as PDF-files, concentrate on bomb-making, explain, among other things, how to extract explosive materials from missiles and land mines, or provide country-by-country lists of "explosive materials available in western markets."[16] A much larger handbook is nicknamed *The Encyclopedia of Jihad*, a multi-volume document of thousands of pages issued by al-Qaeda. These documents are neither written nor published in a concerted fashion, nor are they authorized by the network's leadership. But this lack of systemic control does not preclude organized and remarkably sophisticated forms of knowledge creation, as users of open-source software and their for-profit competitors are well aware of. An example for such a sophisticated outlet is a periodical published by al-Qaeda in Saudi Arabia. In early 2004, the Military Committee of the Mujahideen in the Arabian Peninsula came out with its first issue of the *Al-Battar Training Camp* (mu'askar al-battar), an online magazine that spotlights on military matters. It complements *The Voice of Jihad* (saut al-jihad), the other online magazine published by al-Qaeda in Saudi Arabia since 2003, which focuses on ideology. Each edition of the periodical contains articles on a broad range of issues, such as typologies of "targets in the cities" and their advantages and disadvantages, maintaining and using an Uzi, building a shelter that is not visible from the air, or assembling deadly roadside bombs, so-called improvised explosive devices (IEDs). The first issue of the magazine outlines the publication's rationale:

> Preparing [for Jihad] is a personal commandment that applies to every Muslim. . . . Because many of Islam's young people do not yet know how to bear arms, not to mention use them, and because the agents of the Cross are hobbling the Muslims and preventing them from planning [Jihad] for the sake of Allah – your brothers the Mujahideen in the Arabian Peninsula have decided to publish this booklet to serve the Mujahid brother in his place of isolation, and he will do the exercises and act according to the military knowledge included within it. . . . The basic idea is to spread military culture among the youth with the aim of filling the vacuum that the enemies of the religion have been seeking to expand for a long time.
>
> (Al-Qaeda, "Mu'askar al-Battar," 1, translated by MEMRI, Special Dispatch Series, 637, 6 January 2004)

The spreading of military culture and the use of instrumental knowledge by terrorist groups is characterized by a remarkable pragmatism. In the early 1990s, Louis Beam, a white supremacist from Aryan Nations, an American neo-Nazi group on a war footing with the federal government, wrote *Leaderless Resistance*, a classic pamphlet in extremists' circles. The text argues that resistance movements should organize themselves as leaderless "cells" because a "pyramid" structure would be "an easy kill" for government agencies. Instead of a vulnerable and dangerous "unity of organization," he calls for a "unity of purpose."[17] Despite his ideological incompatibility with Islam, Beam's text is referenced on radical Islamist websites.[18] The conceptual knowledge assets available electronically, in the words of one Israeli researcher who has tracked Islamic websites for many years, resemble an entire "open university for Jihad."[19]

Systemic learning

In strictly non-hierarchical and decentralized organizations the creation and dissemination of systemic knowledge assets is a problem. A hierarchical command and control structure seems a necessary requirement for both authorization as well as officially sanctioned dissemination of systemic knowledge. But militant networks cannot rely on official communication channels such as DoD directives or doctrinal publications. The security risk for the organization would be too significant, even if it operated in a highly professional manner. Given the dispersed and networked character of militant Islamic movements and many insurgent groups, there is no hub, no central authority that, in the bureaucratic sense of authority, has control over actions of the organization's members. This narrow view, however, risks ignoring an important systemic dynamic. The dynamic theory of knowledge creation recognizes emotions, attitudes, and motivations as important routine knowledge assets. Thus, if extremist's celebrities, such as Al-Zawahri or the spiritual rector, Osama Bin Laden, appear on television, a feeling of unity, power, and invincibility is induced in the entire movement or organization, however loose it may be. The seventh edition of the periodical *Mu'askar al-Battar* illustrates this. Abu Thabit al-Najdi argues in his article's opening remarks that god will send "someone like the Shaykh Ayman al-Zawahri," Bin Laden's deputy, to punish America. Al-Najdi then points to the role of television:

> While Americans declare that they are close to capturing him [al-Zawahri] in Wazirstan, we hear his voice on Al-Jazeera TV encouraging the Pakistanis to work against this operation to make it a failure. There has been great reaction to his message.

But systemic communication can go beyond creating a feeling of unity, and also involve operational decisions.

In an audio statement in October 2003, Osama bin Laden called his followers to attack Italy, Spain, and Great Britain, because those countries would support

America in Iraq. In November 2003, Italian soldiers in Nasiriya were attacked, followed by bombings on synagogues and British targets in Istanbul in the same month. In March 2004, Madrid was struck, killing 201 victims and later causing Spain to withdraw its troops from Iraq.[20] Some experts point to a document that was circulated on the internet just as Bin Laden was promoting the attacks in October 2003. The paper, dedicated to Yusef al-'Ayyeri, a captured former head of al-Qaeda in Saudi Arabia, stressed the significance of victory in Iraq, but realized the strength of American resolve. It identified the upcoming elections in Spain as one of the coalition's vulnerabilities and called for "painful strikes" against Spanish troops: "We have to take advantage of the national elections in Spain, which will be held in the near future – in March 2004," the author argues. The Spanish government will not even be able to absorb two to three hits "before public pressure will force them to withdraw their troops," as Guido Steinberg quotes from the original document.[21] It remains unclear whether the document guided the Madrid bombings and it is unlikely that the network's senior leadership exerted command and control in a strict sense, but with all probability the operational planning before Madrid was at least inspired by such messages. Systemic knowledge assets then change or reinforce motivations and provide guidance to self-activating parts of the overall network, using the internet and television networks as semi-official channels. The media are, in Boyd's terminology, a component of the network's orientation phase. An audiotaped or televised statement, some may object, is only a one-way communication, often without clear operational instructions, that leaves room for interpretation – just the same limitations nevertheless apply to DoD directives or joint doctrinal publications.

Experiential learning as well as systemic communication is difficult for virtual organizations. The absence of physical training camps as well as clear command and control structures cannot fully be substituted by new forms of two-way internet-based or one-way media-based communications, although the new information environment offers imperfect alternatives. Conceptual learning performed with the help of media and the internet presumably is the dominant mode of innovation as well as a requirement for continuity of performance in many jihadist networks. Conceptual learning, in general, is superior in speed and innovative momentum to systemic learning. In the absence of bureaucratic structures and cumbersome hierarchies, self-recruited communities-of-practice are an accelerator of learning, although its outcome is probably suffering a high likelihood of errors and mistakes. The flattened hierarchy in terrorist networks thus may have an accelerating effect on decision making, innovation, but also on unlearning and organizational forgetting. Al-Qaeda's organizational form indeed may allow the network to run faster learning loops.

The internet, service and email providers, software firms, mobile phone companies, producers of high-end consumer electronics, and global mass-media organizations are part of the societies Islamist extremists are trying to destroy. The production and maintenance of the critical information infrastructure of terrorist organizations, in other words, has been outsourced and merged with that of western societies whom they consider their enemies, particularly the United

States. In order to attack and punish America, global Islamist extremists probably discuss their plans using Hotmail accounts, their cells and sub-networks communicate through Yahoo!'s groupware, they debate their ideology in conference calls via Skype, supporters transfer funds with the help of PayPal, activists run their websites with Apache webservers, host them on AOL, the mujahideen draft their belligerent manuals and periodicals with Microsoft Word, publish them as ebooks in Adobe PDF-format, and their radicalized followers find the publications with the Arabic language interface of Google – each product manufactured by an American company.[22] In sum, jihadist and other violent networks have begun to digitalize the creation and maintenance of their routine knowledge assets. And they use the modern information environment created by their adversary to run their experiential, conceptual, and even parts of their systemic learning loops. Al-Qaeda has undergone a virtual metamorphosis and assumed the survival strategy of an organizational parasite.

Militant Islamic organizations' transformational strategy of *using* their enemy's infrastructure is sharply contrasted by a US military which focuses its own transformation on *destroying their enemy's infrastructure and* capability to fight. The "war against terror" is a war against capabilities, the enemy often remains elusive. The United States is waging an existential war against its adversaries, with the ultimate objective to capture or annihilate terrorists physically, not to get into a mindset or penetrate a decision cycle. The very phrase "war on terror" captures this deficiency. Al-Qaeda is also waging an existential war against its adversary, but the instrument it applies is, just inversely, predominantly psychological. It seems that Bin Laden and his followers have taken in the accumulated wisdoms of Sun Tzu and Clausewitz much more consequently than the commander-in-chief and his subordinates in the unified commands. Franks's Red Force Tracker during Operation Iraqi Freedom was an imprecise and time-delayed snapshot of *physical* enemy formations on the battlefield, and the "transformation" of the armed forces tries to eliminate the remaining imprecision and time-lag as well as to optimize Blue Force Tracking, an essential tool of control and awareness in a hierarchical top-down organization. CNN and the *New York Times* by contrast are al-Qaeda's Red Force Tracker, and they provide a precise and real-time insight into the *psychological* state of mind of its adversary. The terrorist group's transformation into a dispersed and decentralized network of networks, resembling an ideology as much as an organization, where the operational initiative comes from entrepreneurial lower levels, largely removes the need for Blue Force Tracking. The US military tries to destroy the infrastructure of its adversary and struggles to enter his decision loop; radical Islamic groups use their adversary's information infrastructure to attack his decision loop, despite their enemy's striking military superiority.

In the struggle against terrorism, or the "long war", and in its next military operation, journalists will again be embedded, be it with American or allied troops, with the enemy's units, as unilaterals in Baghdad, Mogadishu, Kabul, or as editors and columnists in New York, London, Moscow, or Beijing. Warring parties will attempt to embed and integrate the media into their strategy and use the internet as an operating platform, and these attempts will be shrewd and sophisticated. The US military is beginning to come to grips with this trend, but many western governments and their hierarchically structured armed forces simply lack the recent experience and the right frames of reference to *systemically* grasp the new challenges. So does the public and many opinion leaders, some of whom are quick to scold their security services for suspected manipulation efforts and pour scorn on their government's supposedly fabricated disinformation campaigns. Sometimes they may be right to do so. But critics thereby often overestimate their government's strategic sophistication while they underestimate an army's risk of inadvertent mistakes in a highly stressful tactical environment. Intentional deception of the electorate as well as torture or violence against civilians in theater should under no circumstances be accepted, and under all circumstances be condemned and prosecuted. But focusing lop-sided criticism too quickly on infringed press freedoms, American or allied "propaganda" efforts, and almost as a reflex to bemoan truth as "the first casualty of war" is too narrow, too naïve, and too shortsighted – and not only that it is not useful, the resulting erosion of public resolve might even be in the interest of those who do not reign with their public's approval. Reporting the facts can mean helping one party, and the odds are high that reporting the facts will mean helping the non-democratic party. In retrospect, pre-emptive attackers might on occasion strike the right target, but pundits are well advised to engage only on the basis of solid investigative journalism, and after weighing the consequences of their action upon publication. Whose interest do they serve? Precisely because the public domain is understood by the enemies of liberal democratic values as part of today's battlespace, that battlespace – the public and even more so a critical and responsible press, vital institutions in any democracy – equally needs a sophisticated understanding of media operations.

At the heart of this lies a dilemma, in which two of liberalism's core tenets clash: freedom of expression and non-partisanship. Both principles are dear to a free and independent press, and vital to liberal societies. The problem is confounded by an asymmetry of visibility and awareness. Suspected infringements on free speech are highly visible and easy to criticize in an open, democratic system that subscribes to freedom of speech and exposes its government's inner workings to public scrutiny – in fact this book could not have been written about a closed system. Such infringements are likely to be attacked fiercely, and there is a long civic tradition in North America and Europe in doing so. But information operations in the public domain that use the twenty-first century's media environment both as an operational platform and as an instrument of war can be done nearly covertly, even if their outcome is highly publicized. This is a more recent phenomenon, and civic awareness of it, sensibility, and historical templates are largely missing. If, as happened in the past, western governments attempt to draw the public's attention to their adversary's skillful psychological operations, they are likely to be accused of trying to distract from their own blunders or incompetence. And in such situations both may be factually right, the government and its critics. In the virtual battlespace, non-democratic actors have several structural advantages: they do not subscribe to liberal values, they are not accountable to an electorate, they are not limited in their choice of means by laws, they do not have to expose their policies in a transparent system, and they are often not organized in a hierarchical fashion – all that puts them in a very comfortable position to exploit their enemy's weaknesses, vulnerabilities, and mistakes. Western-style democracies, exposed on their moral high ground, are both ill-protected against media operations and less prone to engage in them. But accountability, integrity, and credibility are any information's thrust, and here democracies have a distinct advantage over militant networked organizations and autocracies. They should not be treated as equals.

Appendix

List of interviews

Aukofer, Frank	Pool reporter in the Persian Gulf War (Desert Shield)
Bell, Hiram, Jr	Colonel, US Army, commandant, Defense Information School, Fort George G. Meade
Birmingham, Mike	Lieutenant Colonel, US Army, public affairs officer, 3rd Infantry Division, during Operation Iraqi Freedom (OIF)
Brooks, Vincent	Brigadier general, US Army, Central Command spokesman during OIF
Clarke, Victoria	Assistant Secretary of Defense for Public Affairs, (ASD/PA), during Operation Enduring Freedom (OEF) and OIF
Copeland, Peter	Reporter on the Panama invasion and the Persian Gulf War for Scripps Howard News Service, general manager and editor during OIF
Cullin, Brian	Captain, US Navy, Plans Officer, Navy Chief of Information, head of the Pentagon's "Iraq PA planning cell" before OIF
Curtin, Joe	Colonel, US Army, Media Operations, Army public affairs during OIF
Dao, James	Pentagon Correspondent for the NYT, embedded with the 5th Special Forces Group in OIF
Davis, Andrew	Brigadier general, US Marine Corps, acting Chief of Information during OEF an OIF
DeFrank, James	Colonel, US Air Force, director of Press Operations in the ADS/PA's office during OEF and OIF
Galloway, Joseph	Decorated Vietnam War correspondent, Knight Ridder, coauthor of *We Were Soldiers Once, and Young . . .*
Hammond, William	Military historian, Fort McNair, Washington, DC
Kreisher, Otto	Copley News Service
Kuehl, Daniel	Professor, director of the Information Strategies Concentration Program (ISCP), National Defense University, coauthor of the Gulf War Air Power Survey

Lorch, Donatella	War correspondent in Operations Desert Storm and Restore Hope, OEF, and others
McCreary, Terry	Rear Admiral, US Navy, Special Assistant for Public Affairs to the chairman of the Joint Chiefs of Staff during OEF and OIF
Malcom, Scott	Lieutenant Colonel, US Army, public affairs officer in the 5th Special Forces Group during OIF
Mazzetti, Mark	Participant of a media boot-camp, embedded in OIF with the 1st Marine Expeditionary Force for *US News and World Report*
Naylor, Sean	Correspondent, *Army Times*, covered for instance Bosnia, Somalia, OEF (including Operation Anaconda), and OIF
Nessen, Ron	War correspondent in Vietnam, White House spokesman for the Ford administration
Pasquarett, Michael	Professor, Strategic Studies Institute (SSI), Army War College, Carlisle, host of a 2003 conference on military-media cooperation in OIF in Carlisle
Perry, Tony	*Los Angeles Times*, embedded with the 1st Marine Division in OEF, later in OIF
Pullen, James R.	Colonel, US Army, public affairs officer in Somalia
Rounds, Tom	Squadron leader, Royal British Air Force, main coordinator of the embedded media program at the Ministry of Defence in London during OIF
Shea, Jamie	Nato spokesman during Operation Allied Force in Brussels
Shields, Guy	Colonel, US Army, director, Coalition Press Information Center Kuwait, during OIF
Skiba, Kahterine	Milwaukee Journal Sentinel, embedded in OIF with the US Army's 101st Airborne Division
Smullen, Bill	Colonel, US Army, Special Assistant for Public Affairs to the chairman of the Joint Chiefs of Staff during Operation Desert Storm
Thomas, Dave	Commander, US Navy, Deputy Director of Plans in the ASD/PA's office, pool escort officer in Panama
Thomas, Rick	Colonel, US Army, public affairs officer, Coalition Forces Land Components Command (CFLCC), during OIF
Whitman, Bryan	Deputy ASD/PA during OEF and OIF
Williams, Pete	ASD/PA during Panama and the Persian Gulf War
Wright, Richard	Institute for Defense Analysis, author of the Pentagon's After Action Report: *Assessment of the DoD Embedded Media Program*

Notes

1 Introduction

1 B. Trainor, "The Military and the Media: A Troubled Embrace," *Parameters*, 1990, December, p. 2.
2 G.W.C. Westmoreland, "Vietnam in Perspective," *Military Review*, 1979, vol. 59, 1, p. 35.
3 US Department of Defense, *Doctrine for Public Affairs in Joint Operations*, JP3–61, 1997, p. A1.
4 In the same period, ten unilateral reporter lost their lives. The killed embedded reporters were *The Atlantic Monthly*'s Michael Kelly, NBC's David Bloom, Christian Leibig of the German magazine *Focus*, and Julio Parrado from the Spanish paper *El Mundo*; all were embedded with the 3rd Infantry Division. R.K. Wright, *Assessment of the DoD Embedded Media Program*, IDA-Paper P-3931, Alexandria, Virginia: Institute for Defense Analysis, 2004, p. VI-24.
5 DeFrank, James, interview by author, Pentagon, 27 February 2004.
6 US Department of Defense, *Transformational Planning Guidance*, 2003, April, p. 3.
7 US Department of Defense, *Dictionary of Military and Associated Terms*, JP 1–02, 2004, US Department of Defense, *Doctrine for Joint Urban Operations*, JP 3–06, 2002, p. 8.
8 J.Q. Wilson, *Bureaucracy: What Government Agencies Do and Why They Do It*, New York: Basic Books, 1989.
9 H. Münkler, "Den Krieg wieder denken. Clausewitz, Kosovo und die Kriege des 21. Jahrhunderts," *Blätter für deutsche und internationale Politik*, 1999, vol. 44, 6, p. 687, H. Münkler, *Über den Krieg*, Weilerswist: Velbrück Wissenschaft, 2003, p. 252.
10 The term propaganda is problematic. It is both too fuzzy and too morally prejudiced to qualify as an analytic term and will not be used in this text. The US military uses "propaganda" mostly to refer to the information campaigns of its adversaries and sometimes to describe information activities by US agencies. The official definition of propaganda is "any form of communication in support of national objectives designed to influence the opinions, emotions, attitudes, or behavior of any group in order to benefit the sponsor, either directly or indirectly." US Department of Defense, JP 1–02, p. 425. This definition is not useful, it makes it impossible to draw a line between propaganda and diplomacy.
11 J.G. March, and H. Simon, *Organizations*, Cambridge: Blackwell, 1958, 1993, W.H. Starbuck, and F.J. Milliken, "Executives' Perceptual Filters: What They Notice and How They Make Sense," in D.C. Hambrick (ed.) *The Executive Effect: Concepts and Methods for Studying Top Managers*, Greenwich, Conn: JAI Press, 1988.
12 T. Kuhn, *Structure of Scientific Revolutions*, Chicago: Chicago University Press, 1962.
13 C. Argyris, and D.A. Schön, *Organizational Learning: A Theory of Action Perspective*, Reading: Addison-Wesley, 1978.

14 B. Hedberg, "How Organizations Learn and Unlearn," *Handbook of Organizational Design: Vol. 1.*, Oxford: Oxford University Press, 1981.

15 P.M. Senge, *The Fifth Discipline. The Art and Practice of the Learning Organization*, New York, 1990.

16 R.L. Daft, and K.E. Weick, "Toward a Model of Organizations as Interpretations Systems," *Academy of Management Review*, 1984, vol. 9, 2, 284–95.

17 I. Nonaka, "A Dynamic Theory of Organizational Knowledge Creation," *Organization Science*, 1994, vol. 5, 1, 14–37, M. Polanyi, *The Tacit Dimension*, London: Routledge and Kegan Paul, 1966.

18 Ikujiro Nonaka uses "knowledge asset" to account for the fact that organizational knowledge often is created entirely from scratch and cannot be reduced to "memory" of past experiences. I. Nonaka, R. Toyama, and P. Byosière, "A Theory of Organizational Knowledge Creation: Understanding the Dynamic Process of Creating Knowledge," in M. Dierkes, A. Berthoin Antal, I. Nonaka, and J. Child (eds) *Handbook of Organizational Learning and Knowledge*, Oxford: Oxford University Press, 2001.

19 The most publicized example for strategic damage that has been amplified by its media coverage is the Abu Ghraib prison scandal. Some of these images will make it into history books and become icons of the Iraq War. Note that no reporter was involved in taking the pictures.

20 W. Sidle, *Report of the CJCS Media–Military Relations Panel*, Washington: Department of Defense, 1984.

21 Poll conducted by the Times Mirror Center, "Military, Media Rate High in Poll," *Chicago Tribune*, 25 March 1991, p. 5.

22 Williams, Pete, quoted in J.B. Brown, "Media Access to the Battlefield," *Military Review*, 1992, July, 10–20, p. 15.

23 B. Levitt, and J.G. March, "Organizational Learning," *Annual Review of Sociology*, 1988, vol. 14, p. 322.

24 S.B. Glasser, "Media and Military Try Experiment in Openness," *Washington Post*, 7 March 2003, A14.

25 H.G. Gole, "Don't Kill the Messenger: Vietnam War Reporting in Context," *Parameters*, 1996, Winter, p. 152.

26 M. Gordon, and B. Trainor, *Cobra II: The Inside Story of the Invasion and Occupation of Iraq*, London: Atlantic Books, 2006, J. Mann, *Rise of the Vulcans: The History of Bush's War Cabinet*, New York: Penguin, 2004, T.E. Ricks, *Fiasco. The American Military Adventure in Iraq*, New York: Penguin, 2006, B. Woodward, *Plan of Attack*, New York: Simon & Schuster, 2004.

27 J.G. March, and J.P. Olsen, "The Uncertainty of the Past: Organizational Learning under Ambiguity," *European Journal of Political Research*, 1975, 3, p. 48.

28 This definition is a modification of the one used by M.C. Fiol, and M.A. Lyles, "Organizational Learning," *Academy of Management Review*, 1985, vol. 10, 4, 803–13. Fiol and Lyles' concept is in line with Argyris's and Schön's definition of organizational learning with centers on the "restructuring of the organizational theory-of-action." Argyris, and Schön, *Organizational Learning*, p. 29.

29 C. von Clausewitz, *On War*, translated by M. Howard and P. Paret, Princeton, NJ: Princeton University Press, 1832, 1976, p. 128.

30 US Department of Defense, *Doctrine for Joint Operations*, JP 3–0, 2001, p. II-2. In matters military, three levels of analysis – or levels of war – are usually distinguished: the tactical, the operational, and the strategic. The decision to invade Iraq and launch an attack from the south is strategic, the decision to detonate a particular palace or government building is an operational one, and the decision to use a particular weapon system is tactical.

31 This text uses the US government's official terminology to refer to the defense establishment. DoD components, or simply DoD, refers to the entirety of the Office of the

Secretary of Defense (OSD), the military departments or services (the Army, the Air Force, the Marine Corps, the Navy, and the Coast Guard when operating under the department of the Navy), the Joint Chiefs of Staff and chairman, the Unified Combatant Commands, the defense agencies, and DoD field activities.

32 The most influential periodicals are the Army's *Military Review* and *Parameters*, the Air-Force's *Airpower Journal*, the Navy's *Naval Institute Proceedings*, and the Marine's *Marine Corps Gazette*. *Joint Forces Quarterly*, a joint journal, is published by the National Defense University.

33 Nonaka, "A Dynamic Theory of Organizational Knowledge Creation," I. Nonaka, *The Knowledge-Creating Company*, New York: Oxford University Press, 1995.

2 Perspectives on military learning

1 US War Department, *Lessons Learned and Expedients Used in Combat*, Pamphlet No. 20–17, 1945, p. 3.
2 K. Lang, "Military Organizations," in J.G. March (ed.) *Handbook of Organizations*, Chicago: Rand McNally, 1965, p. 838.
3 Kuehl, Daniel, interview by author, NDU, Washington, DC, 28 January 2004.
4 M. Weber, *Wirtschaft und Gesellschaft*, Tübingen: Mohr Siebeck, 1922, 1977, p. 551.
5 S.P. Rosen, *Winning the Next War: Innovation and the Modern Military*, Ithaka: Cornell University Press, 1991.
6 Clausewitz, *On War*, p. 75.
7 G.E. Rothenberg, "Maurice of Nassau, Gustav Adolphus, Raimondo Montecuccoli, and the 'Military Revolution' of the Seventeenth Century," in P. Paret (ed.) *Makers of Modern Strategy: from Machiavelli to the Nuclear Age*, Oxford: Clarendon Press, 1990, pp. 40–2. The detailed descriptions of early drill manuals compare to today's "Tactics, Techniques, And Procedures," shortened by the American military to TTPs. P. Johnston, "Doctrine is not Enough: The Effect of Doctrine on the Behavior of Armies," *Parameters*, 2000, vol. 30, 3.
8 R.C. Cassibry, "Development of Doctrine," *Military Review*, 1956, vol. 36, 2, 25–30.
9 I.B. Holley, "Concepts, Doctrines, Principles: Are You Sure You Understand These Terms?" *Air University Review*, 1984, July–August.
10 Johnston, "Doctrine is not Enough," p. 31.
11 US Department of Defense, JP 1–02.
12 US Army, *Battle Focused Training*, FM 7–1, 2003, p. G-15.
13 US Army, *Operations*, FM 100–5, 1993, p. 1–1.
14 R.D. Downie, *Learning from Conflict: The U.S. Military in Vietnam, El Salvador, and the Drug War*, Westport: Praeger, 1998, p. 26.
15 A. Toffler, and H. Toffler, *War and Anti-War*, New York, 1993, p. 52.
16 Lang, "Military Organizations," p. 839.
17 D.D. Avant, "The Institutional Sources of Military Doctrine: Hegemons in Peripheral Wars," *International Studies Quarterly*, 1993, vol. 37, 4, 409–30, D.D. Avant, *Political Institutions and Military Change: Lessons from Peripheral Wars*, Ithaca: Cornell University Press, 1994, Downie, *Learning from Conflict: The U.S. Military in Vietnam, El Salvador, and the Drug War*, Lang, "Military Organizations," B. Posen, *The Sources of Military Doctrine: France, Britain, and Germany between the World Wars*, Ithaka: Cornell University Press, 1984, S. van Evera, "The Cult of the Offensive and the Origins of the First World War," *International Security*, 1984, vol. 9, 1, K.M. Zisk, *Engaging the Enemy: Organization Theory and Soviet Military Innovation, 1955–1991*, Princeton: Princeton University Press, 1993.
18 E.A. Cohen, *Supreme Command:. Soldiers, Statesmen, and Leadership in Wartime*, New York: The Free Press, 2002, pp. 225–51.
19 S. Huntington, *The Soldier and the State*, Cambridge, MA: Harvard University Press, 1957, p. 76.

20 S.P. Rosen, "New Ways of War: Understanding Military Innovation," *International Security*, 1988, vol. 13, 1, p. 142; also Avant, *Political Institutions and Military Change*, p. 132, E.L. Katzenbach, Jr, "The Horse Cavalry in the Twentieth Century," in R.J. Art and K. Waltz (eds) *The Use of Force: International Politics and Foreign Policy*, Boston: Little Brown, 1971.

21 van Evera, "The Cult of the Offensive and the Origins of the First World War," J. Snyder, *The Ideology of the Offensive*, Ithaka: Corell University Press, 1984, S. Sagan, "1914 Revisited," *International Security*, 1986, vol. 11, 2.

22 Posen, *The Sources of Military Doctrine*, p. 227.

23 Cohen, *Supreme Command*, p. 184.

24 S.J. Kaufman, "Organizational Politics and Change in Soviet Military Policy," *World Politics*, 1994, vol. 46, April, p. 362.

25 G.T. Allison, and P. Zelikow, *Essence of Decision: Explaining the Cuban Missile Crisis*, Boston: Little Brown, 1971, 1999, p. 172.

26 The figure of 1.2 million dollars is an estimate of the Institute for Defense Analysis. Wright, *IDA-Paper P-3931*, p. S6.

27 D.T. Macmillan, "Technology: The Catalyst for Doctrinal Change," *Air University Review*, 1977, November–December.

28 S.J. Cimbala, and J.J. Tritten, "Joint Doctrine – Engine of Change?" *Joint Forces Quarterly*, 2003, vol. Winter 2002–03.

29 J.J. Tritten, "Revolutions in Military Affairs: From the Sea," *Military Review*, 2000, March–April, p. 80.

30 Rosen, "New Ways of War," p. 136.

31 Ibid., p. 141.

32 Ibid., p. 142.

33 Ibid., p. 167. Structurally Rosen's argument is similar to Thomas Kuhn's paradigm shifts in the history of sciences. Both scholars emphasize the generational turnover – be it in the military organization or in the scientific community – that needs to occur in order to jettison old thinking. Kuhn, *Structure of Scientific Revolutions*.

34 K.B. Bickel, *Mars Learning: The Marine Corps Development of Small Wars Doctrine, 1915–1940*, Boulder, Colorado: Westview, 2001, p. 15.

35 March, and Simon, *Organizations*.

36 W. Murray, "Innovation: Past and Future," *Joint Forces Quarterly*, 1996, 12, p. 54, W. Murray, "Thinking About Innovation," *Naval War College Review*, 2001, vol. 54, 2, p. 125.

37 N. Aylwin-Foster, "Changing the Army for Counterinsurgency Operations," *Military Review*, 2005, November–December, p. 10, see also Lieutenant Colonel John Nagl's study of counterinsurgency doctrine, and its focus on strategic culture. J.A. Nagl, *Counterinsurgency Lessons from Malaya and Vietnam: Learning to Eat Soup with a Knife*, New York: Praeger, 2002.

38 Downie's approach illustrates both assumptions. He argues that "doctrine is the formal expression of an organization's standard operating procedures and norms." Accordingly, Downie regards changes in doctrine as "acceptable evidence of organizational learning." Downie, *Learning from Conflict: The U.S. Military in Vietnam, El Salvador, and the Drug War*, pp. 23–7. Nagl, who follows Downie's approach, argues that "doctrinal change is in many ways a trailing indicator of institutional learning," and an "efficient way to track the development of learning in military organizations." Nagl, *Counterinsurgency Lessons from Malaya and Vietnam: Learning to Eat Soup with a Knife*, pp. 7–8.

39 Bickel, *Mars Learning*, p. 4.

40 Ibid., p. 5.

41 D.M. Drew, "Informal Doctrine and the Doctrinal Process: A Response," *Air University Review*, 1984, September–October.

42 See Rosen, "New Ways of War".

43 Bickel, *Mars Learning*, p. 238.
44 Johnston, "Doctrine is not Enough," p. 30.
45 Cimbala, and Tritten, "Joint Doctrine," p. 91.
46 Johnston, "Doctrine is not Enough," p. 30.

3 A model of strategic innovation

1 John Boyd, who rose to considerable acclaim among strategic and military thinkers, never published his writings. G.T. Hammond, *The Mind of War: John Boyd and American Security*, Washington, DC: Smithsonian Books, 2004, pp. 155–175, R. Coram, *Boyd: The Fighter Pilot who Changed the Art of War*, New York: Back Bay Books, 2002, pp. 327–44.
2 A. Toffler, *The Third Wave*, New York: Bantam, 1980.
3 R. Henry, and C.E. Peartree, "Military Theory and Information Warfare," *Parameters*, 1998, August, G. Pounder, "Opportunity Lost: Public Affairs, Information Operations, and the Air War against Serbia," *Airpower Journal*, 2000, Summer, p. 59.
4 Toffler, and Toffler, *War and Anti-War*, p. 147.
5 Nonaka, "A Dynamic Theory of Organizational Knowledge Creation," p. 14.
6 Calling the model a "theory of knowledge creation" arguably is too narrow. The model includes not only the *creation* of knowledge, but incorporates the dissemination, authorization, and implementation of knowledge. Nonaka, *The Knowledge-Creating Company*.
7 Polanyi, *The Tacit Dimension*, p. 4.
8 M. Polanyi, *Personal Knowledge*, Chicago: University of Chicago Press, 1962, p. 50.
9 Polanyi, *The Tacit Dimension*, p. 16.
10 A graph in the appendix to US Department of Defense, JP 3–0 illustrates the joint doctrinal hierarchy.
11 For details of the driving analogy, see H. Tsoukas, "Do We Really Understand Tacit Knowledge?" in M. Easterby-Smith and M.A. Lyles (eds) *Handbook of Organizational Learning and Knowledge Management*, Malden: Blackwell, 2003.
12 Nonaka, *The Knowledge-Creating Company*, p. 60.
13 Levitt, and March, "Organizational Learning," p. 327.
14 T.R. Franks, *American Soldier*, New York: HarperCollins, 2004, p. 80.
15 Ibid., p. 80.
16 US Department of Defense, JP 1–02.
17 R. Cyert, and J.G. March, *A Behavioural Theory of the Firm*, Englewood Cliffs, NJ: Prentice-Hall, 1963.
18 Hedberg, "How Organizations Learn and Unlearn," p. 9.
19 Nonaka, "A Dynamic Theory of Organizational Knowledge Creation."
20 I. Nonaka, R. Toyama, and N. Konno, "SECI, Ba and Leadership: a Unified Model of Dynamic Knowledge Creation," *Long Range Planning*, 2000, vol. 33, p. 14.
21 Nonaka, Toyama, and Byosière, "A Theory of Organizational Knowledge Creation: Understanding the Dynamic Process of Creating Knowledge," p. 497.
22 Brown and Duguid's concept of "learning-in-working" as well as the "on-the-job-training" are analogous to internalization. J.S. Brown, and P. Duguid, "Organizational Learning and Communities-of-Practice: Toward a Unified View of Working, Learning, and Innovation," *Organization Science*, 1991, vol. 2, 1.
23 Nonaka, Toyama, and Byosière, "A Theory of Organizational Knowledge Creation: Understanding the Dynamic Process of Creating Knowledge," p. 503.
24 Clausewitz, *On War*, S. Tzu, *The Art of War*, translated by S.B. Griffith, Oxford: Oxford University Press, 1963. For a discussion of Clausewitz's reception in the US armed forces see C. Bassford, *The Reception of Clausewitzian Theory in Anglo-American Military Thought*, Purdue, 1991, T. Rid, "Vom künftigen Kriege," *Österreichische Militärische Zeitschrift*, 2004, 2, 181–6.

25　Bell, Hiram, interview by author, DINFOS, Fort Meade, 7 June 2004; US Marine Corps, *Combat Camera and Visual Information in Expeditionary Operations*, MCWP 3–33.7, 2002, p. I-8.

26　Nonaka, Toyama, and Byosière, "A Theory of Organizational Knowledge Creation: Understanding the Dynamic Process of Creating Knowledge," p. 495.

27　An example is the "soda-straw" metaphor, extensively used in the Pentagon during the embedded media program's planning phase. In Nonaka's terminology, the precondition to create such new knowledge and metaphors for organizational members is to share the same "ba." I. Nonaka, R. Toyama, and A. Nagata, "A Firm as a Knowledge-creating Entity: A New Perspective on the Theory of the Firm," *Industrial and Corporate Change*, 2000, vol. 9, 1, p. 1.

28　Nonaka, Toyama, and Konno, "SECI, Ba and Leadership," p. 20.

29　D.A. Levinthal, and J.G. March, "The Myopia of Learning," *Strategic Management Journal*, 1993, vol. 14, 95–112.

30　Pasquarett, Michael, interview by author, Army War College, Carlisle, PA, 24 February 2004.

31　Nonaka, Toyama, and Byosière, "A Theory of Organizational Knowledge Creation: Understanding the Dynamic Process of Creating Knowledge," p. 495.

32　US Army, FM 7–1, p. IV-3.

33　K.J. Gunzelman, "Evolution of Military Learning," *Military Review*, 2000, November–December, p. 26.

34　US Army, FM 7–1, p. C-1.

35　Nonaka, Toyama, and Byosière, "A Theory of Organizational Knowledge Creation: Understanding the Dynamic Process of Creating Knowledge," p. 497.

36　A. Berthoin Antal, "Die Dynamik der Theoriebildungsprozesse zum Organisationsler-nen," in H. Albach, M. Dierkes, A. Berthoin Antal, and K. Vaillant (eds) *Organisationslernen - institutionelle und kulturelle Dimensionen*, Berlin: WZB, 1998.

37　E.H. Schein, "How Can Organizations Learn Faster? The Challenge of Entering the Green Room," *Sloan Management Review*, 1993, vol. 34, 2, p. 87.

38　Johnston, "Doctrine is not Enough," p. 37.

39　M. Dierkes, *Handbook of Organizational Learning and Knowledge*, Oxford: Oxford University Press, 2001, p. 4.

40　See F. Aukofer, and W.P. Lawrence, *America's Team, the Odd Couple: A Report on the Relationship between the Military and the Media*, Nashville: The Freedom Forum First Amendment Center, 1995.

41　US Air Force, *Information Operations*, AFDD 2–5, 2002, p. 28.

42　Clausewitz, *On War*, p. 87.

43　US Department of Defense, JP 3–0, p. III-40.

44　G. Shields, "Media Gatekeeper and Troubleshooter," in B. Katovsky and T. Carlson (eds) *Embedded: The Media at War in Iraq*, Guilford, Conneticut: The Lyons Press, 2004, p. 75.

45　Allison, and Zelikow, *Essence of Decision*, p. 170.

46　US Department of Defense, JP 3–06, pp III-37.

47　US Department of Defense, *Joint Doctrine for Information Operations*, JP 3–13, 1998, p. I-13.

48　Ibid., p. 7.

49　March, and Simon, *Organizations*.

50　Nonaka *et al.*, for instance, argue that progressive management styles such as his middle-up-down process hardly take place in "the military-like hierarchy of the top-down model." Nonaka, Toyama, and Byosière, "A Theory of Organizational Knowledge Creation: Understanding the Dynamic Process of Creating Knowledge," p. 504. Kier, writing specifically on doctrinal change, refers to military organizations as "'total' institutions." E. Kier, "Culture and Military Doctrine: France Between the Wars," *International Security*, 1995, vol. 19, 4, p. 69.

51 Bickel, *Mars Learning*, Rosen, *Winning the Next War*, and Berthoin Antal, "Die Dynamik der Theoriebildungsprozesse zum Organisationslernen," Nonaka, *The Knowledge-Creating Company.*

52 Berthoin Antal, "Die Dynamik der Theoriebildungsprozesse zum Organisationslernen," pp. 27–9.

53 Daft, and Weick, "Toward a Model of Organizations as Interpretations Systems," p. 288.

54 Brown, and Duguid, "Organizational Learning and Communities-of-Practice," p. 73.

55 OL literature knows several labels which essentially refer to the same concept. Nonaka speaks of "communities of interaction," Brown and Duguid prefer "communities-of-practice," others use "communities of interpretation." I opt for CoPs because it is the most widespread term. I. Nonaka, "A Dynamic Theory of Organizational Knowledge Creation" *Organizational Science*, 1994, vol. 5, p. 15, Brown, and Duguid, "Organizational Learning and Communities-of-Practice," p. 68.

56 Kilner used the CompanyCommand.com project as an example for a community-of-practice. P. Kilner, "Transforming Army Learning Through Communities of Practice," *Military Review*, 2002, May–June, 21–7.

57 Quoted from CompanyCommand.com, accessed 9 February 2004, 1338 EST.

58 In the context of a massive troop rotations into and out of Iraq – where knowledge transfer was an stated objective – the *Washington Post* ran an article about "CompanyCommand.com." The article in the *Post* triggered increased traffic, and the site was subsequently restricted for public access. T.E. Ricks, "Soldiers Record Lessons From Iraq," *Washington Post*, 8 February 2004, A1.

59 Kilner, "Transforming Army Learning Through Communities of Practice," p. 25.

60 Ibid., p. 21.

61 W.H. Starbuck, and B. Hedberg, "How Organizations Learn from Success and Failure," in M. Dierkes, A. Berthoin Antal, I. Nonaka, and J. Child (eds) *Handbook of Organizational Learning and Knowledge*, Oxford: Oxford University Press, 2001, p. 337.

62 Ibid., p. 338.

63 B. McCaffrey, "Lessons of Desert Storm," *Joint Forces Quarterly*, 2000, 27, p. 14.

64 G.P. Huber, "Organizational Learning: The Contributing Processes and Literatures," *Organization Science*, 1991, vol. 2, 1, p. 147.

65 De Holan *et al.* point to the difference between intentional and unintentional unlearning. They suggest the term "organizational forgetting." P.M. de Holan, N. Phillips, and T.B. Lawrence, "Managing Organizational Forgetting," *Sloan Management Review*, 2004, vol. 45, 2, p. 45.

66 E.H. Schein, "How Can Organizations Learn Faster? The Challenge of Entering the Green Room" *Sloan Management Review*, 1993, vol. 34, 85–92.

67 US Department of Defense, *Doctrine for Public Affairs in Joint Operations*, JP 3–61 (Final Coordination, August 23), 2002, p. I-8.

68 Hedberg, "How Organizations Learn and Unlearn," p. 4.

69 This argument is mirrored in the Popper-Kuhn debate of the 1960s. Thomas Kuhn argued that scientific discoveries happen during crises and as paradigm-shifts, in which one paradigm might entirely contradict its predecessor (he coined the term "incommensurability"). Karl Popper insisted that scientific knowledge would constantly grow and enlarge, based on what is already scientifically proven and known. My organizational learning argument is analogous to Kuhn's position. The key difference to organizational theory, however, is the fluidity of the external environment. Both Kuhn and Popper assumed that the external environment of science does not change, but only humans' understanding of it. Organizational theory, by contrast, does not assume stable environments. Kuhn, *Structure of Scientific Revolutions*, I. Lakatos, and A. Musgrave, *Criticism and the Growth of Knowledge*, Cambridge: Cambridge University Press, 1970.

70 Fiol and Lyles, "Organizational Learning," p. 808.
71 Argyris, and Schön, *Organizational Learning*, p. 3.
72 Fiol and Lyles, "Organizational Learning," p. 808.
73 Nonaka, "A Dynamic Theory of Organizational Knowledge Creation," p. 19.
74 Nonaka uses the same three levels of hierarchy to illustrate what he calls "middle-up-down management," although he arrives at very different conclusions. Nonaka, Toyama, and Byosière, "A Theory of Organizational Knowledge Creation: Understanding the Dynamic Process of Creating Knowledge,"
75 de Holan, Phillips, and Lawrence, "Managing Organizational Forgetting," p. 46.

4 Disasterous public affairs: Vietnam

1 Kalb, Bernard, quoted in P. Knightley, *The First Casualty: From the Crimea to Vietnam: The War Correspondent as Hero, Propagandist and Myth Maker*, New York: Harcourt Brace Jovanovich, 1975, p. 381.
2 The 11th Infantry Brigade had been awarded a Special Commendation for 128 enemy killed at My Lai before Seymour Hersh uncovered the grisly details of the massacre. For details see ibid., pp. 391–2.
3 D. Halberstam, *The Best and the Brightest*, New York: Ballantine, 1969, p. 248.
4 W.S. Murray, "A Will to Measure," *Parameters*, 2001, Autumn, 134–47.
5 W.M. Hammond, *Public Affairs: The Military and the Media, 1962–1968*, Washington, DC: Center of Military History, 1988.
6 Knightley, *The First Casualty*, p. 398.
7 P. Braestrup, *Battle Lines*, New York: Priority Press, 1985, p. 64, J.J. Fialka, *Hotel Warriors: Covering the Gulf War*, Hopkins University Press: Baltimore, 1991.
8 W.M. Hammond, "The News Media and the Military," in J.E. Jessup (ed.) *The Encyclopedia of the American Military*, New York: Seritumis, 1994, p. 2101.
9 Nessen, Ron, interview by author, Brookings Institution, Washington, DC, 15 January 2004.
10 Nessen, interview.
11 C.R.B. Rigg, "How Not to Report a War," *Military Review*, 1969, June, p. 20.
12 The insignia of such a press card read as follows: "The bearer of this card should be accorded full co-operation and assistance ... to assure the successful completion of his mission. Bearer is authorized rations and quarters on a reimbursable basis. Upon presentation of this card, bearer is entitled to air, water and ground transportation under a priority of 3." Knightley, *The First Casualty*, p. 403.
13 Braestrup, *Battle Lines*, p. 64.
14 D.B. Stockwell, *Press Coverage in Somalia: A Case for Media Relations to be a Principle of Military Operations Other Than War*, Masters Thesis: DINFOS, 1995.
15 C.L. Powell, and J.E. Persico, *My American Journey*, New York: Random House, 1995, p. 120.
16 Cronkite, Walter, quoted in D. Oberdorfer, *Tet!*, New York: Garden City, 1971, p. 158.
17 Cronkite, Walter, on CBS News Special, 27 February 1968, 2200 EST. Find the full text of the news transcript in ibid., pp. 250–1.
18 Jack Welch, General Electric's former CEO, describes in his memoirs how a remark was used in some of the company's internal meetings: "Don't Walter Cronkite me!," meant that someone reported the bad news but did not say how to fix it. The adage, Welch states, was "understood by everyone." J. Welch, *Jack: Straight from the Gut*, New York: Warner Business Books, 2001, p. 43.
19 Johnson, Lyndon B., quoted in J. Neuman, *Lights, Camera, War*, New York: St. Martin's Press, 1996, p. 179.
20 Ibid., p. 85.

21 H.G. Summers, "Lessons: A Soldier's View," in P. Braestrup (ed.) *Vietnam as History: Ten Years After the Paris Peace Accords*, Washington, DC: University Press of America, 1984, p. 110.
22 US Department of Defense, JP 3–06, pp. III-40.
23 Gole, "Don't Kill the Messenger," p. 151.
24 Brown, "Media Access to the Battlefield," p. 12.
25 G.W.C. Westmoreland, "Vietnam in Perspective," pp. 37–8.
26 Braestrup, *Battle Lines*, pp. 69–70.
27 Ibid., p. 69.
28 Trainor, "The Military and the Media: A Troubled Embrace".
29 Gole, "Don't Kill the Messenger: Vietnam War Reporting in Context."
30 Ibid.
31 J.M. Shotwell, "The Fourth Estate as a Force Multiplier," *Marine Corps Gazette*, 1991, July, p. 72.
32 S.C. Stearns, "Unit-Level Public Affairs Planning," *Military Review*, 1999, December–February
33 Ibid.
34 M. Belknap, "The CNN Effect: Strategic Enabler or Operational Risk?" *Parameters*, 2002, 3, p. 104.

5 Restrictive public affairs: Grenada, Panama, and the Persian Gulf

1 Reagan, Ronald, quoted in Braestrup, *Battle Lines*, p. 83.
2 Ibid., p. 92.
3 N. Schwarzkopf, *It Doesn't Take a Hero*, New York: Bantam, 1992, p. 287.
4 R. Reagan, *An American Life*, New York: Simon & Schuster, 1990, p. 455.
5 Ibid., p. 454.
6 Gergen, David, quoted in Braestrup, *Battle Lines*, p. 90.
7 R.H. Cole, *Operation Urgent Fury: Grenada*, Washington, DC: Joint History Office, Department of Defense, 1997.
8 The media reported that the three reporters were "evacuated" from the island, Washington Post Foreign News Service. P. Gailey, "U.S. Bars Coverage of Grenada Action; News Groups Protest," *New York Times*, 26 October 1983, A1.
9 Metcalf notes merely, without mentioning Cody's name, that "my PAO escorted him below." J. Metcalf, III, "The Mother of the Mother," *United States Naval Institute Proceedings*, 1991, vol. 118, 8, E. Cody, "U.S. Forces Thwart Journalists' Reports," *Washington Post*, 28 October 1983.
10 Metcalf, "The Mother of the Mother," p. 57.
11 Ibid., p. 57.
12 Quoted in Braestrup, *Battle Lines*, p. 90.
13 Metcalf, "The Mother of the Mother," p. 58.
14 Major Donald Blank, who was part of the JIB staff in Barbados, quoted in Braestrup, *Battle Lines*, p. 93.
15 Brown, "Media Access to the Battlefield," p. 12.
16 B. Baker, "Wanted: A Professional Press," *Proceedings*, 1984, July, p. 75.
17 R.L. Upchurch, "Wanted: A Fair Press," *Proceedings*, 1984, July, p. 72.
18 As quoted in B. Baker, "Wanted: A Professional Press," p. 76.
19 H.F. Noyes, "The Media's Role in Grenada," *Media Military Review*, 1987, January, pp. 26–7.
20 The image is reprinted in R.L. Upchurch, "Wanted: A Fair Press," *Proceedings*, 1984, July, p. 73. Reagan's remark is an early illustration of how the media can penetrate the administration's decision loop in a beneficial way.
21 Cheney, Richard, quoted in F.S. Hoffman, Review of Panama Pool Deployment, December 1989, Washington, 1990, p. 7.

22 Cheney, Richard, quoted in R.H. Cole, *Operation Just Cause: Panama*, Washington, DC: Joint History Office, Department of Defense, 1995, p. 47.

23 Hoffman, Review of Panama Pool Deployment, December 1989, p. 5.

24 Ibid., p. 9.

25 Public Affairs After Action Report, TRADOC Lessons Learned Collection Phase II, September 1990, reprinted in US Army, *Public Affairs Tactics, Techniques and Procedures*, FM 3–61.1, 2000.

26 Merida, Kevin, quoted in Neuman, *Lights, Camera, War*, p. 208.

27 S. Komarow, "War-Gaming with Lieutenant General William Wallace," in B. Katovsky and T. Carlson (eds) *Embedded: The Media at War in Iraq*, Guilford, Connecticut: The Lyons Press, 2004, p. 83.

28 Thomas, Dave, interview by author, Fort McNair, Washington, DC, 9 February 2004.

29 Hoffman, Review of Panama Pool Deployment, December 1989, p. 2.

30 Francis, Fred, in a memo quoted in W. Boot, "Wading Around in the Panama Pool," *Colombia Journalism Review*, 1990, March–April, p. 18.

31 Thomas, D., interview, Copeland, Peter, interview by author, Scripps Howard News Service, Washington, DC, 29 January 2004.

32 Copeland, interview.

33 Ibid.

34 J. Vasquez, "Panama: Live from the Marriott!" *Washington Journalism Review*, 1990, March, p. 44.

35 Powell, and Persico, *My American Journey*, p. 419.

36 Ibid., p. 431–3.

37 Hoffman, Review of Panama Pool Deployment, December 1989.

38 C.L. Powell, *DoD National Media Pool Planning Requirements*, Directive 182305Z: Department of Defense, 1990.

39 Ibid.

40 M. Sherman, "Informing through the JIB," *Proceedings*, 1991, August, 59–61.

41 The precise numbers are difficult to determine. Many journalists registered multiple times in different Joint Information Bureaus to get more benefits and access, M. Moore, *A Woman at War*, New York: Scribner's, 1993.

42 B. Baker, "Last One in the Pool," *Proceedings*, 1991, August, p. 71.

43 Schwarzkopf, *It Doesn't Take a Hero*, p. 398.

44 Ibid., p. 398.

45 Ibid., p. 400.

46 Ibid., p. 510.

47 Ibid., p. 510.

48 Powell, and Persico, *My American Journey*, p. 514.

49 Powell, Colin as quoted in Hammond, "The News Media and the Military," p. 2108.

50 R. Atkinson, *Crusade: The Untold Story of the Gulf War*, London: HarperCollins, 1993, p. 160.

51 Ibid., p. 160. Officially the pool system worked as follows:

> Under the operating rules of pools, each member of a combat correspondent pool would observe and record (in words, pictures, or video) what he or she saw in the field. Public affairs escort officers would review those words, pictures, and video footage for security and conformity to ground rules. Once cleared, the reports would be sent back to the JIB in Dhahran, where they would become available to all other reporters, faxed to the JIB in Riyadh, and dispatched to each pool reporter's parent news organization.
>
> R.L. Olson, *Gulf War Air Power Survey Volume 3: Logistics; Support*, Washington, DC: Government Printing Office, 1993, p. 173.

52 Sherman, "Informing through the JIB," p. 59.

53 Ibid., pp. 60–1.

54 Copeland, interview.
55 Ibid.
56 Many military officers (and journalists) I interviewed recommended the short book as valuable background reading, Fialka, *Hotel Warriors*, p. 5.
57 Davis, Andrew, interview by author, API office, Reston, Virginia, 17 February 2004.
58 Quoted in R.F. Machamer, "Avoiding a Military–Media War in the Next Armed Conflict," *Military Review*, 1993, April, p. 44.
59 Fialka, *Hotel Warriors*, p. 26.
60 See ibid., p. 15. Fialka provides a detailed account of Army officers preventing the few reporters from doing their job properly.
61 Major Cook, quoted in ibid., p. 16.
62 V.H. Krulak, *First to Fight: An Inside View of the U.S. Marine Corps*, Annapolis, MD: Naval Institute Press, 1999, p. 15; Davis, interview.
63 Davis, Interview.
64 Shotwell, "The Fourth Estate as a Force Multiplier," p. 77.
65 Carlson, Eric, quoted in Fialka, *Hotel Warriors*, p. 27.
66 P. Arnett, *Live from the Battlefield*, New York: Simon & Schuster, 1994, p. 384.
67 W. Goodman, "Critic's Notebook: CNN in Baghdad: Danger of Propaganda vs. Virtue of Reporting," *New York Times*, 29 January 1991, 11.
68 Neuman, *Lights, Camera, War*, p. 217.
69 R.J. Blanchfield, *Gulf War Air Power Survey Volume 4: Weapons, Tactics and Training; Space Operations*, Washington, DC: Government Printing Office, 1993, section "Iraqi PSYOP."
70 For details see Atkinson, *Crusade*, chapter 10.
71 Middle East Watch. *Needless Deaths in the Gulf War*, Washington, DC: Middle East Watch, 1991, pp. 128–9.
72 Pounder, "Opportunity Lost," p. 60, Powell, and Persico, *My American Journey*, p. 499.
73 W.S. Murray, *Gulf War Air Power Survey Volume 2: Operations; Effects and Effectiveness*, Washington, DC: Government Printing Office, 1993, section "Attacking the Core of Iraq's Military Power."
74 Olson, *Gulf War Air Power Survey Volume 3: Logistics; Support*, p. 135.
75 US Department of Defense, *Principles for DoD News Media Coverage*, DoDD 5122.5, 1992.
76 P.J. Brown, "The DoD and the Flyaway Dish," *Proceedings*, 1991, August, p. 63.
77 McIntyre, Jamie, quoted in M.S. Galloucis, "Military–Media Relations: One Officer's Perspective," *Military Review*, 1999, September–October, p. 78.
78 Sean Naylor, coauthor of a book on great tank battles, was unable to find any first-hand photographs of the fight. Naylor, Sean, interview by author, Capitol Hill, Washington, DC, 30 March 2004.
79 Shotwell, "The Fourth Estate as a Force Multiplier," p. 71.
80 DeFrank, interview.

6 Experimental public affairs: Somalia, the Balkans, and Afghanistan

1 Davis, interview.
2 Belknap, "The CNN Effect," p. 106.
3 Lorch, interview.
4 Ibid.
5 US Marine Corps, *Marine Corps Public Affairs*, MCWP 3-33.3, 2000, p. II-5.
6 C.W. Ricks, *The Military–News Media Relationship: Thinking Forward*, Carlisle, PA: Army War College, 1993.
7 Stockwell, *Press Coverage in Somalia*, p. 21, N. Gowing, *Real Time Television Coverage of Armed Conflicts and Diplomatic Crises: Does it Pressure or Distort Foreign Policy Decisions?*, Working Paper: The Shorenstein Center, 1994, p. 48.

8 Information as given by Stockwell, who interviewed Hassan in October 2003, Stockwell, *Press Coverage in Somalia*, p. 21.

9 Ibid., p. 8.

10 Gramm, Phil, quoted in Neuman, *Lights, Camera, War*, p. 14.

11 McCain, John, quoted in B. Clinton, *My Life*, London: Random House, 2004, p. 551.

12 Lake, Anthony, quoted in Gowing, *Real Time Television Coverage*, p. 48. The remark is a good illustration of the OODA loop. The Somali warlord succeeded to get into the White House's OODA loop and to give the President a new orientation (by changing his advisors' perception of the situation on the ground) as well as to limit options to decide (by putting pressure on him through Congress).

13 Clinton, *My Life*, pp. 551–4.

14 Gordon, and Trainor, *Cobra II*, p. 66.

15 Ricks, *The Military–News Media Relationship*, p. 6

16 A. Zinni, and F. Lorenz, "Media Relations: A Commander's Perspective," *Marine Corps Gazette*, 1995, December, p. 69.

17 US Marine Corps, MCWP 3–33.3, pp. 2–5.

18 US Department of Defense, *Doctrine for Public Affairs in Joint Operations*, JP 3–61, 1997, p. III-1.

19 C.C. Krulak, "The Strategic Corporal: Leadership in the Three Block War," *Marine Corps Gazette*, 1999, January, p. 20.

20 F.J. Stech, "Winning CNN Wars," *Parameters*, 1994, Autumn, 37–56.

21 Stockwell, *Press Coverage in Somalia*, p. 1.

22 US Marine Corps, MCWP 3–33.3. In the debate about the "CNN effect," two such effects need to be distinguished. "Media images of starving Somalis got the world into Somalia and media images of a dead U.S. soldier being dragged though Mogadishu streets got the world out of Somalia," as Stockwell put it. This statement, although contested, sums up the two CNN effects: inbound pressure is of political significance, outbound pressure is militarily relevant (the military has no control over the first, and only some control over the second). The seemingly new effect – mostly the inbound one – spawned debate beyond the narrow circles of military periodicals: Does the media drive foreign policy? Political science and media studies have debated that question since the 1990s. L. Freedman, "Victims and Victors: Reflections on the Kosovo War," *Review of International Studies*, 2000, vol. 26, 335–58, J. Mermin, "Television News and American Intervention in Somalia: The Myth of a Media-Driven Foreign policy," *Political Science Quarterly*, 1997, vol. 112, 3, 385–403, Neuman, *Lights, Camera, War*, T. Rid, "Revolution in Reporting Affairs. Der Krimkrieg und seine Bedeutung für die Geschichte der Kriegsberichterstattung," *Österreichische Militärische Zeitschrift*, 2003, 3, P. Robinson, "The CNN Effect: Can the News Media Drive Foreign Policy?" *Review of International Studies*, 1999, vol. 25, 301–9, J. Mermin, *Debating War and Peace: Media Coverage of US Intervention in the Post-Vietnam Era*, Princeton: Princeton University Press, 1999.

23 Thomas, Rick, in M. Pasquarett, *Reporters on the Ground: The Military and the Media's Joint Experience During Operation Iraqi Freedom*, at Army War College, Carlisle, PA, 3–5 September 2003.

24 Naylor, interview.

25 T. Ricks, "U.S. Brings to Bosnia Tactics that Tamed Wild West," *Wall Street Journal*, 27 December 1995, A7.

26 R.J. Newman, "Burned by the Press: One Commander's Perspective," in V.C. Franke (ed.) *Security in a Changing World*, Westport: Praeger, 2002, p. 116.

27 D.G. Hernandez, "'Embedding' Leads to Restrictions," *Editor & Publisher*, 25 May 1996, 10.

28 US Department of Defense, *Public Affairs Guidance on Embedding Media During Possible Future Operations/Deployments in the US Central Command's Area of Responsibility*, PAG1, 2003.

29 Nash, William, quoted in Newman, "Burned by the Press," p. 123.
30 Shields, Guy, interview by author, Pentagon, 10 March 2004.
31 DeFrank, interview.
32 W.K. Clark, *Waging Modern War: Bosnia, Kosovo, and the Future of Combat*, New York: Public Affairs, 2001, p. 272.
33 Ibid.
34 Pounder, "Opportunity Lost,"
35 Detailed figures of the incident are difficult to determine. There is confusion about the number of aircraft involved, the number of bombs dropped, and the number of casualties. For a more detailed discussion see the Final Report of the Nato Bombing Campaign by the *International Tribunal for the Former Yugoslavia*. CNN initially reported "85 dead," 14 April 1999, 1911 EDT.
36 J. Shea, "Kampf der Fernsehbilder," *message*, 2001, 1.
37 S. Livingston, "NATO-Fehler im Kosovo," *message*, 2001, 1.
38 Shea, Jamie, interview by author, 27 June 2005, by telephone.
39 B.S. Lambeth, *NATO's Air War for Kosovo: A Strategic and Operational Assessment*, Santa Monica: Rand, 2001, p. 145.
40 For a detailed discussion of the information battle-space in the Kosovo War see Pounder, "Opportunity Lost," p. 60.
41 US Air Force, AFDD 2–5, p. 27.
42 2J. Shea, *The Kosovo Crisis and the Media: Reflections of a Nato Spokesman*, at Atlantic Council of the United Kingdom, Reform Club, London, 15 July 1999.
43 Clark, *Waging Modern War*, p. 444.
44 Shea, Jamie, quoted on CNN, "Nato Hits Yugoslav Political Institutions for 3rd Day," 23 April 1999, 0104 EDT.
45 Clark, Wesley, quoted in C.R. Whitney, "Generals Vow to Hit Serb TV but Nato Civilians Say No," *New York Times*, 9 April 1999, A8.
46 Shea, *The Kosovo Crisis and the Media*.
47 Shea, interview.
48 A. Campbell, "Communications Lessons for NATO, the Military and the Media," *RUSI*, 1999, vol. 144, 4, p. 36.
49 Ibid., p. 34.
50 Shea, *The Kosovo Crisis and the Media*.
51 Crowley, P J, quoted in Pounder, "Opportunity Lost," p. 67.
52 J. Holm, "Get Over It! Repairing the Military's Adversarial Relationship with the Press," *Military Review*, 2002, January–February, p. 61.
53 Clark, *Waging Modern War*, p. 443.
54 Pounder, "Opportunity Lost," p. 57.
55 M. Hills, and R. Holloway, "Competing for media control in an age of asymmetric warfare," *Jane's Intelligence Review*, 2002, vol. 14, 5, p. 20.
56 Shea, interview.
57 Shea, *The Kosovo Crisis and the Media*.
58 Rodgers, Walter, quoted in J. McIntyre, "The Relationship After Sept. 11: A Media View," in N. Ethiel (ed.) *The Military, the Media and the Administration: An Irregular Triangle*, Chicago: McCormick Tribune Foundation, 2002, p. 149.
59 Ibid., p. 145.
60 Sarah Chayes quoted on PBS, www.pbs.org, accessed on 16 January 2003.
61 Deppendorf, Ulrich, quoted in E. Becker, "In the War on Terrorism, a Battle to Shape Public Opinion," *New York Times*, 11 November 2001, p. A1.
62 W.S. Ross, "First Lady to Address Taliban Abuses against Women," *Washington File*, 16 November 2001.
63 C. Morello, "Tight Control Marks Coverage of Afghan War; Curbs Exceed Those of Past; Broader Access is Promised," *Washington Post*, 7 December 2001, A43.
64 Davis, interview.

65 Perry, Tony, interview by author, by telephone, 12 November 2004.
66 S. Sandler, *"Cease Resistance: It's Good for You": A History of US Army Combat PSYOP*, Fort Bragg: US Army Special Operations Command, 1996.
67 Davis, interview.
68 V. Clarke, Meeting with DoD National Media Pool Bureau Chiefs, *Transcript*, 29 November 2001.
69 Lorch, Donatella, interview by author, ICFG, Washington, DC, 25 February 2004.
70 Naylor, interview.
71 S. Naylor, *Not a Good Day to Die*, New York: Penguin, 2005, p. 50, 139.
72 Quoted by Naylor, interview.
73 Ibid.
74 Ibid.
75 Reeder, Melanie, quoted in T.L. Miracle, "The Army and Embedded Media," *Military Review*, 2003, September–October, p. 42.
76 Thomas, Rick, interview by author, by telephone, 5 May 2004.
77 McCreary, Terry, quoted in J. Neuman, "Pentagon Plans to Deploy Journalists in Iraq," *Los Angeles Times*, 4 December 2002, p. A14.
78 Cox, Larry, quoted in J. Laurence, "Embedding: A Military View," *Columbia Journalism Review*, 2003, 2.

7 Retrieving past experiences?

1 Mazzetti, Mark, interview by author, US News and World Report, Washington, DC, 3 February 2004.
2 See Wright, *IDA-Paper* P-3931, p. VII-9.
3 Whitman, Bryan, interview by author, by telephone, 11 March 2004.
4 Clausewitz, *On War*, p. 75.
5 C. Bassford, *Clausewitz in English: The Reception of Clausewitz in Britain and America 1815–1945*, New York: Oxford University Press, 1994.
6 Tzu, *The Art of War*, p. 77.
7 Franks, *American Soldier*, p. 311.
8 US Marine Corps, *Warfighting*, MCDP 1, 1997, pp. 4, 14.
9 In the German version of *On War*, *Vom Kriege*, Clausewitz uses the word *Gewalt*. The extension of the term in German includes violence as well as force. Peter Paret argues that for Clausewitz the "use" of force also implied the "threat of use." P. Paret, "Clausewitz," in P. Paret (ed.) *Makers of Modern Strategy: from Machiavelli to the Nuclear Age*, Oxford: Clarendon Press, 1990, p. 190.
10 Clausewitz quoted in one of the highest-order joint doctrines US Department of Defense, JP 3–0, p. III-22. See the original phrase at Clausewitz, *On War*, p. 596.
11 US Department of Defense, JP 1–02.
12 Tzu, *The Art of War*, p. 84.
13 US Department of Defense, *Joint Doctrine for Information Operations*, JP 3–13 (First Draft, July 8), 2004.
14 US Department of Defense, JP 3–0, p. III-23.
15 Pounder, "Opportunity Lost," pp. 58, 72.
16 US Marine Corps, MCDP 1, p. 46.
17 US Department of Defense, JP 3–61, p. 6.
18 Ibid., p. III-2.
19 Alternative names are CIB, PIC, APIC: coalition information bureau, press information center, or allied press information center.
20 US Department of Defense, JP 3–61, p. III-10.
21 US Army, FM 3–61.1, p. III-28.
22 US Department of Defense, JP 3–61 *(Final Coordination, August 23)*.

23 US Department of Defense, *Development of Proposed Public Affairs Guidance (PPAG)*, DoDI 5405.3, 1991.

24 US Department of Defense, JP 3–61, p. III-12.

25 US Army, *Public Affairs Operations*, FM 46–1, 1997, p. 25.

26 Davis, interview.

27 US Marine Corps, MCWP 3–33.3, p. 2–13.

28 Ibid., p. 1–4.

29 Ibid., p. III-18, emphasis in original.

30 US Department of Defense, JP 3–61, p. III-6.

31 US Department of Defense, *Principles for DoD News Media Coverage*, DoDD 5122.5, 2000.

32 US Department of Defense, JP 3–61, p. 6.

33 US Department of Defense, *Doctrine for Joint Psychological Operations*, JP 3–53, 2003, p. 9.

34 US Department of Defense, JP 3–61, JP 3–61 *(Final Coordination, August 23)*, p. III, emphasis in both originals.

35 US Code Collection, Title 22, Chapter 18, Subchapter V, §1461.

36 US Department of Defense, JP 3–61, JP 3–61 *(Final Coordination, August 23)*.

37 US Air Force, *Air Force Basic Doctrine*, AFDD 1, 1997, p. 31.

38 US Department of Defense, JP 1–02.

39 US Department of Defense, JP 3–13 *(First Draft, July 8)*.

40 US Air Force, *Air Force Basic Doctrine*, AFDD 1, 2003, p. 46.

41 Ibid., p. 46.

42 T. Bui, *Following Ho Chi Minh: Memoirs of a North Vietnamese Colonel*, translated by J. Strowe and D. Van, Honolulu: University of Hawaii Press, 1995, T. Bui, "How North Vietnam Won the War," *Wall Street Journal*, 3 August 1995, A8.

43 US Department of Defense, JP 3–13 *(First Draft, July 8)*, p. III-2.

44 Ibid., p. I-5.

45 US Air Force, AFDD 2–5, p. 27.

46 Ibid., p. 27.

47 Franks, *American Soldier*, p. 649.

48 US Air Force, AFDD 2–5, p. 27, with an almost identical wording in US Department of Defense, JP 3–61 *(Final Coordination, August 23)*, p. I-5.

49 "Es kann nämlich nur derjenige überraschen, welcher dem anderen das Gesetz gibt." C. von Clausewitz, *Vom Kriege*, Berlin: Ullstein, 1832, 1980, p. 186. The English translation, remarkably, uses "impose will" instead of "give the law." Clausewitz, *On War*, p. 200.

50 B.H. Liddell Hart, *Strategy*, London: Faber & Faber, 1954.

51 US Department of Defense, JP 3–13, p. II-6.

52 Rid, "Revolution in Reporting Affairs".

53 US Army, FM 3–61.1.

54 US Department of Defense, JP 3–61 *(Final Coordination, August 23)*, p. I-6.

55 Ibid., p. I-7.

56 US Department of Defense, JP 1–02.

57 US Department of Defense, JP 3–13 *(First Draft, July 8)*.

58 US Department of Defense, JP 3–61 *(Final Coordination, August 23)*, p. I-10, emphasis in original.

59 DeFrank, interview.

60 Clarke, Victoria, interview by author, by telephone, 18 May 2006.

61 Whitman, interview.

62 B. Whitman, "The Birth of Embedding as a Pentagon War Policy," in B. Katovsky and T. Carlson (eds) *Embedded: The Media at War in Iraq*, Guilford, Connecticut: The Lyons Press, 2004, pp. 205–6.

63 This idea is inspired by Nonaka's middle-up-down management model, but deviates

significantly from it. Nonaka, "A Dynamic Theory of Organizational Knowledge Creation," Nonaka, Toyama, and Byosière, "A Theory of Organizational Knowledge Creation: Understanding the Dynamic Process of Creating Knowledge".

64 Clarke, interview.
65 Cullin, Brian, interview by author, Washington Navy Yard, Washington, DC, 18 February 2004.
66 Birmingham, Mike, interview by author, Pentagon, 6 April 2004.
67 Mann, *Rise of the Vulcans*, pp. 43–4.
68 Franks, *American Soldier*, p. 649.
69 Many pundits and experts external to the military – including the author of this study – opined and hypothesized publicly that "co-option" would be one of the embedded media planners' strategic rationales. Although the possibility remains that this thought occurred to single individuals in the Department of Defense involved in the process, the co-option hypothesis cannot be maintained after a thorough examination of the Pentagon's decision making and the military's implementation of the program. T. Rid, "Präventive Medienstrategie der USA. Militärische Öffentlichkeitsarbeit im Banne eines Krieges," *Neue Zürcher Zeitung*, 10 February 2003, 5.
70 Cullin, interview.
71 Cullin, interview.
72 DeFrank, interview.
73 Clarke, interview.
74 Clarke, interview.
75 Clarke, paraphrasing Rumsfeld in interview by author.
76 Franks, *American Soldier*, p. 644.
77 Wilkinson, James, quoted in J. Keen, "Information 'War Room' Deploys its Own Troops," *USA Today*, 18 December 2001, p. A14.
78 Wilkinson, James, quoted in T. Shanker, and E. Schmitt, "Firing Leaflets and Electrons, US Wages Information War," *New York Times*, 2003, p. A1.
79 Franks, *American Soldier*, p. 641.
80 An F16 is a falcon fighter bomber; an M16 is a 5.56 mm infantry rifle.
81 Franks, *American Soldier*, p. 640.
82 Thomas, interview.
83 Franks, *American Soldier*, p. 644.
84 DeFrank, interview.
85 T. McCreary, "Command Support of Public Affairs Activities in Potential Future Military Operations," *SECDEF-CJCS P4 Message* 2003.
86 Ibid.
87 US Department of Defense, *PAG1*, Cullin, interview.
88 Ibid.
89 Mazzetti, interview.
90 US Department of Defense, *PAG1*.
91 Birmingham, interview.
92 Birmingham, interview.
93 Pasquarett, *Reporters on the Ground*, p. 118.
94 Ibid.
95 Ibid.
96 Shields, interview.
97 Wright, *IDA-Paper* P-3931, p. IV-9.
98 Thomas, interview.
99 Thomas, interview.
100 Thomas, Rick, quoted in A.C. Shepard, *Narrowing the Gap: Military, Media and the Iraq War, Cantigny Conference Series*, Chicago: McCormick Tribune Foundation, 2004, p. 31.
101 Thomas, interview.

102 Wright, *IDA-Paper* P-3931, appendices.

103 Thomas, interview.

104 US Department of Defense, *PAG1*.

105 Birmingham, interview.

8 Strategic public affairs: Iraq

1 Franks, *American Soldier*, p. 523.

2 Ibid., p. 705.

3 Gordon, and Trainor, *Cobra II*, pp. 164–81.

4 Probably Franks is hinting at President Bill Clinton's reaction to the US embassy bombings in Dar-es-Salaam, Tanzania, and Nairobi, Kenya, where more than 200 people were killed. As a response, Clinton had TLAMs launched against a suspected chemical weapons facility in Sudan and training camps in Afghanistan. Franks repeatedly remarks in his memoirs that the reaction was ineffective and ill-advised.

5 Franks, *American Soldier*, p. 717.

6 G.W. Bush, "President Bush Addresses the Nation," *The White House Oval Office*, 19 March 2003, 2216 EST.

7 Davis, interview.

8 Franks, *American Soldier*, p. 572.

9 W. Murray, and R.H. Scales, *The Iraq War. A Military History*, Cambridge, MA: Harvard University Press, 2003, p. 94.

10 Ibid., p. 95, Franks, *American Soldier*, p. 577.

11 Lorch, interview.

12 Whitman, "The Birth of Embedding as a Pentagon War Policy," p. 206.

13 Davis, interview.

14 Thomas, interview.

15 M. Pasquarett, *Perspectives on Embedded Media*, Carlisle, PA: Army War College, 2004, p. 5.

16 N. Gowing, *Information in Conflict: Who Really Commands the High Ground?*, at Liddell Hart Center for Military Archives, London, 2 March 2000.

17 Ferrell, Terry, in M. Pasquarett, "Reporters on the Ground: The Military and the Media's Joint Experience During Operation Iraqi Freedom," *Center for Strategic Leadership. Issue Paper*, 2003, 08.

18 Clarke, interview.

19 Franks, *American Soldier*, p. 698.

20 Glasser, "Media and Military Try Experiment in Openness," p. A14.

21 Eisenhower, Dwight, quoted in US Department of Defense, JP3–61, p. I-1.

22 Franks, *American Soldier*, p. 722.

23 Davis, Andrew, interview.

24 Steve Komarow, from USA Today, is an example: "I probably had the best big-picture view of the army ground war that any reporter could possibly have," we wrote after the war. Komarow, "War-Gaming with Lieutenant General William Wallace," p. 80.

25 Most journalists who were embedded, in contrast to those not embedded, well understood that problem. Sean Naylor pointed out some of his problems during a conference in Carlisle: "from my little soda straw, it was just an odd thing. I couldn't write a trend story out of that. I'm just in one tiny slice of the battle." Naylor, Sean, quoted in Pasquarett, *Reporters on the Ground*.

26 The Iraqis did not have a three-tiered information campaign. No reporters were embedded with Iraqi units. The arrangement that comes closest to embedding were minders, employed by the ministry of information, constantly attending the journalists they were assigned to. A. Garells, *Naked in Baghdad* New York: Farror, Straus, and Giroux, 2003, 10–16.

27 CNN, "U.S. like Al Capone, says Iraq," 21 March 2003, 1054 EST.
28 Only later Sahaf would be nicknamed "Comical Ali," or "Baghdad Bob," and turned into a ridiculed cartoon figure. In fact, his complete loss of any credibility in the following weeks illustrates the success of the embedded media program.
29 Franks, *American Soldier*, p. 530.
30 Brooks, Vincent, interview by author, Pentagon, 10 March 2004.
31 Brooks, interview.
32 Ibid.
33 Franks, *American Soldier*, p. 766.
34 Ibid., p. 787.
35 Ibid., p. 788.
36 Ibid., p. 722.
37 Mellman, Todd, in Pasquarett, *Reporters on the Ground*.
38 Starnes, Glenn, in Pasquarett, *Reporters on the Ground*.
39 US Army, 3rd Infantry Division, *After Action Report Operation IRAQI FREEDOM*, 3ID AAR, 2003, p. 42.
40 Ibid., p. 43.
41 Mazzetti, Mark, interview. See also the account of Lacey, a reporter embedded with the 101st Airborne Division, J. Lacey, "Who's Responsible for Losing the Media War in Iraq?" *Proceedings*, 2004, October, p. 39.
42 Gordon, and Trainor, *Cobra II*, pp. 375–90.
43 Schwartz, Eric, quoted in Center for Army Lessons Learned, *On Point: The United States Army in Iraq*, 2004.
44 Task Force 1–64 AR, Summary of Unit Actions from 20 March to 11 April 2003, Operation Iraqi Freedom.
45 Perkins, David, in Pasquarett, *Reporters on the Ground*.
46 Perkins, David, in ibid.
47 D. Zucchino, "Was with Iraq/The Front Lines; A Daylight Dast," *Los Angeles Times*, 6 April 2003, p. A1.
48 Perkins, David, in Pasquarett, *Reporters on the Ground*.
49 Perkins, David, interview with PBS, 26 February 2004.
50 Ibid.
51 Perkins, David, quoted in D. Zucchino, *Thunder Run: Three Days in the Battle for Baghdad*, New York: Atlantic Books, 2004, p. 80.
52 "It would have been not only a tactical loss, but I think a strategic loss if we pulled out the city" Perkins said in the PBS interview, "because then the Iraqis could spin it: 'They came in the city, we defeated them, we pushed them out, we kicked them out.'"
53 Perkins, David, quoted in Zucchino, *Thunder Run*, p. 130.
54 Malcom, Scott, interview by author, by telephone, 11 May 2006.
55 CBS newscast, video provided by Scott Malcom, precise date unknown.
56 Malcom, Scott, "Your Dissertation," *e-mail*, 12 May 2006.
57 The meaning of the term "truth" as DeFrank is using it when he says "the truth was our friend" is descriptive – journalistic facts corresponding to military events – rather than normative (as in: "this is the true way of reporting a war").
58 Perkins, David, in quoted Pasquarett, *Reporters on the Ground*, p. 75.
59 Ibid., p. 87.
60 US Army, *3ID AAR*, p. 44.

9 The friendly learning loop

1 The most important contributions to the IO debate were J. Arquilla, and D. Ronfeldt, "Cyberwar is Coming!" *Comparative Strategy*, 1993, vol. 12, 2, 141–65, J. Arquilla, and D. Ronfeldt, *In Athena's Camp: Preparing for Conflict in the Information Age*, Santa Monica: Rand, 1997, A.F. Krepinevich, "Cavalry to Computer: The Pattern of

Military Revolutions," *The National Interest*, 1994, vol. 37, Fall, 30–42, Krulak, "The Strategic Corporal: Leadership in the Three Block War," M. Libicki, *What is Information Warfare?*, Washington, DC: National Defense University, 1995, J.S. Nye, and W.A. Owens, "America's Information Edge," *Foreign Affairs*, 1996, vol. 75, 2, 20–36, Stech, "Winning CNN Wars," Toffler, and Toffler, *War and Anti-War*. Murray provides a valuable critical counterpoint to the "new technocratic view," W. Murray, "Clausewitz out, Computer in. Military Culture and Technological Hubris," *The National Interest*, 1997, vol. 48, Summer, 57–64.

2 Shea, interview.
3 Ibid.
4 S. Babst, "Der Kosovo-Krieg, die Nato und die Medien," *Europäische Sicherheit*, 2000, vol. 49, 3, 63–6, Campbell, "Communications Lessons for NATO, the Military and the Media," Clark, *Waging Modern War*, Pounder, "Opportunity Lost".
5 Franks, *American Soldier*, p. 662.
6 Interviews with Bell, Hiram; Birmingham, Mike; Brooks, Vincent; Cullin, Brian; Curtin, Joe; Davis, Andrew; DeFrank, James; Kuehl, Daniel; Naylor, Sean; Pasquarett, Michael; Rounds, Tom; Shields, Guy; Thomas, Rick; Whitman, Bryan; Wright, Richard.
7 "Communities of interaction contribute to the amplification and development of new knowledge. . . . Gradually, concepts which are thought to be of value obtain a wider currency and become crystallized [as explicit knowledge]. Nonaka, "A Dynamic Theory of Organizational Knowledge Creation," pp. 15–16.
8 McCreary, interview.

10 The adversarial learning loop

1 Terrorism is a tactical or strategic instrument, not an actor or adversary. Militant substate organizations may or may not engage in terrorist operations, and they may or may not be Islamic. The adjective "terrorist" should be used with caution and reluctance, particularly in conjunction with Islam. Al-Qaeda is the most prominent militant Islamic organization, and many experts argue that it turned from an organization into an ideology. "Al-Qaeda" is here used as a placeholder for various rump or splinter groups that associate themselves to the base organization.
2 For a thought-provoking description of this development see T.L. Friedman, *The World is Flat: A Brief History of the Twenty-first Century*, New York: Farrar, Straus and Giroux, 2004.
3 H. Binnendijk (ed.) *Transforming America's Military*, Washington, DC: National Defense University Press, 2002.
4 Lang, "Military Organizations," p. 838.
5 D.A. Macgregor, *Transformation Under Fire: Revolutionizing How America Fights*, Westport, Connecticut: Praeger, 2003, p. 4.
6 Binnendijk (ed.) *Transforming America's Military*, p. 17.
7 Murray, and Scales, *The Iraq War*, p. 95.
8 J. Stern, "The Protean Enemy," *Foreign Affairs*, 2003, vol. 82, 4, p. 27.
9 G. Weimann, *Terror on the Internet: The New Arena, the New Challenges*, Washington, DC: The United States Institute of Peace, 2006.
10 Marc Prensky, of games2train, a firm that promotes the educational use of computer games, describes today's 40-plus generation as "digital immigrants" who, like newcomers everywhere, had to adapt to their digital surroundings. "Digital natives," by contrast, grew up surrounded by the new global information environment and are culturally accustomed to it. M. Prensky, "Listen to the Natives," *Educational Leadership*, 2005, vol. 63, 4, p. 8.
11 Weimann, *Terror on the Internet*, pp. 107–8.
12 Stern, "The Protean Enemy," p. 28.

13 S. Coll, and S.B. Glasser, "Terrorists Turn to the Web as Base of Operations," *Washington Post*, 7 August 2005, A1.
14 MEMRI Dispatch 637, 6 January 2004.
15 Weimann, *Terror on the Internet*, pp. 123–45.
16 Quoted in Coll, and Glasser, "Terrorists Turn to the Web as Base of Operations" p. A1.
17 L. Beam, "Leaderless Resistance," *The Seditionist* 1992, vol. 12.
18 Stern, "The Protean Enemy," p. 30.
19 Paz, Reuven, quoted in F. Symon, "Keeping Track of Terrorists on the Web," *Financial Times*, 26 August 2005.
20 G. Steinberg, *Der nahe und der ferne Feind. Das Netzwerk des islamistischen Terrorismus*, München: Beck, 2005, p. 94.
21 For a detailed analysis see ibid., p. 97.
22 The original editions of the *Mu'askar al Battar* magazine, for instance, are written on a Microsoft Windows Arabic operating system, see the PDF file's document properties. See also Y. Musharbash, *Die neue Al-Qaida. Innenansichten eines lernenden Terrornetzwerks*, Köln: Kiepenheur & Witsch, 2006.

Select bibliography

Allison, G.T. and P. Zelikow, *Essence of Decision: Explaining the Cuban Missile Crisis*, Boston: Little Brown, 1971, 1999

Argyris, C. and D.A. Schön, *Organizational Learning: A Theory of Action Perspective*, Reading: Addison-Wesley, 1978

Arnett, P., *Live from the Battlefield*, New York: Simon & Schuster, 1994

Arquilla, J. and D. Ronfeldt, *In Athena's Camp: Preparing for Conflict in the Information Age*, Santa Monica: Rand, 1997

Atkinson, R., *Crusade: The Untold Story of the Gulf War*, London: HarperCollins, 1993

Aukofer, F. and W.P. Lawrence, *America's Team, the Odd Couple: A Report on the Relationship between the Military and the Media*, Nashville: The Freedom Forum First Amendment Center, 1995

Aylwin-Foster, N., "Changing the Army for Counterinsurgency Operations," *Military Review*, 2005, November–December, 2–15

Bassford, C., *The Reception of Clausewitzian Theory in Anglo-American Military Thought*, Purdue, 1991

Beam, L., "Leaderless Resistance," *The Seditionist* 1992, vol. 12

Bickel, K.B., *Mars Learning: The Marine Corps Development of Small Wars Doctrine, 1915–1940*, Boulder, CO: Westview, 2001

Binnendijk, H. (ed.), *Transforming America's Military*, Washington, DC: National Defense University Press, 2002

Braestrup, P., *Battle Lines*, New York: Priority Press, 1985

Brown, J.S. and P. Duguid, "Organizational Learning and Communities-of-Practice: Toward a Unified View of Working, Learning, and Innovation," *Organization Science*, 1991, vol. 2, 1

Cassibry, R.C., "Development of Doctrine," *Military Review*, 1956, vol. 36, 2, 25–30

Clark, W.K., *Waging Modern War: Bosnia, Kosovo, and the Future of Combat*, New York: Public Affairs, 2001

Clausewitz, C. von, *On War*, translated by M. Howard and P. Paret, Princeton, NJ: Princeton University Press, 1832, 1976

Clausewitz, C. von, *Vom Kriege*, Berlin: Ullstein, 1832, 1980

Clinton, B., *My Life*, London: Random House, 2004

Cohen, E.A., *Supreme Command: Soldiers, Statesmen, and Leadership in Wartime*, New York: The Free Press, 2002

Cole, R.H., *Operation Just Cause: Panama*, Washington, DC: Joint History Office, Department of Defense, 1995

Cole, R.H., *Operation Urgent Fury: Grenada*, Washington, DC: Joint History Office, Department of Defense, 1997

Coram, R., *Boyd: The Fighter Pilot who Changed the Art of War*, New York: Back Bay Books, 2002

Cyert, R. and J.G. March, *A Behavioural Theory of the Firm*, Englewood Cliffs, NJ: Prentice-Hall, 1963

Daft, R.L., and K.E. Weick, "Toward a Model of Organizations as Interpretations Systems," *Academy of Management Review*, 1984, vol. 9, 2, 284–95

Downie, R.D.. *Learning from Conflict:. The U.S. Military in Vietnam, El Salvador, and the Drug War*, Westport: Praeger, 1998

Fialka, J.J., *Hotel Warriors: Covering the Gulf War*, Hopkins University Press: Baltimore, 1991

Fiol, M.C. and M.A. Lyles, "Organizational Learning," *Academy of Management Review*, 1985, vol. 10, 4, 803–13

Franks, T.R., *American Soldier*, New York: HarperCollins, 2004

Friedman, T.L., *The World is Flat: A Brief History of the Twenty-First Century*, New York: Farrar, Straus and Giroux, 2004

Garrels, A., *Naked in Baghdad*, New York: Farrar, Straus and Giroux, 2003

Gole, H.G., "Don't Kill the Messenger: Vietnam War Reporting in Context," *Parameters*, 1996, Winter, 148–53

Gordon, M. and B. Trainor, *Cobra II: The Inside Story of the Invasion and Occupation of Iraq*, London: Atlantic Books, 2006

Halberstam, D., *The Best and the Brightest*, New York: Ballantine, 1969

Hammond, W.M., *Public Affairs: The Military and the Media, 1962–1968*, Washington: Center of Military History, 1988

Hedberg, B., "How Organizations Learn and Unlearn," *Handbook of Organizational Design: Vol 1.*, Oxford: Oxford University Press, 1981

Huntington, S., *The Soldier and the State*, Cambridge, MA: Harvard University Press, 1957

Johnston, P., "Doctrine is not Enough: The Effect of Doctrine on the Behavior of Armies," *Parameters*, 2000, vol. 30, 3, 30–40

Katzenbach, E.L., Jr, "The Horse Cavalry in the Twentieth Century," in R.J. Art and K. Waltz (eds) *The Use of Force: International Politics and Foreign Policy*, Boston: Little Brown, 1971

Kilner, P., "Transforming Army Learning Through Communities of Practice," *Military Review*, 2002, May–June, 21–7

Knightley, P., *The First Casualty: From the Crimea to Vietnam: The War Correspondent as Hero, Propagandist and Myth Maker*, New York: Harcourt Brace Jovanovich, 1975

Krepinevich, A.F., "Cavalry to Computer: The Pattern of Military Revolutions", *The National Interest*, 1994, vol. 37, Fall, 30–42

Krulak, C.C., "The Strategic Corporal: Leadership in the Three Block Wa,r, *Marines Magazine*, 1999, January

Krulak, V.H., *First to Fight: An Inside View of the U.S. Marine Corps*, Annapolis, MD: Naval Institute Press, 1999

Kuhn, T., *Structure of Scientific Revolutions*, Chicago: Chicago University Press, 1962

Lakatos, I. and A. Musgrave, *Criticism and the Growth of Knowledge*, Cambridge: Cambridge University Press, 1970

Lang, K. "Military Organizations," in J.G. March (ed.) *Handbook of Organizations*, Chicago: Rand McNally, 1965

Levinthal, D.A. and J.G. March, "The Myopia of Learning," *Strategic Management Journal*, 1993, vol. 14, 95–112

Levitt, B. and J.G. March, "Organizational Learning," *Annual Review of Sociology*, 1988, vol. 14, 319–40

Liddell Hart, B.H., *Strategy*, London: Faber & Faber, 1954

Mann, J., *Rise of the Vulcans: The History of Bush's War Cabinet*, New York: Penguin, 2004

March, J.G. and J.P. Olsen, "The Uncertainty of the Past: Organizational Learning under Ambiguity," *European Journal of Political Research*, 1975, 3, 147–71

March, J.G., and H. Simon, *Organizations*, Cambridge: Blackwell, 1958, 1993

Mermin, J., *Debating War and Peace. Media Coverage of US Intervention in the Post-Vietnam Era*, Princeton: Princeton University Press, 1999

Moore, M., *A Woman at War*, New York: Scribner's, 1993

Murray, W., "Innovation: Past and Future", *Joint Forces Quarterly*, 1996, 12, 51–60

Murray, W., "Clausewitz out, Computer in: Military Culture and Technological Hubris," *The National Interest*, 1997, vol. 48, Summer, 57–64

Nagl, J.A., *Counterinsurgency Lessons from Malaya and Vietnam: Learning to Eat Soup with a Knife*, New York: Praeger, 2002

Naylor, S., *Not a Good Day to Die*, New York: Penguin, 2005

Neuman, J., *Lights, Camera, War*, New York: St. Martin's Press, 1996

Nonaka, I., "A Dynamic Theory of Organizational Knowledge Creation," *Organization Science*, 1994, vol. 5, 1, 14–37

Nonaka, I., *The Knowledge-Creating Company*, New York: Oxford University Press, 1995

Oberdorfer, D., *Tet!*, New York: Garden City, 1971

Paret, P., "Clausewitz", in P. Paret (ed.) *Makers of Modern Strategy: from Machiavelli to the Nuclear Age*, Oxford: Clarendon Press, 1990

Polanyi, M., *Personal Knowledge*, Chicago: University of Chicago Press, 1962

Polanyi, M., *The Tacit Dimension*, London: Routledge and Kegan Paul, 1966

Powell, C.L and J.E. Persico, *My American Journey*, New York: Random House, 1995

Prensky, M., "Listen to the Natives," *Educational Leadership*, 2005, vol. 63, 4

Reagan, R., *An American Life*, New York: Simon & Schuster, 1990

Rid, T., "Revolution in Reporting Affairs. Der Krimkrieg und seine Bedeutung für die Geschichte der Kriegsberichterstattung," *Österreichische Militärische Zeitschrift*, 2003, 3

Rosen, S.P., *Winning the Next War: Innovation and the Modern Military*, Ithaka: Cornell University Press, 1991

Schein, E.H., "How Can Organizations Learn Faster? The Challenge of Entering the Green Room," *Sloan Management Review*, 1993, vol. 34, 2, 85–92

Schwarzkopf, N., *It Doesn't Take a Hero*, New York: Bantam, 1992

Starbuck, W.H., and B. Hedberg, "How Organizations Learn from Success and Failure," in M. Dierkes, A. Berthoin Antal, I. Nonaka and J. Child (eds) *Handbook of Organizational Learning and Knowledge*, Oxford: Oxford University Press, 2001

Stech, F.J., "Winning CNN Wars," *Parameters*, 1994, Autumn, 37–56

Steinberg, G., *Der nahe und der ferne Feind. Das Netzwerk des islamistischen Terrorismus*, München: Beck, 2005

Stern, J., "The Protean Enemy," *Foreign Affairs*, 2003, vol. 82, 4

Toffler, A. and H. Toffler, *War and Anti-War*, New York, 1993

Trainor, B., "The Military and the Media: A Troubled Embrace," *Parameters*, 1990, December, 2–11

Tzu, S., *The Art of War*, translated by S.B. Griffith, Oxford: Oxford University Press, 1963

Weber, M., *Wirtschaft und Gesellschaft*, Tübingen: Mohr Siebeck, 1922, 1977

Weimann, G., *Terror on the Internet: The New Arena, the New Challenges*, Washington, DC: The United States Institute of Peace, 2006

Wilson, J.Q., *Bureaucracy: What Government Agencies Do and Why They Do It*, New York: Basic Books, 1989

Woodward, B., *Plan of Attack*, New York: Simon & Schuster, 2004

Wright, R.K., *Assessment of the DoD Embedded Media Program*, IDA-Paper P-3931, Alexandria, Virginia: Institute for Defense Analysis, 2004

Zucchino, D., *Thunder Run: Three Days in the Battle for Baghdad*, New York: Atlantic Books, 2004

Index